The Developing Child in the 21st Century

A global perspective on child development

Second edition

Sandra Smidt

Routledge
Taylor & Francis Group

LONDON AND NEW YORK

Second edition published 2013
by Routledge
2 Park Square, Milton Park, Abingdon, Oxon OX14 4RN

Simultaneously published in the USA and Canada
by Routledge
711 Third Avenue, New York, NY 10017

Routledge is an imprint of the Taylor & Francis Group, an informa business

First published by Routledge 2006

British Library Cataloguing in Publication Data
A catalogue record for this book is available from the British Library

Library of Congress Cataloging in Publication Data
Smidt, Sandra, 1943–.
    The developing child in the 21st century: a global perspective on child
    development/Sandra Smidt. – Second edition.
    pages cm
    1. Children.   2. Child development.   I. Title.
    HQ767.9.S625 2013
    305.231 – dc23
    2012047336

ISBN: 978-0-415-65865-2 (hbk)
ISBN: 978-0-415-65866-9 (pbk)
ISBN: 978-0-203-48364-0 (ebk)

Typeset in Bembo and Gill Sans
by Florence Production Ltd, Stoodleigh, Devon, UK

The first edition was dedicated to the memory of my father, Harry, my aunt, Gessy and my friend, Hilda, all of whom dreamed of a more just world. This book is still for them with regrets that the dream is still just that.

Contents

Preface

In this second edition of this book, written seven years after the original, the world has changed. We have seen a change of government in the United Kingdom and in the United States; a huge economic crisis enveloping Europe; the economic and political development of China, Brazil, India and South Africa; tumultuous uprisings throughout the Arab world and several extreme and shocking events, from the tsunamis in Thailand and Japan to earthquakes in Italy and Haiti and beyond. In some countries the divide between rich and poor has narrowed and in others increased. But children continue to develop and learn and grow as they have always done. What is significantly different now is our knowledge and understanding of neuroscience. So what you will get in this edition is a new Chapter 9 to reflect this, together with some other changes including an updated section on street children and the insertion of some relevant facts in the form of asking you, the reader, 'Did you know . . .?' You will find these scattered throughout the text, in italics. The boxed piece of text labelled 'Questions' has been replaced by a less school-like list of issues arising from the chapter that you may want to think about.

In 1996 I was in South Africa and became involved in working for a project on Early Childhood Education. This was in the early days of the post-apartheid government and the project was aimed at defining the minimum norms and standards that could be required of those working with children of preschool age. I was delighted to be involved in this project and came to it full of the confidence I had gained in the UK as an early childhood 'expert'. I had worked as a teacher and a headteacher, as a local authority inspector and as a lecturer in education at more than one university. Early in the project I was asked to work with a South African colleague looking particularly at what we would include in our programme about children's learning and development. For me this was clear. We would need them to think about the work of the great theorists – people like Piaget, Bruner, Vygotsky and others. My colleague and friend, Ann Short, insisted we would need to take account of factors I had not before considered – things like nutrition, health and poverty. Although I was, of course, aware of the impact of these on children's development I was firmly rooted in a Western psychological tradition and it took three days of constant, intense and furious discussion for us to agree to pool our expertise, our experience and our philosophies to come up with a less narrow view. It was from this life-changing experience that the idea of this book arose. So the book is an attempt to re-examine what we now know about how children develop and learn, taking account of a range of perspectives and ideologies.

In writing the book it was difficult to find a term to define what constitutes countries like England or France or the USA, as opposed to countries like South Africa or China or Peru. In the literature some authors refer to North and South, with the North referring to Europe and North America, for example, and the South to countries like South Africa and so on. Other writers prefer to talk of the Majority and the Minority worlds with the Minority world applying to the poorer countries and the Majority to the more wealthy. I have chosen to refer to the developed world and the developing world not because these are accurate terms. It is clear that if one includes countries like China or Nigeria or Mexico, for example, in the developing world one implies that these countries are not developed and that, of course, ignores centuries of development. I use these terms, really, to define the privileged and powerful blocks of Europe, North America and the United Kingdom as opposed to the often poor, often repressed and often ignored countries.

In writing the book I have sought to discuss concepts that are sometimes difficult to explain and understand, and to use as many examples as I can find to illustrate these in order to make them more accessible to readers. There is always a tension between academic writing and accessible writing and like many authors I try to bridge this divide. As an educationalist I am also concerned to offer models of learning for those reading the book and have chosen to revisit themes throughout the book. So you will find reference to concepts like 'intersubjectivity', for example, in the least expected places. As you are reading you might feel irritated at reading something that feels familiar to you in a new context. I hope you will accept that this is a technique to try and make the links between ideas more transparent.

I very much enjoyed writing the first edition of this book because it gave me the opportunity to bring together some of the themes that have dominated my personal and my professional life – an abiding interest in children and childhoods; an extreme anger at injustice, oppression and poverty, and a passion for the work of writers, painters, theorists and others who have worked and continue to work to improve the world for those who will inherit it. The second edition, written at a time of crisis throughout the world, has been more difficult.

Note: To avoid using the clumsy 'he or she' or the more usual 'he', I have elected to use 'she' throughout this second edition.

Chapter 1

Children and childhoods

In this opening chapter we examine what is meant by child development, which leads us to look at how important both history and culture are to any understanding of child development. We will start by looking at childhood, as a concept, and examine its origins and the importance of thinking about childhood as a space or a phase separate from adulthood. As we do this we will also look at how concepts of 'the child' have developed and how they do not remain static over time or place. Closely allied with concepts of childhood per se are aspects of reality such as poverty and rights and we touch on these. We develop a workable image of the child of the twenty-first century and touch on the notion of 'good parenting'.

Child development: which child? What development?

It is evening in the Zocalo in Oaxaca in Mexico. The street sellers and the shoe-shine boys and the mariachi are out in the streets. Three-year-old Cristina is there, too, as she is every day and every evening. Her mother has a stall that sells plastic inflatable toys and giant balloons, which billow above the stalls in the breeze. Cristina is cruising the streets, as she does every evening. All the stall-holders and the food sellers and the musicians know her: she is a member of the market community that inhabits the square. As she roams around munching on bits of food given to her, chatting to people, looking at the things on display she keeps her mother within view although she is perfectly safe. All the adults there treat her as though she were their child. This is her world. This is her childhood.

In Ho Chi Minh City, Hung is in the arrivals hall of the airport. He holds up a card on which his wares are displayed – books of postcards of Vietnamese scenes, bracelets made of strips of plastic, comic books. It is 2.30 in the afternoon and his school day has ended. He goes early in the morning and finishes in time to get in a whole afternoon's selling – and, more importantly, speaking English – at the airport and in the streets. He is 7 years old and his English is fluid and fluent. He tells people he has learnt it from the tourists who arrive at and leave from the airport. He is known to the other sellers at the airport and to the taxi drivers and to the police who threaten to move him on, but his cheery smile seems to protect him from authority. He says he is saving up the money he earns (after he has given most of it to his mother) to buy a mobile phone. This is his world and his childhood.

Jinjing is 4 years old and lives in a village in rural China. She goes to kindergarten everyday although this year on 9 April there were such severe traffic problems that she could not get to the kindergarten and was taken instead to the village teaching spot – an open-air space where teachers had gathered to teach the children. She is an only child and her father is a tool dresser and works in the streets. Her mother does whatever part-time work she can get and the family is poor. But they do enjoy going to the wet market and to cultural events in the nearest town. Jinjing has many friends at kindergarten and they often play together in the courtyards where their houses are set.

Lindelwa lives in KwaZulu Natal in South Africa. She is 5 years old. Her mother died of HIV/AIDs last year and she hasn't seen her father for many years. He works far away. Her older brother Vusi is sick and so is her uncle. Three people in the house next door have died of AIDS. Lindelwa lives with her grandmother and she goes to school whenever she can. It is a long walk to school but Lindelwa loves going to school and she wants to get an education so that when she grows up she can become a doctor and find a cure for the terrible illness that is devastating her community. Her grandmother thinks this is a wonderful plan and she has talked to the teachers at the school who say they will help Lindelwa in every way they can. Hers is a difficult childhood and a difficult life.

(Personal observation notes)

Four different children: four different childhoods. This can be multiplied and multiplied and one would still not have any real sense of just how individual and different childhoods are. This is a book about child development. You may question why another book about child development is needed. After all there are dozens around, from the famous classical texts of researchers and theorists from the developed world like Piaget and Vygotsky, to simpler primers written for a range of audiences. This book aims to explore some of the ideas of the recognised authors and to consider how they contribute to our knowledge of children today not only in the developed world but also more globally. This is a book that adopts a position which goes beyond the psychological and the individual and considers findings from other fields and domains that contribute to our understanding of how children in both the developed and the developing worlds grow and learn. A consideration of child development at the start of the twenty-first century cannot afford to ignore the realities of life for the majority of the world's children.

We start by considering what we mean by 'child development'. Superficially, child development can be described as a discipline that looks at how children develop from conception to the end of childhood. The definition of when childhood ends, however, is not as simple as it might appear. In the United Nations Convention on the Rights of the Child, childhood is deemed to end at the age of 18 unless, under the law applicable to the child, majority is attained earlier. The discipline of child development aims to identify, describe and predict patterns in children's growth, which includes intellectual (or cognitive), linguistic, physical, social, behavioural and emotional development. Because all aspects of development are interrelated, child development is seen as being holistic.

Important themes emerge from this and embedded in these are a number of assumptions:

1   Since development is seen as holistic (where all aspects of development are conceived of as being interrelated) it is evident that *something that affects one aspect of development may affect others*. For example, children who fail to thrive physically are sometimes expected to fail in other areas. In some cases this is so, but the question to ask is whether this is a given.

2   Development is thought to be *continuous and cumulative* and the early years are almost always described as vital to later development. For example, children who have a difficult start in life are often expected to be less likely to succeed in life. Again, there is evidence to suggest that this is often the case, but as the next point illustrates it is not always so.

3   Development is sometimes considered to have a certain *plasticity* that allows for children to adapt and adjust to adverse events and circumstances. Evidence suggests that some children who have a difficult start in life overcome enormous difficulties, and conversely children who have a privileged start in life sometimes struggle to adapt to later hardships.

Development, then, is a complex and dynamic construct and is sometimes described as though it exists outside of history and culture. The theme of this book is that development cannot be fully understood outside of a historical and a cultural context. Criticisms are often made of the books written about child development on the basis that they adopt an almost totally Western view of children and of their development. When one considers that there are significantly more children growing up in the developing world than there are in the developed world the primacy of the views of North American and European writers remains a concern.

The changing representations of children

The early Renaissance painter, Caravaggio, scoured the streets of Italian towns and cities, sketching the faces and postures of people he encountered. In his paintings – almost always of religious subjects and themes – the faces – smiling, weeping, anguished, joyous – of the people he had sketched appear as Salome or Jesus or Herod. Through the use of line and colour and light he was able to represent anger, disbelief, awe, horror, fear, love – every possible emotion. And the bodies of the people in his paintings are clearly human, capable of movement and repose. His skills were unequalled. And yet, when it came to drawing infants or babies – most often cherubs – this eye for detail and truth and reality seemed to desert him. The babies are unlike any babies you will see anywhere. They are – in proportion and expression – miniature adults. The question of why this is so is a fascinating one and it does not take much imagination to realise that this was not because he was unable to draw babies in proportion. Clearly, this most exceptional of painters could reproduce anything he had seen. It seems likely that the reproduction of babies in his work relates more clearly to the concepts he held of infants. Leonardo da Vinci's babies are chubby and rosy-cheeked and idealised in his paintings, but in his anatomical drawings they are accurate and exact. It seems that in these scientific drawings he drew what he saw whilst in some of the paintings his ideas about babies and small children overcame this. It is tempting to conclude that at that time and throughout much of Europe infants were seen as miniature versions of adults – as adults in waiting. And indeed an analysis of medieval European paintings does seem to suggest as much.

By contrast, during Victorian times the perceived and romanticised innocence of childhood was very evident in images of children. It is interesting to situate this view in the context of growing industrialisation and the development of new capitalist endeavours. Children were often depicted in pastel colours, prettified, with softened edges and these images were later transposed to be used in advertising. A famous example is of John Millais's painting of *Bubbles* (1886), which was later used to sell Pears' soap and is an image some of you may be familiar with.

What seems evident is that images of childhood have changed over time and do change with place. This means that the conceptions people have of childhood will relate to not only to childhood itself but also to attitudes to children, to their positions in the family and society, to how they learn and develop morally, intellectually and emotionally, and to what their rights are.

It was the work of the author Philippe Aries that first drew attention to how notions of children and childhood have changed over time. In his seminal work *Centuries of Childhood* (1962) he suggested that the concept of childhood was a new one that did not exist in medieval times. He studied medieval icons and used them to show how images of Jesus as an infant always showed him as a shrunken adult and linked that to the concept of the *homunculus* (little man). He went on to argue that, beyond infancy where the child was seen as totally dependent, there was no concept of a child per se, and consequently no real concept of childhood as a specific phase of life. He believed that the concept of childhood developed slowly in the upper classes in the sixteenth and seventeenth centuries and only appeared fully in society in the twentieth century. In his argument young people between the ages of 7 and 15 were regarded as adults: they were required to work as apprentices in the fields and later in the factories, and entered into what we might regard as adult life at very young ages. The great painters of the Renaissance did not paint realistic infants not because they lacked skill but because they perceived of babies as adults in waiting.

Aries went on to examine how the developing concept of the child and of childhood changed the position of young people in society. He argued that with the concept of childhood came a theory of the innocence of the child. Children were to be protected from the dreadful realities of life – from birth and death, sex and world events. Where children had once been merely apprentice adults, age itself was of no consequence, but with the development of childhood as a concept children were increasingly segregated by age. Along with the concept of the child and of childhood came thoughts about leisure and play and work and family roles.

For Aries the changes that came about between the fifteenth and seventeenth centuries could be ascribed to three factors. First there was a change to what was happening within families as children became perceived of as more vulnerable and more valued and in need of protection. Second, at a later stage, children were seen as being in need of discipline and training. Third, with the development of schooling, children's ages were seen as significant and schools were seen as the institutions where children belonged. These changes gradually spread from the upper and middle classes until they affected all classes.

Aries's arguments have been challenged by various authors including Shulamith Shahar (1990) who, in her study of childhood in the Middle Ages, concluded that some thinkers did conceive of childhood as being made up of several separate stages. She criticised Aries for using very limited sources (things like the diaries and letters and pictures from primarily French aristocratic homes) in order to describe childhood per se. Her point was that the majority of children were not written about and this is a theme of much of the work that followed.

Later historians, including Heywood (2001), have shown how modern concepts of childhood arose through the different discourses and practices relating to child labour, to criminality and to welfare. The development is sometimes summed up as the path from the child as miniature adult, to the child as sinner, to the child as property, to the child as school pupil.

British childhood over time: an illustration

We are talking about childhood as a social construct – which means that the ideas of what childhood is and what children are like are created by adults. It requires little extrapolation from this to see that the adults who construct images of childhood do so within a specific time and place, responding to the economic, political, religious, class and political influences and challenges in place. We will use evidence of how views of childhood and children changed over time within Britain over the past two centuries.

It was in the eighteenth century that a public debate began about children and about how they should be thought of, nurtured, disciplined and educated. There were two competing strands operating. At one extreme were the harsh views of John Wesley, the Methodist leader, who urged parents to break the will of the child so that it could be subject to the will of God and at the other extreme the views of Rousseau and his followers. In his famous and influential book *Emile* (1762), Rousseau wrote of the child as being imbued with goodness – the natural child. He urged teachers and parents to treat the child like a child – which was revolutionary in the sense that although the child was seen as being prepared for adulthood, childhood was given some status as a phase in its own right.

The notion of the natural child evolved into the notion of the romantic child as the Romantic poets Blake, Coleridge and Wordsworth began to explore the essence of the being, the development of self. Although there were variations in the details of how these poets conceived of this, essentially childhood was a state of innocence and a model of what would – inevitably – be lost during later life. The childhoods being reflected here bear little relation to the reality of life for the majority of children in Britain at the time, reflecting the extremely precious and sentimentalised childhoods of the rich. For the poor children harsher views grew up around the impact of industrialisation, the effect of the French Revolution and the growth of capitalism. The effect of this on the lives of children included a focus on original sin, and parents were urged to teach their children that they were evil. The *Evangelical Magazine* in 1799 referred to children as being 'sinful polluted creatures'. The founder of the Sunday School movement, a woman called Hannah More, carried this even further, believing that children brought into the world a 'corrupt nature and evil disposition' (cited in Hendrick, 1997). Despite these negative views of children, More had an abiding belief in the importance of educating and rearing children.

As the eighteenth century drew to a close child labour predominated. But this began to change as factory children and chimney sweeps and apprentices in the cotton mills began to be seen as slaves being denied their childhood. It was now that a new construction of childhood began to be apparent and the use of children as free labourers died out. The concept of childhood as a specific time and phase characterised by a concern for the welfare and protection of children began to grow. Fears grew for the safety of children in work, for their weakness as compared with adult workers. In an attempt to define what qualities children had, and the span of childhood, in 1883 a Royal Commission declared that childhood ended at age 13. Although all of this was concerned with the universality of childhood there were clear perceptions that the childhoods of the rich and the poor still varied widely and much attention was paid to the so-called 'delinquent' child. Out of this grew the great education reforms that resulted in compulsory schooling. By the mid nineteenth century the concerns were mainly on establishing norms and images and the role of the state in determining aspects of childhood was fixed.

And what of today's child? Trond Waage, special adviser to the UNICEF Research Centre, gave a talk in Glasgow in November 2005 where he stated his views about the image of the child in modern Western societies. He said that today's children are in conflict for many reasons. For one, they have been through a gender revolution that has meant that their schooling has given them the same opportunities as one another, regardless of gender. For a while they had the opportunity to pursue education without a concern about the cost to their parents. Today, in England at least, that has gone. They have a developed understanding of the global world due to the development of the internet, the mobile phone, social networking and more. So today's children cannot follow well-trodden paths but have to be in charge of their own futures more than children in the past. They live in an intensely consumerist world where even toys are invested with symbolic values – they become expressions of love or pride. Children are often made aware of their rights – sometimes their rights seem to dominate those of all others in their world. Many are concerned that today's children have no sense of the real lives and needs and concerns of others in their own community, let alone those further removed (Waage, 2005).

The portrayal of children

When we talk about 'representations' here we are thinking of representation in its cultural sense and about the socially available images and concepts through which children are thought about and portrayed by others. As we have seen, images of painting reveal quite clearly how the concept of childhood in the Western world has changed and developed. Higonnet (1998) describes how children in paintings have moved from those sentimentalised and romanticised representations of painters like Millais and Gainsborough. Higonnet believes that childhood is defined largely by what it is not: it is not adulthood. These are idealised images of children – children without class or gender or culture. You will still find images like these on calendars and birthday cards, on biscuit tins and on adverts that seek to represent children as part of happy families living uncomplicated lives of innocence. So childhood itself is portrayed as being 'not adulthood' – without difficulties or problems.

Towards the end of the twentieth century, however, these images themselves were being challenged for their perceived sexual preoccupation. Parents themselves became nervous of photographing or painting their own children naked. You may have read of a case in the United States where the director of an arts centre was charged with (and later released) promoting obscenity after staging a photographic exhibition by the controversial artist Robert Mapplethorpe.

If you take the time to examine current images of children you will see a different view of childhood. Children from different cultures and classes, ethnic groups and genders are presented. Sometimes these children are shown as victims but this is certainly not always so. What some theorists believe is happening here is that a new image of child-hood is being promoted. Christensen (1999) believes that this new image of childhood is one in which aspects of power relationships between adults and children are played with and where children are often portrayed as the strong, the able, the competent as compared to the weak, embarrassing adults. This is depicted in some of the jokey cartoons or in recent films showing 'adult' babies and infantile adults. This fictional reversal of rules and of roles is almost always temporary, with power eventually restored to its 'proper' place – i.e. with the adults.

In China at the time of Confucius there was no such thing as a children's playground. Children from wealthy families were looked after by wet-nurses and taught by private tutors. They were constrained by the regulations and formalities of high society at the time. In paintings of children from the Song court we see these well-bred children having time for entertaining themselves. By contrast (and as in many societies) the children of the peasants grew up in the fields and did not go to school. They spent their time alongside their parents and their areas of play were the places of work for their parents. Illustrations from traditional agricultural manuals show children playing alongside their working parents. An example cited by Bai (2005) shows women working in a room where silkworms are breeding while two little children play with silkworms in a basket.

Moving away from popular images, the images of children in paintings also reflect a changed view of childhood. Paula Rego, born in Portugal, and still painting, includes in her work disturbing images of children and of women. The images are drawn on her own experiences, often of poverty and cruelty, and imbued with her strong political sensitivities. In 1992 she was invited by the Folio Society to produce a new illustrated version of J.M. Barrie's *Peter Pan*. The pictures reveal images of Peter and Wendy in a relationship imbued with sexuality. The young people are neither innocent nor depraved. They are adolescents in the grip of development. The images are disturbing perhaps because they show aspects of the lives of children that many painters have been reluctant to depict. But the realities of the lives of children often include things that are deeply disturbing.

The ways in which children are portrayed in literature and on film give further illustration of the prevailing philosophies of children and childhood. We are all familiar with how children – particularly poor boys – are portrayed in the Victorian novels of Charles Dickens. One such boy, Oliver Twist, is to be both admired and feared: a poor boy subject to tremendous trials but overcoming adversity through his own 'pluckiness'. In France, Gavroche in Victor Hugo's *Les Misérables*, is represented in a similar way. In North America Mark Twain gave us a picture of a street child, Huckleberry Finn – a free spirit representing, according to Twain, all that should be avoided for mothers and all that should be aimed at for boys.

Moving into the early twentieth century, representations of the lives of children change. In literature, in art and later in film and cartoon we find representations of children who did not fit into the conventional mode of Western childhoods – e.g. not only those who were poor heroes but also those living on the streets, being without a family, involved in adult work. Jorge Amado's heroic street child in Brazil was Pedro Bala in his book *Capitães de Areia*. This was paralleled in some of the films that were produced particularly in Europe after 1945. In Hollywood the depictions of children in film remained largely sentimentalised and offered a somewhat saccharine version of childhood: by dramatic contrast films produced in post-war Italy moved to revealing the brutal realities of the lives of children. Basil Davidson, writing in the *New Statesman* in 1951, drew attention to how determined Italian film makers were to depict the reality of life for many in Italian cities and in the countryside. A milestone in cinema depictions of children was *Bicycle Thieves*, which showed the impact on one child of massive unemployment, and the effects of deep poverty and utter despair. From India, too, came films about childhood showing the effects of poverty and deprivation – like Satyajit Ray's *Apu Trilogy*, made up of *Pather Panchali* (Song of the Little Road), *Aparajito* (The Unvanquished) and *Apur Sansar* (The World of Apu).

Along with changing representations of childhood came changes to the language used to discuss children and childhoods and a developing understanding of children's interests and preoccupations. Bai (2005) tells us that in classical China there were no words to describe children's playthings. It was only when Froebel's ideas about play in education were introduced into China at the beginning of the twentieth century that the Chinese invented a word to describe the 'gifts' given to the children of the affluent to play with. In the fields, however, children picked up the things around them and used them to their own purposes. These were their playthings or toys. At the same time some adults were designing things for children to play with and as in Western society today these were often miniatures of things in the adult world. Toy lanterns are a case in point. So children's games developed, often reflecting popular customs and rites.

In the famous nursery schools of Reggio Emilia the ways in which language is used reveal their very particular view of children and of childhood. The word for 'play' ('giocare' in Italian) is used but less frequently than words like culture and competent and challenging and critical. All children are seen as competent children, all set in the context of their culture, all raising and answering questions. So learning includes being able to make and challenge meaning, to construct metaphors and explore paradoxes, to develop and use individual symbols and codes in the process of learning to decode the established symbols and codes of their culture and society. The educators in Reggio Emilia are clear that childhood itself is a value-laden construct and Rinaldi explains how political the concept is as she tells us that 'childhood does not exist, we create it as a society, as a public subject. It is a social, political and historic construction' (Rinaldi, 2006: 13). This relates closely to the work of Foucault, who looked at how knowledge and power are intertwined in the dominant discourses. The dominant discourse about childhood in the Western world relates to our notions of child development, the importance of play and stages of development. These very concepts then contribute to how we think about the child – the whole thing being cyclical. Knowledge and power legitimise one another.

Western concepts of childhood

The way in which childhood is perceived in the developed world today is as a very distinct and separate phase of development from adulthood. The very discipline of child development as a separate subject illustrates this. Those theorists whose work we will examine later in this book, particularly those who see childhood as being a linear process of moving from dependence to independence, from immature thought to rational thought, encourage the growth of this concept of childhood. In much of the developed world childhood itself is now separated out into different phases – early childhood, childhood and adolescence, for example. For each phase there are ideas about what children should and shouldn't be doing, how they should and should not behave and what their world should be like. Childhood is perceived of as a time of exploration of the world, moving towards adulthood, protected by the family and the state and free from the pressures of economic demands and work. Remember, however, that we are talking about a minority rather than the majority of children.

Did you know that in the developing world in 2012 one in six children (an equal number of boys and girls) between the ages of 5 and 14 are involved in work? (http://www.childinfo.org/labour.html)

Powerful in the development of childhood as a unique phase are the advertisers, the manufacturers and the producers of things designed and made specifically for children. Cross (2004), in his analysis of the underpinning philosophy for the development of children as consumers, describes it as 'wondrous innocence'. He argues that the roots of this lie in the romantic view of childhood expressed in the nineteenth century and in the changing views of the middle classes in the USA and also in Europe. This view of childhood does not mesh well with views of educators or psychologists: nonetheless the influence of it is pervasive and powerful.

Cross (2004) analyses the development as having started in the first three decades of the twentieth century with the growth of magazines for middle-class women. These magazines reached millions of readers and promoted the notion of the child as central to the life and happiness of the adults. The image of the child they promoted was that of the individual, sheltered and scientifically raised child. Adverts consequently promised children (and their parents) brighter, happier, more fulfilled futures if they bought the product. So buying the correct soap could protect the child from illness; ensuring the child had access to a particular toy would promise future opportunities. Buying an insurance policy would guarantee against future hardship and so on. So the child emerged as an independent being with needs different from those of the parents.

As advertising took hold and a market of specialised goods flourished, so adverts appeared encouraging children to 'teach' their parents. Towards the middle of the century adverts often featured father–son bonding as a theme for buying. Fathers, like their sons, would enjoy electric train sets, for example. Girls were often featured as prospective users of beauty products and shown with their mothers in female-bonding around their appearances. Over the twentieth century Western childhoods came to be treated as imitations of adulthood with children being overwhelmed by miniature versions of 'real life'. No longer was it enough for children to play with sticks and lengths of fabric and empty boxes and sand and water: children were offered miniature ironing boards, guns, tables and chairs, washing machines. Children's clothes increasingly began to resemble the clothes being worn by their parents and children's fashion became an enormous growth industry. Younger and younger children were encouraged to dress glamorously or casually but in the fashion of the day: to acquire jewellery and use facial products; to consider their nails and have more than one pair of shoes; to explore fantasy worlds through electronic toys.

In schools and other settings for young children it was thought that the wider the range of bought equipment, the better the education children would receive. That was the implied message and often this was linked to the messages being drawn through the media about what current research into brain activity indicated. Children need to be stimulated and the more varied the stimuli the better the learning. This is something that we challenge throughout this book.

You will recall that we looked briefly at the image of childhood held by educators in Reggio Emilia. For them, the image of a child is, above all, a cultural – and hence a social and political – construct that allows those who hold that image to recognise or ignore some qualities and potentials in children and from that to develop expectations and contexts that will develop the potentials or negate them. Rinaldi says, 'What we believe about children thus becomes a determining factor in defining their social and ethical identity, their rights and the educational contexts offered them' (Rinaldi, 2006: 83). This is something to be considered when reading what follows.

Representations of global childhoods

Many in the developing world find the images of childhood in that world deeply offensive. You will be used to images of children as victims – of war, of ethnic cleansing, of poverty, of disease, of natural disasters, of work and of cruelty. The intention behind these images is ostensibly to make an emotional appeal to the rich. In 2005 there was what was described as a celebration of Africa in the media. Images of the poor and deprived dominated and Africa was portrayed as a single entity with all of its people as suffering and stereotyped. Africa is, as you must know, a vast continent made up of many nations, cultures, languages, beliefs, values, levels of wealth and poverty and with a complex and rich (if not always enriching) history. It is important to remember, however, that using such images merely reinforce the centuries-old creation of the superiority of the developed over the developing world.

In many developed countries, including the UK and the USA, there are rich as well as poor children. In these countries the gap between rich and poor is vast and it could be argued that the concept of childhood in these and other countries is a privilege of the rich and practically non-existent for the poor. This was the finding of Goldstein (1998), who explained that rich children in Brazil share many of the experiences of children in the developed world. They go to school, although for those involved in paid labour this is to a limited extent. Poor children in Brazil, however, are required to contribute to the economy of the family and cannot go to school – except for some who may attend sporadically and infrequently. Some are cut loose from their families and have to live on the streets. Remember that this was in 1998.

Think, too, of the millions of children in sub-Saharan Africa who, as a result of the AIDS pandemic, are themselves heads of families. But can we say that for these children childhood does not exist? Clearly there are aspects of their lives that are terrible and urgently need to be improved, but if we deny them the existence of a childhood we characterise childhood as the domain of the rich. I am persuaded by the arguments of Prout (2005) who suggests that we need to broaden our concept of childhood to include the childhoods of the poor as well as those of the rich. In other words, childhood itself cannot be seen as a single simple concept but one that has to take on the diversity of the reality of childhoods across the world. This is an important theme of this book.

Rosemberg (2005) added another dimension to the argument. In her study of childhood and inequality in Brazil she pointed to the dominance of presenting what is problematic – being poor, being black, being indigenous, being 'the other' – and asks why there is no focus on what it means to be white, to be of European origin, to speak the dominant language. Very rarely do we question how the dominant status of one group is maintained over generations. That would require us to examine what it is we have to do to maintain our position vis-à-vis the rest of the world. Rosemberg noted that many recent developments (increased urbanisation, access to television, drop in infant mortality and fertility rates, for example) contribute to the concept of childhood in Brazil. Parents are now reconsidering their patterns of child-rearing. They now see young children as intelligent and the role of the father is being reconceptualised.

In 2009 Marco Kisil analysed how provision for young children in Brazil is being changed through government plans to develop programmes of early childhood development. Poverty still exists, of course, and progress is slow, but there are some interesting and important initiatives that lend hope for the future. For example, in 2003 in one of the southern states a programme was launched aimed at enabling family members to learn to pay more attention to what their young children are doing and saying. Today there are 222 local authorities taking part in another project, which was inspired by the Cuban programme called *Educa a tu Hijo*. This involves staff members visiting families at home to help them understand about child development and how to meet the developmental needs of their children. In addition, there is a programme in the north-east of Brazil that looks at rural children in poor areas (Health Exchange News, 2009).

Gupta (2005) examined concepts of childhood in mountain villages in the Himalayas. She found that the mountain communities were, on the whole, functioning well and that the impact of modernity on them was not helping them move forward, as anticipated, but rather making these traditional societies more fractured. The result is that the communities are losing confidence in their own abilities, their own styles of child-rearing, their own value systems. Gupta's view is that the space of traditional societies must be restored so that their confidence is regained and they can take their own initiatives.

Penn (2005) spent some time in Kazakhstan and highlighted the advantages to children of living in the old Soviet system. Children had freedom and mobility, showed respect for their elders, were part of extended families where child-rearing was shared. Children were thought of as valuable to society – principles upheld both by Soviet society and Central Asian nomadic culture. With the breakdown of the Soviet Union the kindergartens for children, the health services, the water and sanitation facilities broke down. Alongside this has come the impoverishment of women and children – not only in Kazakhstan but also in many of the countries that were part of the Soviet Union. In the first five years after transition the amount of gross domestic product spent on social security has decreased by about 90 per cent, and education and health spending by more than 50 per cent. Families are unable to protect children from the negative outcomes associated with this, despite the traditional pride families take in children.

Did you know that inequality in terms of income distribution in 2012 was greatest (meaning the gap between rich and poor was extremely wide) in five African countries and lowest in Denmark, Japan and Sweden? This is according to the Gini Index, which measures equality (where an index value of 0 represents absolute equality). No country attains or even nearly reaches this target. Income inequality, worldwide, is still with us.

Images of childhood and poverty

One of the most significant and neglected factors in discussions of child development is that of poverty. The United Nations Children's Fund report, published by UNICEF in 2005, stated that 90 per cent of the world's wealth was owned by only 10 per cent of the world's population. It appears that the poor of the world are getting poorer and many believe that this is caused by the International Monetary Fund and the World Bank imposing a free-market economy on the economies of Africa, Asia and South America. What this means is a cut in state expenditure on vital issues like health, welfare and education, reversing state ownerships of various things and removing or lowering barriers to free trade. For some countries these measure have been effective, but for many they have resulted in debt and retrenchment. Prout (2005) tells us that:

> Between 1998 and 1993 the real income of the world's poorest five per cent actually fell by over a quarter (UNICEF, 1996). In 1990 the annual income per person in high-income countries was 56 times greater than in low-income countries: by 1999 it was 63 times greater (UNICEF, 2001). The number of people struggling to survive on less than $1 per day (the international measure of absolute poverty) rose by ten million for every year of the 1990s.
>
> (Prout, 2005: 18)

The ways in which poverty itself are depicted and the effect that poverty has on the lives of children and families is something deserving attention. For the millions of children across the developing world, living without clean water, sanitation, health care or enough food, life is difficult. Parents often struggle to know how to deal with the problems they face. Often these parents are characterised as inadequate or uncaring when in reality they are merely overwhelmed by what life has dealt them. Descriptions of the lives of such families abound: Nancy Scheper-Hughes (1993) writes of the neglect and resulting high infant mortality rate in the *favelas* of Northeast Brazil and Phillipe Bourgois (1998) of similar issues in the *barrios* of New York where he worked with Puerto Rican families.

Poverty is also an issue in the developed world and current economic policies are ensuring that the divides between the rich and poor in the USA, Japan and Europe are still increasing. This was recently and poignantly illustrated by the impact of the earthquake and subsequent tsunami that devastated much of the rural and coastal regions of highly developed Japan. Many of those worst affected were the poorest and weakest people – the elderly, the ill and children. The state did intervene but was hampered in its success by the terrible nuclear accident that followed. In Japan as in some other developed countries the existence of a form of welfare state provides some protection from the more heinous effects of poverty. Nonetheless the differences between the most affluent and the poorest continue to grow and there has been a particular impact on children. In the OECD study carried out by Oxley *et al.* in 2001, of 17 developed countries, 12 showed a growing inequality between the children of the rich and the poor. A more recent OECD report (2011) presents some more optimistic findings, such as that growth in the developed world has outpaced that in advanced economies for more than ten years; China, which once accounted for over one-third of global poverty, now accounts for less than one-sixth. It became the leading trade partner of Brazil, South Africa and India and was set to surpass Germany as the world's largest trading nation in 2010.

Today poverty is becoming more and not less of an issue. I wrote the previous sentence in 2005 and it is sad that this is even more true now, in 2013. Tony Blair, Labour prime minister at the time, had promised to end child poverty by 2020. He did not succeed but the Labour government did manage to give nearly a million children a more secure childhood and a better future. But in 2012 the Centre for Social Justice published a paper called *Rethinking Child Poverty* that totally misrepresented what had been achieved by the Labour government and reframed poverty as being an issue about morality and behaviour, citing things like poor parenting, adult addiction, worklessness and family breakdown as the causes. So lack of money is seen as a symptom rather than as a cause of poverty. In England, as in much of the developed world in 2012, poverty not only remains an issue but is perceived as being nothing requiring the help of the state (*Observer*, 2012).

Penn (2005) argues that even within the poorest groups there are some positive aspects associated with poverty. She points to the findings of Rahnema and Bawtree (1997), who found that within poor communities life was not meaningless, but grounded in a valuable non-consumerist way of living. There may be some truth in this, although critics find it a somewhat romanticised view of poverty. We must not abandon the battle against child poverty.

Representations of children: children as players

We have seen how childhood has been an intensively regulated phase of life with decisions about the lives of children made almost entirely by adults. It was only towards the end of the last century that the view of children as social beings – as players in their own life stories – began to be accepted as a principle. This was evidenced by the rights of children being encoded in Article 12 of the UN Convention on the Rights of the Child, which states:

> States Parties shall assure to the child who is capable of forming his or her own views the right to express those views freely in all matters that affect the child, the views of the child being given due weight in accordance with the age and maturity of the child.
>
> For this purpose, the child shall in particular be provided the opportunity to be heard in any judicial and administrative proceedings affecting the child, either directly, or through a representative or an appropriate body, in a manner consistent with the procedural rules of national law.

Mayall *et al.* (1996) have looked at children's views on health and worked with them in schools, treating them as social actors. Children are a minority group in the sense that they lack power to influence their own lives. They may well have views and even be able to articulate these and be heard. But the decisions to be made remain remote from them. There are a range of constraints that stop them from being full participants. What Mayall *et al.* do is to link the sociological study of children in schools to a political agenda that goes beyond the notion of rights.

Some slow progress is being made in the area of children as actors, as people begin to reflect on how the previously dualistic versions of childhood (for example, as a time of innocence vs. as a time of evil) made it difficult for children to be perceived of as anything other than dependent. However, now, in countries throughout the world children are becoming social actors for justice. Some of the examples of this come from South Asia where 45 per cent of the population lives below the income required to meet minimum daily needs and where the disparities between rich and poor are becoming some of the widest in the world (Mahbub ul Haq, 1999). Children are beginning to ask out loud questions about fairness and justice. How fair and just a society is, is determined by who has the power and how it is used. Social justice implies justice for the poor, the marginalised, the exploited, the oppressed and the denied. Redistribution of wealth goes some way towards addressing these inequalities, but the notion of rights is important too. Children are emerging from their invisibility as both active citizens and social actors.

Raman (2000) points out that understanding the concept of childhood cannot be separated from understanding the wider context.

> The very definition of the selfhood, subject hood and personhood is deeply scripted by the larger context. The impact of macro-structures and processes operating at a wider societal level affect groups differentially determining the life-choices of groups and individuals.
>
> (Raman, 2000: 12)

O'Kane (2002) uses this to analyse how concepts of childhood have changed in South Asia. Culturally children in South Asia were not encouraged to express their views or to take part in decision making processes at any level. Children, she says, were seen as the property of their parents. Through the development of some children's collective organisations like the Bal Mazdoor Union (a union of child workers in Delhi) and Bhima Sangha (a union of working children in South India), both of which have been in existence for more than a decade, children have found a voice to express concerns about grave events. A case in point was the killing of 15-year-old worker Zaffar Imam by his employer in 1994, the deaths of three street children at the Government Observation Home at Delhi Gate, also in 1994, and the brutal killings of Gond tribal women and children in Nagpur. All of these cases were discussed by the children and this has been documented (Reddy, 2000 and White, 2001). The impact of this on the views of parents and the community are worth considering. How will views of childhood change over the coming decades? Theis (2001) suggests that there is an ongoing paradigm shift in relation to children and to childhoods. Changes at many levels will result from this – changes to theory and practice, attitudes and language, laws and rights.

Craig (2003) offers us some interesting case studies of projects aimed at involving children and young people working on sensitive issues including racism. One of these relates to work being done in Germany with Turkish mothers and children, and McIvor (1995) has reported on a project where disabled children in Morocco are challenging their dependent status and critically examining how they are both portrayed and viewed by others. People involved in immigration work in the UK are beginning to be aware of the silence of those children and young adults living in situations of great uncertainty and this is surely a field worth researching.

Becoming a good parent

Much has been said and written about the importance of parents in considerations of how children learn and develop. We do not have space here to explore patterns of child-rearing and parenting across time and cultures, but we do have time to consider how images of 'parenting' affect how we conceive of children and their development. We have seen how dominant Western views of child development have been and discussed how much of the work has been done with white middle-class children and their families. Underpinning much of the work has been the assumption that 'everybaby' lives in a home with two parents – a mother and a father. We know that this idealised family is reality for the minority of the world's children and have seen how poverty and disease impact on family structures.

Along with this has been the widely held view that the role of parents – particularly of mothers – is crucial in deciding the success of children. Intervention programmes, developed in response to the idea that poor children need the rich to intervene to provide more stimulation for the children (not to address poverty and inequality per se) offer advice to parents such as 'Speak to your children; read to them; use English with them; play games with them'. Lamb (1999) suggests that what is conveyed through the psychological literature about parenting includes the following:

- Children need to have two parents – one of each gender.
- Parents should divide up family responsibilities between them with the mothers being home makers, care-takers and child-rearers (because they are better suited to these roles) and the father earning the living.
- Young children should be cared for primarily within the family and by family members.
- White middle-class parents have superior parenting skills and thus have children who are more likely to excel.

You will know that even within the developed North this model of the idealised family is uncommon. Hochschild (2001) wrote about the care chain in America where middle-class American mothers employed women immigrants from the South to care for their children while the children of these migrant workers were left behind. We find this pattern here in the UK today, when many Eastern European women have come here to work in order to earn more money to support the children they have left behind. This pattern of well-to-do people depending on the poor to care for children at the expense of their own children is documented across time and place.

Currently in the UK there are many projects designed to 'teach' parents how to 'parent'. This is clearly based on some image of 'the good parent' and this, by definition, is a monocultural, over-simplified and Western model.

An image for the twenty-first century?

We have looked, briefly, at how the concepts of childhood and children change over time, place and circumstance. We have seen that how children are represented sometimes gives an indication of how they are perceived within a culture or group, remembering always that often only certain children are represented in literature or art or film. We have considered the pervasiveness of Western ideas in many discussions about children and their development and seen how vital aspects like poverty are ignored or discussed in pejorative ways, suggesting that simple solutions can solve the immense problems created.

We need an image of the child to work with for the purposes of this book. The image suggested by Loris Malaguzzi, founding father of the Reggio Emilia preschools, offers a meaning making child, situated in a culture, coming from a rich history and being enabled to make meaning, represent feelings and ideas and challenge existing structures. The image we hold of the child, is, as we have said, one of the factors that will determine how we conceive of development. Here is our twenty-first century child, drawn on the model suggested by Rinaldi (2006).

From birth she is engaged in building a relationship with the world and intent on experiencing it so that she develops a complex system of abilities, strategies for learning and ways of organising relationship. So she is able to make her own personal maps for her own development and orientation – social, cognitive, emotional and symbolic. She is making meaning from events from very early on and she will share her meanings through representations and language. She will make and take and share meanings through stories. She is a competent and active and critical child – thus one who might be described by the word challenging. Challenging is often used as a negative term but we use it to suggest that the child is challenging because she can produce change and movement in the various systems with which she is involved. These include the family, the setting, the school, the society. She is a player in her society. The child makes culture, values and rights and is competent in learning and in living. This child can explore a range of realities, can construct metaphors, seeing what is like what and why that matters. She can make and explore paradoxes, seeing what is different and why that matters. She can invent symbols and codes and use these to help her learn to decode the conventional means of symbolisation prevalent in her culture and community. Living within a community, she will learn from all those around her through interaction, watching, listening, being an apprentice and being a teacher.

Things to think about

- How do history and culture affect your understanding of child development?
- In what ways do poverty and rights affect the ways in which you think about how children develop and learn?
- How do you feel about seeing childhood as a separate and distinct phase? Does it allow you to take a broader view of development that encompasses the experience of all?
- Do you think that the dominance of privileged groups continues over generations? What do you see as the effects of this? Do you see this dominance as having an effect on how people in the developing world perceive their own customs, values, traditions and cultures?
- Should we, in the developed world, change, and if so how?

Chapter 2

The child as meaning maker
Making sense of the physical world

In this chapter we start to investigate the field of child development, which is often described as being a scientific exploration of how children learn and develop. In doing this we examine the work of Jean Piaget, one of the key theorists in the field of child development, and examine what he said about how the human infant, from birth onwards, begins to make meaning in order to understand the world and the objects in it. Piaget had a tremendous impact on our understanding, but his work has been criticised on a number of grounds. We look at his work and his critics.

> In a restaurant a small child and her older sister are each given a balloon attached to a long shiny thread. The older child is interested in the balloon and stares intently at it watching how it moves when she pulls the string. The younger child immediately puts the thread in her mouth and uses her tongue and her lips to explore it. What questions can she be asking as she does this? She is clearly using her tongue and lips which are very sensitive to get a feeling of the sleekness of the thread. It is only by chance that she notices the balloon attached to her thread when her sister laughs when the two balloons collide. The look of amazement on her face is wonderful.
> (Personal observation notes, 2002)

From conception to birth

It takes about 40 weeks from conception to birth. For nine months the human infant inhabits its first environment. Housed in the mother's watery womb the foetus develops as cells divide and multiply to become organs – the eyes, ears, heart and lungs, brain and pancreas, stomach and bowels – until the human foetus is ready to live independently and outside of the womb. Born into a world of light and noise and smell and sensation the infant starts to demonstrate an extraordinary capacity to learn and develop from the moment of birth. Indeed, there are many theorists who suggest that there is evidence of learning even before birth. Some of this is described here.

Although it is dark in the womb there is evidence that if a bright light is shone on the foetus in the womb three months before birth, the foetus responds by making a sudden movement. This suggests that the foetus is able to use sight to detect a change in the light in the womb. Similarly, if a heavy object is placed on the womb the foetus tends to push against it with some part of her own body. This suggests that the foetus is able to both detect and respond to pressure. The womb is not a silent place. The foetus is able to hear the sounds of the mother's heartbeat and the rumble of the amniotic fluid and the sound of voices. From the response of infants to the sound of the mother's voice immediately after birth there is evidence that before birth the foetus is able to tune in to the pitch and intonation patterns of the mother's voice (Karmiloff-Smith, 1994).

After nine months of sharing the mother's physiology, the baby releases hormones into the mother's bloodstream and it is this that triggers labour. Birth itself is regarded by many as traumatic, and there is evidence that immediately after birth the infant is more alert and awake than she will be for some time to come. The reason for this is that the infant's adrenaline levels have soared to enable the baby to cope with the traumatic changes from the relative quiet and gloom of the womb, through the birth canal and into the unfamiliar, bright and noisy world. It is at this stage in much of the developed world that certain medical tests are carried out on infants. These tests aim to check that the baby is responding appropriately to a range of stimuli.

The child as empty vessel?

In Chapter 1 we looked at how views of children and of childhood change over time and place. The human infant born anywhere in the world from Africa to North America and beyond, actively seeks to discover and understand the world that she inhabits. We are so accustomed to thinking about human infants as active learners that we struggle to understand how they could, for so many years, have been viewed as no more than blank slates or empty vessels.

One of the earliest thinkers in the field of child development was Burrhus Skinner. He was an American psychologist who followed the school of behaviourism, which emphasised the importance of the external world on development. He was interested in what could be seen and heard and tested and not interested in feelings or motives or intentions. His focus was on the observable aspects of behaviour at the expense of the hidden internal processes. For him, the child was the sum total of her genetic inheritance, past history and current situation. In summary, he believed that responses to an action can either increase or decrease the likelihood of that action being repeated. An action that is regarded as desirable (like saying thank you) can be reinforced by a reward – a kiss or a smile or a sweet, for example. This positive reinforcement, repeated again and again, is what helps the child learn that saying thank you is a good thing to do. Swearing, on the other hand, might be negatively reinforced by a reprimand, being sent to bed without supper or even being smacked. The child learns that swearing should not be repeated. It is a model of learning and development that depends on the child doing something and the subsequent response from the adult that determines whether the action is rewarded or not. Those familiar with the work of Pavlov will recognise this model of learning: Pavlov used the term *operant conditioning* to describe it. The organism (in the case of Skinner, the child) does something (the stimulus) and the adult involved responds (the response). This stimulus–response model is both simple and crude and cannot account for the subtle and complex aspects of learning.

The child as active learner?

It is important to note that Jean Piaget was the first Western theorist to consider the infant as more than a blank slate waiting to be written on. By training he was a biologist and he used his investigations of how organisms adapt to the environment to inform the studies he made of children's cognitive development and thinking. Through acute observations of his own children he concluded that the human infant was actively seeking to make sense. He noted that the human infant is born with the ability to adapt to and learn from the environment. This is not surprising to us but was revolutionary at the time. Essentially, then, learning is the result of interaction between the child and the environment. Through this interaction the child takes information from the environment and uses this to change what Piaget called *'mental structures'*. He believed that cognitive development took place through three processes, which he called *accommodation, assimilation* and *equilibrium*. The language he used makes his theories seem daunting, but with some unpicking they become more accessible.

Assimilation can be thought of like this:

- The infant takes in or assimilates every new experience or event and adds this to an existing and ever-growing store of memories and/or understandings.
- Through these repeated additions the infant is later able to classify and order experiences and meaning.

Accommodation means that:

- Sometimes an experience or event challenges some earlier understanding and when this happens some mental adjustment has to be made.
- Something about a new experience may mean that the child has to accommodate an earlier understanding in order to adapt to the environment.

For Piaget accommodation was a *higher-order cognitive process* than assimilation and he saw it as the process that allows human beings to become the effective problem-solvers they so patently are. Piaget believed that the goal of every child, every learner, was cognitive equilibrium. It is important to state that cognitive equilibrium or balance can only ever be partially achieved as a stepping stone to more adequate forms of knowing. Piaget used the phrase *'active learner'* to indicate his theory that the human infant is never passive in the learning process but is mentally or cognitively active and pro-active in seeking to make sense of the world.

Meadows (1993) gives an amusing example to help readers understand the difficult concepts of assimilation and accommodation. She adds an additional dimension that she calls organisation. Her example relates to an experienced cook who has a history of having successfully cooked both carrots and potatoes. She has boiled, roasted, fried and mashed potatoes and made them into chips. She has boiled carrots, grated them for salad and made them into soup. So she has used a range of methods for successfully preparing these two vegetables.

A matrix can be drawn up as follows, see Table 2.1. Note that x indicates a successful attempt.

The cook is then introduced to parsnips for the first time. She assimilates parsnips into the carrot category, because they are similar in shape and texture. She is able to boil them and make them into a soup – a rather bland soup, it must be said. She grates them for a salad but they look unattractive. She is also able to assimilate them into her potato category. They mash well, can be chipped or fried and are, says Meadows, delicious roasted.

A second matrix then is given, see Table 2.2.

Table 2.1 Matrix 1: Carrots and potatoes (source: Meadows, 1993: 199)

Method	Carrots	Potatoes
Boiling	x	x
Chipping	Not tried	x
Frying	Not tried	x
Grating, for salad	x	Not tried
Mashing	Not tried	x
Roasting	Not tried	x
Soup	x	Not tried

Table 2.2 Matrix 2: Carrots, potatoes and parsnips (source: Meadows, 1993: 199–200)

Method	Carrots	Potatoes	Parsnips
Boiling	x	x	x
Chipping	Not tried	x	Possible
Frying	Not tried	x	Possible
Grating, for salad	x	Not tried	Maybe
Mashing	Not tried	x	x
Roasting	Not tried	x	x
Soup	x	Not tried	Maybe

Meadows goes on to add that assimilation is always accompanied by accommodation. So the schema of what we might call 'mashable vegetables' now consists not only of potatoes but includes parsnips and with repeated experience of root vegetables (with the possible addition of butter) can be extended eventually to include carrots, Jerusalem artichokes and so on.

Some examples illustrating children using assimilation and accommodation illustrate these concepts and make their meaning more apparent:

> Thandi has had experience of drinking milk from her bottle and does so with ease. We could say that she is a skilled bottle-drinker. She can grasp and lift the bottle, put it to her lips and drink from it. When her carer puts a new bottle in front of her, a bottle that is much larger and full of milk, she attempts to assimilate this new object into her schema of grasping and drinking and in doing this she draws on her experience of bottles. But she finds that although she can grasp the bottle she cannot lift it because it is too heavy. The only way in which she can accommodate to this new situation is to seek help and the only way in which she can do this is to cry. Her mother lifts the bottle for her and they hold it together while she drinks.
>
> Eleni has been drinking from a cup for some time now. When an empty cup is placed in front of her she asks for a drink. Her behaviour demonstrates that she responds appropriately according to her previous experience of a familiar situation and this could be explained as having reached equilibrium.
>
> (Drawn from observation notes of early childhood students, 2003)

The concept of equilibrium or equilibration is a complex one and one that many writers find difficult to explain, partly because Piaget's own definitions seemed to change over time, but it does appear to be closely related to the emphasis in his theory on the fact that all cognition is directed to a *logico-mathematical model*. This is another concept that needs exploration and is at first reading difficult to understand. Piaget considered a logical operation to be an internalised, mental action, part of a logical system. Logical operations are things like *seriation* (being able to organise things in a logical sequence), *classification* (being able to sort things into categories on some logical basis of similarity or difference, inclusion or exclusion) and *numeration*. We will look more closely at each of these:

- *Seriation*   Seriation is said to refer to the understanding of the relationships of position in space and in time. The child explores and comes to understand things like height and length and width. A classic example is when a child demonstrates the ability to work out which stick is longer by using a third stick of intermediate length.

  The two sticks whose length the child is comparing are sticks A and B. Stick C, which is the stick of intermediate length, is clearly shorter than stick A but longer than stick B. The child compares stick A with stick C and makes some judgement about its length and then compares the intermediate stick C to stick B. What is required is that the child can understand, remember and store what has been found out and then apply these double relationship of C with A and C with B. The child can only do this when she has reached the stage of concrete operations.

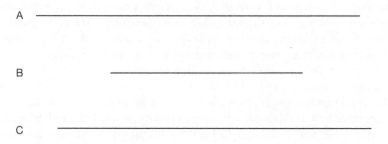

Figure 2.1

- *Classification*   Classification involves the child in being able to consider things like inclusion and exclusion. Piaget's famous (or perhaps infamous) example is one where children are asked questions about a bead necklace made up of seven brown and three white beads. The children are asked 'Are there more beads, or are there more brown beads?' It is important to pay close attention to how the question is phrased. Can you answer this question? In Piaget's terminology the superordinate class (the one that includes everything) is that of beads and the subordinate class (the one that is included in the superordinate class) is that of brown beads. Not surprisingly young children find this nonsensical question difficult to answer and mainly respond by saying there are more brown beads. The analysis of this you may well make is that the younger children are being extremely rational and logical in giving this response because the question makes little sense. But Piaget's explanation is that younger children have not logically recognised the relationship between the set and the subset.

- *Numeration* Numeration is a combination of seriation and classification. Young children count objects, but Piaget believed that it was only with an understanding of both seriation and classification that they come to understand numbers as a sequence and are then able to classify them into sets of classes and sub-classes. Much doubt has been thrown on these concepts and Piaget's findings. They are cited here only to try and explain something about logico-mathematical reasoning.

An important aspect of Piaget's work is often claimed to be that it allowed those studying child development to begin to think about cognitive development as a process. Learning takes place and provides a foundation for future learning. This highlights clearly how children are actively constructing knowledge about the world. The cognitive structures and processes allow them to actively select what about the input is meaningful to them and then to represent, re-represent and transform what they have selected in accordance with their current understanding. Flavell tells us that it is the 'active nature of their intellectual commerce with the environment [that] makes them to a large degree the manufacturers of their own development' (1992: 998).

A linear approach to development

One of the things you will almost certainly already know is Piaget's famous *stage theory*. Observing how children grow and change over time, he saw development as linear (progressing in a line) and suggested there were four major cognitive stages in the development of logic and thinking. He saw these stages as corresponding to four successive forms of knowledge and believed that during each of these stages children were thinking and reasoning in different ways. For Piaget the stages were age related although some writers on Piaget suggest that the ages of attainment he gave were only approximate (Goswami, 2001). This is very much open to debate and this aspect of his work has been much criticised. Nonetheless, his stage theory, in particular, has influenced many aspects of how children are educated in Britain, in the USA and in much of Europe and many people find it difficult to think of learning in a less linear fashion. Piaget's stages are as follows:

1   The sensory-motor period: 0–2 years.
2   The period of pre-operations: 2–7 years.
3   The period of concrete operations: 7–11 years.
4   The period of formal operations: 11–12 years and upward.

We will look at each of these in turn.

The sensory-motor phase

In this phase cognition was seen as being based on physical interaction with the world. Piaget saw thought as developing from action. It is as though infant meaning-seekers use all the means available to them in their earliest development. These are their senses and their own movements and it is these that they use to try and make sense of every encounter with objects, people and events, asking 'What is this?' and then, perhaps, 'What does it do?' and still later, 'What can I do with it?' Anyone familiar with infants will recognise their incessant exploration of the physical world and appreciate Piaget's suggestion that this is neither random nor haphazard, but a construction of meaning. As Goswami puts it, 'sensory-motor behaviours *became* thought' (2001: 260). Central to development in this period is the concept of *object permanence* and it is here, again, that many critics feel unhappy with Piaget's explanations. For Piaget, it is only at the age of about 15 to 18 months that the infant is able to retain the concept of object permanence. This means that the human infant, up to that age, is not able to appreciate that an object or a person, hidden from view, still exists. Piaget suggests that this is because the infant is unable to create and sustain a *cognitive representation* (by which he meant an image or a memory) of the object or person. When the object or person is no longer visible the infant cannot call up a memory or representation of it. For many critics this view is unacceptable, suggesting as it does that true and meaningful cognitive activity is delayed for so long.

Research in the USA suggested that infants as young as 5 months old can make mental images or representations of objects. Luo *et al.* (2003) carried out an experiment on 5-month-old infants; they were shown a tall cylinder moving back and forth behind a low screen. The experimental hypothesis was that the infants would form a prediction based on the experience of seeing two objects and when one or both objects were obscured (or had 'disappeared') the infants would show surprise. This would indicate that they were paying attention to the strange event. The measure for paying attention usually means watching for a longer period of time.

Piaget's views on the inability of the young child to make mental images were related to the view he held that children in the sensory-motor stage were essentially *egocentric* in their thinking. By egocentric he meant they have an inability to perceive the world from the perspective of anybody else. This is another of his ideas that has been seriously challenged.

The pre-operational phase

In this phase (between 2 and 7 years of age), Piaget suggested, ideas about the properties and the relationships of concrete objects developed. And it was here that he found evidence of this egocentrism. He saw the child as solving all problems and interpreting the world in terms of the self. For him the child at this stage was essentially unable to use logical thinking and was locked into a subjective understanding of the world.

The concrete operations phase

During the next stage egocentricity starts to wane; the child begins to be able to *decentre* (or consider multiple aspects of any situation at the same time) and achieves some understanding of *reversibility* (the understanding that any operation or action on an object implies its inverse or its opposite). The development of concrete operational mental structures such as *classification* (grouping things that are the same or similar for some reason), *seriation* (arranging things in some logical sequence or order) and conservation (the understanding that despite apparent visible changes some things remain constant or the same) characterise thinking during this stage.

Some of the most vociferous criticisms of Piaget's work relate to the experiments he devised and conducted to assess how well children were able to conserve ideas of number or mass or weight. Conservation, for him, was a key logical concept that underpins the understanding of invariance and this is essential in understanding, for example, number systems. Put more simply, children cannot manipulate numbers until they know that two is always two. This applies whatever the objects – two cars, two dogs, two children. Whatever the objects, the number remains the same. His classic experiments required the child to compare two initially identical situations, one of which was later changed in some way.

To illustrate this let us look at the conservation of number. A child is shown two rows of beads arranged in an array demonstrating one-to-one correspondence. While the child watches, the adult re-arranges one of the rows of beads, making the spaces between the beads wider so that the arrays are no longer visually identical. Piaget found that most children under the age of about 7 said, when asked, that there were more beads in the array where the beads were more widely spaced. Was this an example of an inability to conserve quantity? Or was there something about the test situation itself that suggested to the child that the adult required an answer other than the obvious one? (Remember, the child had watched the adult moving the beads!)

Margaret Donaldson (1978) was a stern critic of some of Piaget's ideas and she felt that the test itself was flawed. She and a colleague developed a new test (now known as the 'naughty teddy' test) where the children were told that they were going to play a game and were given a cardboard box that contained a teddy bear. The children were told that the teddy had been very naughty and kept escaping from the box to mess up the toys and spoil the game. Two identical rows of conservation beads (just like those described above) were brought out and the children were asked, 'Are there more here or more here, or are they both the same number?' Then the naughty teddy appeared and began to mess about, moving the beads on one array. The teddy was scolded and the children asked the same question again. Most of the children (even those as young as 4) were able to 'conserve'. In this meaningful context, where there was a reason for the beads to have been moved, the children were not trapped by the seemingly nonsensical question asked in the original experiments. They showed that where they could draw on their experience and the context, they could conserve.

The formal operations phase

This final stage is achieved with the child able to generate hypotheses and think scientifically. One of the most significant aspects of thinking at this stage is reasoning by analogy. Analogy is where one thing is said to be like another because of something they have in common. This requires the thinker to reason about what the similarities between objects might be. Young children, you will remember, were said not to be able to do this.

Here is an example cited by Goswami (2001). The analogy is *bicycle is to handlebars as ship is to . . . ?*' (The answer, you will have worked out if you know anything about ships, is 'ship's wheel'.) When Piaget gave a pictorial version of this to young children they gave answers like 'bird' and when questioned found similarities to justify their responses. One example quoted by Goswami is of the child giving a perfectly acceptable response – 'ships and birds are both found on the lake'. Piaget's explanation, however, was that children solved analogies on the basis of associations and their inability to solve some of the analogies he explained as being the result of lack of knowledge. How many young children would have understood that the question related to the way in which bicycles and ships were steered, for example?

Goswami and Brown (1989) carried out a series of pictorial item analogies with very young children and based these on the types of relationships young children would have experienced and hence understood. Again, more recent thinkers like Goswami and Brown ensured that their test situations allow children to draw on context and their own experience. An example of this is *'chocolate is to melted chocolate as snowman is to . . .?'* Or *'play doh is to cut play doh as apple is to . . .?'* Remember that these were in pictorial form. The finding that children as young as 3 are able to think analogically is an interesting one.

Much criticism has been made of the linear and age-related stage theory posited by Piaget. Critics feel that although children do develop and change over time, not all learning is linear and learners often resort to strategies that they have successfully used earlier in life. An example is what adult learners do when they are faced with a new technological gadget. Piaget might have suggested that the experienced learner, operating at the stage of formal operations, might use their prior learning and experience in order to know that the best thing to do might be to read the documents that accompany the new gadget. In effect, often what happens is that learners use their movements and senses in order to try and work out what they can do with the new gadget. Piaget, you will remember, believed that the thinking was different at each stage and that a child could only progress to the next stage once the requirements of the previous stage had been met. It is an approach that focuses on what learners cannot yet do.

Schemas: repeated patterns of action

One of the features of exploration Piaget noted was the tendency of young children to repeat patterns of action or behaviour. Piaget used the term *'schema'* to describe these repeated patterns (although, as Athey (1990) noted, there is some debate over whether there are different meanings for the words 'scheme' and 'schema'). We will describe schemas as patterns of actions (or behaviours) that can be repeated. This repetition allows learners to come to be able to categorise and then classify objects, behaviours and events. Some examples will help to make this clear.

Early patterns of motor behaviour that are repeatable are things like grasping and shaking of objects and tracking and gazing at objects. Later patterns include things like exploring rotation, verticality, enveloping and so on. Much has been written about schemas and how an understanding of them enables educators and others to see the purposefulness of children's sometimes seemingly random and haphazard explorations. You may often hear people talking about children's repeated behaviours as though they are senseless. One of the most important things we learn from Piaget is how to attend to what we see children doing and listen to what they are saying in our search for the meaning-making child. Athey (1990) suggests that the history of a particular schema is important. If early schemas are applied in different contexts and through diverse events, the child will have assimilated a broad range of contents.

Recent developments in neuropsychology are finding links between brain activity and schematic behaviour. Their findings are tentative and their use of the term 'schema' is rather different than ours. If this is an area that interests you, you are referred to the work of people like Arbib *et al.* (1987) and Tse *et al.* (2007).

Hunt, writing as long ago as 1961, believed that it is through schematic behaviour that learning takes place and knowledge is acquired. The assumption is that the more the experiences and the more diverse the experiences, the better the learning. This is something we will return to later in this book. An example might make this clearer:

> Abdul grasps whatever is placed in his hand – his mother's finger, a spoon, a toy. This is a reflex response in this newborn child. With time and experience, however, this reflex grasp becomes elaborated and Abdul can soon reach out, curling and retracting his fingers. Theorists suggest that, as this happens, there are changes in brain function as electrochemical pathways in the brain lay down what may be called a mental map of the grasping response. For Abdul, what is happening is movement and the sensation of grasping different objects. This enables Abdul to develop a disposition or a desire or a habit to grasp objects and within time Abdul uses the grasp purposefully, in order to hold something, and later still Abdul will grasp one object rather than another – making a choice. This is the progression from simple reflex to more complex schema and this is only possible because he has a mental map or a mental representation of the actions.
>
> (Observation note made by an early childhood studies student, 2000)

Making sense of symbols

Piaget was interested in the idea of *symbolic representation* or symbolic functioning. Young children become more and more able to represent things or events they have experienced symbolically. This can be in the form of representational thought – images or ideas that are internal and not accessible to outside view, or external in the form of drawings, models, speech or symbolic play. To begin with children symbolically draw on and represent or re-present (which means to present again) objects or events they have experienced. The educators in the famous nursery schools in the Reggio Emilia region of Italy often talk about the importance of representing and re-representing experiences and ideas. They see this as an essential way in which children can explore ideas and feelings, thoughts and emotions. Piaget, you will remember, retained a focus on the cognitive importance of representation. Representation, then, means the ability to play over and over again, in the mind, the way things look or feel or the patterns of movements made or felt. The term *action images* is used by Athey (1990) to describe the sort of symbolic representation we will all be familiar with where, for example, a child uses a stick to be a gun, a block to be a mobile phone or a bucket to be a hat.

Here is a wonderful example where Gillian Allery (a student on a degree programme in Early Childhood Education in 1998) tracked what Colin (aged 2 years and 7 months) did when playing in the garden of the setting. She noticed him put a football in a mop bucket and use the football as a baby and the mop bucket as a pram. Here is an extract from her observation notes:

> Anabel, aged 4½, came over to Colin.
> 'Can I have the ball, Colin?'

Colin looked at her. He seemed puzzled. She picked the ball up and kicked it away from her.

'Nooo!' Colin cried and ran after the ball . . .

Colin picked up the ball. 'Don't run away, baby. It's all right,' he said lovingly. He then put the ball under his arm and pulled the bucket over to a small chair. He sat down on the chair and put the ball in the bucket. 'Going shops in a minute, baby, shops and sweets, baby, yeah?' he said.

(Allery, 2010: 30)

Coming to understand how one thing can stand for or represent another is important in view of the fact that much that children encounter will be *symbolic*. In the developed world and much of the developing world children will encounter signs and symbols and in the same way as they try to make sense of the physical world they will try to make sense of this symbolic world. Most obviously the symbols they will encounter will include the relatively simple-to-decode pictorial symbols, but also numeric symbols, alphabetic symbols and the many signs and symbols that define a culture. Gunther Kress (1997) uses the terms *semiotics*, *signs* and *symbols* to clarify thinking about this:

- Semiotics is the study of the meaning of systems of signs. (Language is a system of signs and so is clothing.)
- Signs are a combination of meaning and form. (The form of a road sign, for example, is something made of metal and the meaning relates to some information or warning about roads and/or traffic.)
- Symbols encapsulate and convey meaning. (The numeral two means more than one and less than three: the letters c-a-t in English represent the animal cat; the red cross indicates a place where help for the injured or sick can be given.)

You will appreciate from this that the young child, faced with making sense of these systems of signs, is actually confronted with learning how to 'read' the world. This is something else we will return to in later chapters.

From Piaget we have learned that the child is curious and actively trying to understand the objects, people and experiences encountered. Piaget's focus was very much on how knowledge was constructed and his model of the child was close to that of Kant, of the child being born with structures that allow her to make sense of the world. So knowledge is *constructed* through interaction with the environment and developmental change is qualitative and occurs through a series of stages.

Rationality and the child as developing scientist

Cannella and Viruru (2004) argue that Piaget's notion of the importance of *equilibration* supports the notion of the child as miniature scientist. For Piaget, the child identifies some problem in understanding or interpreting an aspect of the world and tries out some hypotheses in an attempt to solve the problem. The importance of logical thinking is highlighted whilst the senses and the emotions are no longer emphasised (Silin, 1995). For Piaget, learning is an individual activity with a focus on concepts. Some writers suggest that this had led to vital aspects of learning and exploration being ignored in favour of this logico-mathematical approach. Critics like Egan (1988) focus on the absence of fantasy, whilst Tobin (1997) adds the absence of pleasure.

Prout and James (1990/1997) state that there are three key themes in Western theories of child development, one of which they call *'rationality'*. Being rational means being able to use logical reasoning and hence being able to think mathematically. According to Piaget, the child only reaches this stage of thought in adolescence and the implications of this is that early thinking is irrational and children are apprentice thinkers in terms of rationality until they reach Piaget's stage of formal operations. For many researchers and theorists this approach represents both an over-simplification of rationality and marginalises children's intellectual capacities. There are examples of very young children demonstrating a deep understanding of issues like injustice, war, fear, danger and so on. Bolloten and Spafford (1998) cite the case study of Saeed, a refugee from the war in Northern Somalia, in a Year 5 class in the UK. He wrote about his experiences as in the example quoted here:

> Once me and my mum had to change our names and lie about who we were so we could go in a house and have enough to eat and sleep there for the night. That night we had to be disguised.
>
> (Bolloten and Spafford, 1998: 120)

During the apartheid years in South Africa children were routinely detained, arrested, tortured and even killed. At the Harare Conference many children testified to their horrific experiences. Here is a small part of the testimony of 12-year-old Moses Madia (re-written by a lawyer to whom he recounted his experiences). He describes sharing a cell with his 14-year-old friend Charlie and explains that he was unable to eat because he felt nauseous:

> and on various occasions dizzy and disoriented. I found it difficult to sleep and consequently I felt very tired with the result that when the nausea occurred I often broke down crying. I have no idea why I was arrested and detained as I have committed no illegal acts, nor been involved in any unrest or violence of any sort.
>
> (Brittain and Minty, 1988: 8)

Here is a child perfectly capable of rational thought and a complex analysis of the horrors he experienced.

After the horrors of apartheid in South Africa, the new government had an enormous number of issues to address and included in these was the protection of the rights of children. Built into the constitution, which was ratified in 1996, was a bill of rights that guarantees children four rights – to survival, to development, to protection and to participation. And the new curriculum developed for all schools set out that the purposes of language in the curriculum include the categories *political* and *critical*. Political gives all children the right to assert or challenge power, persuade others about respecting diverse viewpoints and develop and sustain identities. Critical gives all children the skills to understand and challenge the relationship between language, power and identity and the dynamic nature of culture and resistance to persuasion.

The notion of an 'everybaby'

The type of scientific approach to studying child development we have been examining in this chapter is based largely on observations and experiments carried out in North

America and Europe. It is important to note that only 18 per cent of the world's children live in these areas and the studies were carried out primarily on the children of white middle-class parents – which represents an even smaller percentage. Yet so pervasive have these findings been in schools and universities in the developed world that a notion of universality has emerged. It is as though Piaget's typical child is a model for all children – or what Gottlieb (2004) calls an *'everybaby'*. There are sociologists, cultural psychologists and anthropologists who would question whether universality – which implies ignoring context and history – can scientifically or ethically be applied to a study of children.

You may well be familiar with the notion of developmental milestones. Much has been written about these and the suggestion that children reach particular milestones at particular ages is possibly another feature of 'everybaby'. It is interesting, then, to note that studies in Africa suggest that the ages at which African children reach particular behavioural milestones indicate that they develop at a faster rate than American children. Can this possibly be so? Richter and Griesel (1994) have shown that South African infants have significantly higher psychomotor and mental development scores on the Bayley Scales of Infant Development. Possible reasons put forward to explain such differences include looking closely at child-rearing practices – some of which include things like carrying the infant in an upright position, which may foster earlier neuromuscular development. The details are interesting but the suggestion that development will vary according not only to individual and group but also to culture and context is vital. Two case studies illustrate the wide differences between children of the same age, growing up in different contexts and cultures:

> Two-year-old Zakes is sent to the market to buy things and has routine jobs to do within the context of his African family. For example, he sometimes takes messages to the neighbours and often helps with the cleaning and the cooking of food. Independence is fostered.

> Two-year-old Alex has no role to play within his family. He has his own room, equipped with many toys, and is often to be found watching cartoons on the video. He sleeps in a child's bed, has low chairs to sit on and has no independence.

In Chapter 6 we will explore in depth the impact and importance of culture and context.

The child as individual

Child development studies in the developed world are characterised by the notion of the ideal child as an individual. We are used to considering the importance of each child – thinking about each child's preferences, fears, experiences, strengths and weaknesses. Educators in the developed world promote ideas of self-confidence and self-esteem, separateness and individuality.

But this, too, is not universal. For many children the notion of *the group* and *the community* is essential to thriving and survival. Penn (2001) cites the examples of children in Mongolia who are taught to consider the needs of others and to avoid noise, disturbance and discord. Similarly LeVine (2003) speaks of communities where children are expected to develop self-restraint and mutual tolerance.

Closely associated with the concept of the ideal individual child are notions of consumerism, because the individual child's tastes and needs must be catered for through the provision of specialist toys, foods and possessions. A walk around a nursery school in the developed world will reveal the wide range of materials, equipment and toys specially designed to meet the perceived needs of young children as they make sense of their world. In Southern India, Viruru (2001) describes a typical nursery where frugality is what underpins the pedagogical approach. This is not because there is insufficient money to purchase specialist play materials. Rather, the underpinning philosophy is that material possessions are unimportant and that a good Hindu should not be overwhelmed by worldly goods.

The implications

Piaget, with his strong emphasis on the active learner, presented an image of the generic child as male – a constructor, an explorer and individual in control of his own learning and his environment. This was almost inevitable when one considers the time and place of his work. Nonetheless, critics including Cannella and Viruru (2004) suggest that the female learner – although still potentially acquiring logico-mathematical reasoning – may receive contradictory ideas from society and culture, things associated with independence, individuality, reasoning, negotiation, compromise, passivity and/or dependence. They also argue that the emphasis on individuality may allow for the denial of group issues like gender, class, race and culture. Walkerdine (1988) was convinced that Piaget's logic, although designed to promote a rational and democratic society, also created a generic child 'to meet the egocentric, ethnocentric needs of the European male child' (Cannella and Viruru, 2004: 94). Finally, there is the issue of Piaget's child-centredness, which may create nothing more than an illusion of freedom. The question critics need to ask is whether this freedom applies not only to Piaget's ideal child but also to those who are not male, nor white, nor adult, nor always rational.

Summing up

In this chapter we have looked primarily at the work of Jean Piaget and his thoughts on how children come to make meaning through their explorations of the world. You may have noted that in his work, with its emphasis on the individual child set on a linear path towards rational thought, there is little mention of the role of others in learning. Piaget saw the child as active constructor of knowledge and believed that this constructive process was universal and came about through the interaction between the individual learner and the physical environment. His is a complex theory and a very influential one, despite criticism of many aspects. He is possibly prime amongst the theorists known as constructivists. We have also looked at those who criticised his work and at how the notion of the little scientist, the universal child, does not allow us to account for the huge diversity we encounter when we broaden our palette to encompass all the world's children. In Chapter 3 we turn our attention to the work of theorists who might be described as social constructivists.

Things to think about

• Have you had to re-evaluate your ideas about the contribution made by Piaget to your understanding of child development? If so, in what way?

- What is your response to the notion of the universal child, termed 'everybaby' in this chapter?
- Is your image of the developing infant that of a miniature scientist? If not, what is missing in this image?

Chapter 3

The child as meaning maker
Making sense of the social world

In this chapter we move on to looking at the child as a member of the social world. There are two distinct aspects to this. The first is the role that others (both peers and adults) play in the learning and development of the child and the second is how the child comes to understand the social world. The key theorist whose work we look at in this chapter is the Russian psychologist, Lev Vygotsky. If you find what you learn about him interesting you can read more about his ideas in *Introducing Vygotsky* (Smidt, 2009).

> Fatih and Darinder are both in a nursery. They are 3 years old. They are playing with magnets. An adult is watching them. The children use the magnets to try and pick up objects – a wooden toothpick, a plastic glue pot, a sponge. Nothing happens. Then Fatih tries a paper clip and a metal pencil sharpener and when the sharpener starts to move towards the magnet he is delighted. The adult asks, 'I wonder why that is happening?' Darinder wants to have a go and then says to Fatih, 'Some things worked, didn't they and some didn't.' They decide to sort the things on the table into two piles – those that stick and those that don't. After a while the children use the magnets to pick up all the metal things and they comment that some things are still on the table. The adult asks why and Darinder replies, 'They haven't got the right things, the right bits to make them stick.'
>
> Marianna is crying in a corner of the playground, She is new to the school and doesn't yet speak any English. Four-year-old Bongiwe came to the school six months previously and also spoke no English. She notices Marianna's distress and goes over to one of the teaching assistants and says, 'Marianna – she crying. She sad. No English.'
>
> (Personal observation notes, 1999)

The first example shows the children as little scientists, exploring their environment and supported in their learning by an adult and by one another. The second example shows how children are able to draw on all their experience in order to come to understand not only the ideas and words of other people but also their feelings. In the previous chapter we examined, in depth, the views of one of the so-called founding fathers of Western theories of child development, Jean Piaget. In our examination of some of his key themes we found some that support the portrait we are constructing of the twenty-first century child. Piaget gave us a child who, from birth, is actively engaged in making sense of the world and is intent on experiencing it. She is able to make her own personal maps, which can be considered as schemas (or Piaget's repeated patterns of behaviour) that become internalised and later allow her to remember previous experiences. Piaget's picture is of a child very much situated at any time and in any place. Context and culture play little part and although Piaget gave some weight to both biological factors (what the child inherits) and to social/environmental factors (what the child experiences), the importance of others in the development of the child was rarely addressed.

It is evident that social context was marginalised in much of the psychology written up to the 1970s, when a more critical psychology began to emerge. This new approach was wary of a psychology based on universal laws which were supposed to apply at all places and in all times. Radically, the Russian psychologist Lev Vygotsky, writing in the Soviet Union in the 1920s (but only available in translation into English in the 1960s), adopted a much more social and cultural view of learning and development and this was consistent with his views on Marxist dialectical materialism. His deep concern was to explain development in terms of both biological and social concerns. Central to his approach was the notion of mediated action.

Mediated action: the role of others in learning

By *mediation* Vygotsky was talking about the use of *communicable systems*, by which he meant the ways in which ideas and thoughts are communicated by one person to another person or group of people. What is shared through communicative systems are ideas and thoughts needed for both representing reality and for acting on it. He saw this as the basis of all cognition. This model goes way beyond the simple stimulus response model we discussed in Chapter 1. For Vygotsky the role of others in learning was essential and by others he meant adults but also, and crucially, other children. He believed that during socialisation (where people interact with others) the child is inducted or drawn into the culture and is then able to internalise the means of being part of that culture through the very fact of common participation in activities with others. So, through sharing something with another person, the child takes the first steps in becoming a member of the *shared culture of that interaction*. These ideas are quite difficult to understand at first, but as you read on you will be able to see just what it is that Vygotsky was arguing.

It is society that produces the symbolic tools or the communicative systems of that society. These may be material or linguistic and are what shape the development of thinking. So the child is born into a culture and becomes a full member of that culture through making meaning of all aspects of that culture – its practices and beliefs and values. The child does this through using the communicable systems as tools, which allow the child's thinking to change. Vygotsky said that:

> The inclusion of a tool in the process of behaviour (a) introduces several new functions connected with the use of the given tool and with its control; (b) abolishes and makes unnecessary several natural processes whose work is accomplished by the tool; and (c) alters the course and individual features (the intensity, duration, sequence, etc.) of all the mental processes that enter into the composition of the instrumental act, replacing some functions with others (i.e. it re-creates and reorganises the whole structure of behaviour just as a technical tool re-creates the whole structure of labor operations).
>
> (Vygotsky, 1981: 139–140)

Confused? The language itself is difficult to unpack, but do read on in order to make meaning for yourself. Vygotsky talked a lot about tools and by tools he meant things like the everyday tools we use such as pens and pencils but also things we might be surprised to find called tools – such as words and paintings and music. And because he was interested in how ideas and knowledge were passed on from generation to generation, he was interested in the particular tools that define a culture. For Vygotsky, then, artefacts or *cultural tools* transform mental functioning and affect thinking:

- When the child hears a book, which is a cultural tool, being read to her it creates pictures in her head that may change her thinking.
- When the child sees an adult make marks on paper these raise questions in the child's head about what it is the adult is doing and this may change her thinking.
- When the child hears the mobile phone ringing she might ask who is phoning and why and whose voice might be at the other end.

The development of thinking (or of the mind) comes about through the interweaving of the biological (what the child has inherited) and the appropriation of the cultural or material heritage of the child, which defines the child's society. The artefacts or tools that allow the child entry into the culture have been created by the people in the child's society over time. So this is how children acquire and become part of culture – which includes beliefs, language, norms, artefacts, ways of acting and so on.

This is a difficult concept to grasp but one that makes perfect sense once grasped. A key *symbolic tool is language*. This is clearly a communicative system and it changes the relationships of human beings to one another. There are other tools that we have developed and used and these all shape our thinking. Here are some examples:

- various counting systems;
- mnemonic devices for remembering;
- algebraic symbols;
- paintings and sculptures;
- music;
- maps and diagrams;
- conventional signs.

Examples of people using such tools include:

- the Incas tying knots in strings to create a record of time;
- young children learning to chant nursery rhymes;
- the icons used to show emotional states on mobile phones and computers.

All of these tools have been invented by people operating within the context of their culture.

Vygotsky's theory was based on the premise that all knowledge and all the knowledge-making tools (about which we have been talking) available to a community reside within a socio-historical context. Your community and mine each have a set of beliefs and practices that govern the way in which the world operates and that have been developed over generations and which collectively represent its history. My community includes being an immigrant, being a non-believer, valuing reading and music and education, enjoying Middle Eastern food, speaking English and some other languages, enjoying families and so on. And although I have lived in the UK for more than half my life I am still not a full participant in some very English things – country fairs, the world of the *Beano*, the customs of Eton and more. Your community will probably share some but not all of these beliefs and ways of operating. The ways in which the beliefs and customs are passed down from generation to generation are through the language and the symbolism used to communicate these whilst they are being made part of the culture through participation. I sat alongside my grandfather whilst he chanted Yiddish rhymes. You may have worked alongside your mother making pasta or alongside your siblings at Sunday School or watching your mother dress in her burkha.

According to Vygotsky all children, born into communities, can be viewed as gradually appropriating to themselves the knowledge and the psychological tools of the people who make up their community. This is a way of making the knowledge the child has gained through interaction her own. So the child assumes ownership of this knowledge through internalising it. Vygotsky went on to theorise that this internalisation took place twice, on two planes, first on the social level and later on the psychological level or personal, internal level.

Put more simply, what he was saying was that learning happens first through interaction and then by internalisation. So we learn first through being alongside more experienced others and then we internalise or make mental images or maps of what has been experienced and understood. In light of this we can say that the acquisition of knowledge and the making of meaning may best be viewed as being socially and culturally determined rather than as individually constructed. We are moving away from the lone rational scientist to the collaborative learner. This is an important idea and it is worth reading it again.

Here is an example of 4-year-old children at play, recreating and sharing their culture. It comes from the wonderful work of Vivian Gussin Paley. This group of children are obsessed with 'bad guys'. And there are firm rules relating to these bad guys, all of which have been developed by the children. A bad guy cannot have a birthday or a name or share in any play sequence with a baby. And once he has been spotted he has to be dealt with quickly:

> 'Keep makin' gold', Barney orders. 'You're the walkout guards and the goldmakers. Don't forget. I'm the guard that controls the guns.'
> 'But we control the guns when you sleep', Frederick decides.
> 'No. You make the gold and I control the guns. Anyway, I'm not sleeping because there's bad guys coming. Calling all guards! Stuart, get on. You wanna be a guard? Bad guys! They see the ship because it's already the sun.'
> 'No bad guys, Barney', Mollie cautions. 'The baby is sleeping.'
> 'There hasta be bad bad guys, Mollie. We gots the cannons.'
> 'You can't shoot when the baby is sleeping.'
>
> (Paley, 1988: 19)

Eventually Mollie abandons the play because she insists on the baby being there and you can't have a baby around bad guys.

You can see in this example how hard children work to develop rules related to what they have learned through stories read and told, real events in their lives, the values and beliefs of their homes and societies. The book is worth reading because it clearly illustrates how the children – all the same age and sharing their play culture – use language in order to explore unfamiliar ideas and how they create new and shared meanings for knowledge to be acquired. This is a clear example of one of Vygotsky's key themes – that of children learning from others – either peers or adults.

Barbara Rogoff (2003) takes the argument about mediation a stage further. She argues that development occurs on three rather than on the two planes described by Vygotsky. Rogoff did a lot of work in the USA and with communities in developing countries where she noted how children were more involved in the real life of families and community. This meant that they were active participants in the processes, routines and rituals of adult daily life. She watched as children were inducted into the particular practices of families and communities through what she called *guided participation*. This guided participation was sometimes through being alongside an experienced person watching what they were doing, sometimes through social interaction such as talking about what was being done and sometimes through direct teaching. Her view of development now involves three interacting planes at which development occurs. These are the *individual plane* within the child herself; the *social plane*, involving other people within the community within which the child lives and the actual *sociocultural context* that defines the manner in which these people engage in the processes of making and sharing meaning. So Rogoff extend the sociocultural plane to the individual and social planes:

> Three children are alongside their mother who is making tortillas on the fire. She gives them each a lump of dough and they watch what she is doing and imitate her, throwing the dough, flattening it and rolling it. They watch not only their mother but also one another. Here they are doing and memorising individually as they are involved with other people within the cultural context of making the bread of their community.
>
> (Adapted from the work of Rogoff)

In Rogoff's words, development 'is a process of people's changing participation in the sociocultural activities of their communities' (Rogoff, 2003: 52). This is important because it means that we cannot see development itself as a universal term. Rather, it must involve the acquisition of those skills and knowledge practices that are important to the host (in the sense of the particular) community rather than to a generalised community. Making tortillas requires skills similar but not identical to making bagels, for example.

Piaget versus Vygotsky: is there a dichotomy?

In much of the literature there is an implied division between the thoughts of Piaget and Vygotsky on the importance of the social dimension to learning and development. Piaget focused on the individual child constructing knowledge through her own actions on the world. By contrast Vygotsky insisted that understanding is social in origin. As in many dichotomies this is an oversimplification of the views of both. In many places in his work Piaget explicitly recognised that the social world is a co-equal in the construction of knowledge. As early as 1932 he talked about societies being made up of relationships and being not fixed but incomplete and in 1970 he said: 'there is no longer any need to choose between the primacy of the social or that of the intellect: collective intellect is the social equilibrium resulting from the interplay of the operations that enter into all cooperation' (Piaget, 1970: 114).

Vygotsky was, of course, deeply interested in the importance of the social world but also saw the child as active constructor of knowledge. Some of this is evident when he discussed Piaget's notions of how children acquire language and, as part of this hugely complex process, use *egocentric speech*. By egocentric speech Piaget was talking about the personal narratives or running commentaries that young children often use. Vygotsky noticed that the child's very use of egocentric speech whilst doing something practical affected the child's thinking. So the use of a communicative system (spoken language) was both a tool for learning and later a tool for thinking about what has been learned.

> Three-year-old Minna is playing with dough on the kitchen table. Her mother is in the same room talking to a friend. The adults are intrigued to note that Minna talks aloud all the time she is playing.
> 'I throw it on the table. Whoops. What a noise. I feel it – soft, squishy. Lovely and cold. I throw it again. Whoops! Loud noise . . . Oh no!, some dirty bits here. I'll get a tissue to make it clean again . . . Rub, rub. Look, the tissue bits are sticking to my dough. I'll put it in the fridge to get clean.'
>
> (Personal notes)

The child is talking aloud through her actions, both describing them and analysing them in terms of the effects of what she is doing. At the end of this session (very abbreviated here) she noticed that her attempt to clean the dough with the tissue have not worked and came up with her own, and very individual and delightful theory for what might work – putting the dough in the fridge to get clean.

The zone of proximal development

For Vygotsky learning was the social transmission of knowledge. He believed that all learners operate at two levels. The first is the *performance level* and is what the child demonstrates that she can do without help. The second is the level of *potential development*, which can be achieved with the guidance and support of an adult or in collaboration with a more capable peer. Vygotsky described the gap between these two levels as the *zone of proximal development (ZPD)*. For Vygotsky what was demonstrated at the performance level was what the child has already mastered. What is at the upper level demonstrates functions that are not yet mature but are in the process of becoming so. He famously stated, 'What the child can do with assistance today (s)he will be able to do by herself tomorrow' (Vygotsky, 1978: 87).

It is obvious that this aspect of Vygotsky's work has implications for those involved in teaching. He was interested in the relationship between learning and development and felt that in order for the learning opportunities available to a child to be of use they must be appropriately targeted. This means that offering opportunities at or below the performance level will not bring about learning because the child's cognitive functioning here is stable and mature. Equally, it would be useless to offer opportunities above the top of the ZPD level because the difference from the child's actual level of functioning might be too great. So the art of effective teaching and what is sometimes called 'good learning' (Meadows, 1993) is learning that is only slightly in advance of development. It is worth taking time to think about this. For many of you it will seem too obvious to even state. But in many schools and settings we see children being asked to do things at the performance level over and over again, whilst in other schools and settings children are asked to do things that are not within their reach, even with help. Wertsch and Stone state that teaching is good only when it 'awakens and rouses to life those functions which are in a stage of maturing, which lie in the zone of proximal development' (1985: 165).

The question for educators – and this includes, of course, parents, carers and others involved in the development of the child – is what is it that the adult (or more proficient peer) should do to ensure learning? Another theorist, Jerome Bruner, now enters the frame. In an attempt to understand and explain the ZPD he offered the concept of *'scaffolding'* learning. His explanation was that it is the work of the adult or more proficient learner to act almost as the consciousness of the learner until such time as the learner is in control of her learning. Once the child has achieved this mastery she is able to function independently and the new function or conceptual system becomes 'hers' and she can then use it as a tool. You can see how Bruner builds on much of what Vygotsky has told us. So the educator offers a scaffold of small steps alongside the child to help the child internalise external knowledge and then turn that into a tool to be used for conscious control.

Again, the language and concepts appear difficult, but in effect scaffolding is something that adults and proficient learners often do almost instinctively. Implicit in this model is a gradual move from other-regulation or control to self-regulation as the child moves towards the upper limit of the ZPD. As the child makes this journey the adult, at first, may have to give help and support that is explicit and frequent: later the help will be more abbreviated and less frequent. As you read the example below try and identify just what it is that the adult does to enable the learner to reach her goal.

> Yinka is trying to make a model out of coloured blocks, following a template that arrived in the same box as the blocks. His mum, alongside him, pays attention to what he is doing and gives him detailed and precise advice. 'Look, now you need a blue one,' and 'You need one exactly the same as that one' (pointing).
> Two days later he tries to do the same thing, this time moving more quickly through his construction. Towards the end – where he is required to balance one block on another – his mother offers less explicit advice. 'Can you remember how you did it last time?' and 'What do you think you could do?'
>
> (Personal observation notes)

In this example the child is gradually being helped to internalise what he has done (hence to become conscious of what he can do) and then helped to find ways to know what to do next. He is moving from being largely dependent on the help of someone else to being less dependent on the less explicit and detailed help and will soon need no help at all.

A socio-cultural theory of psychological processes

Like Piaget, Vygotsky was a constructivist in that he saw the child constructing meaning from experience. But over and above that he emphasised that children choose and use tools that are socially constructed. In the preschools of Reggio Emilia the children most often choose to represent their understandings through the visual arts. They select the cultural tools of painting or drawing or making and it is significant that in the preschools there is an artist in residence. Children can visit the artist in the atelier and watch what she is doing. There are also framed paintings displayed throughout the preschools. In the reception classes in England young children are expected to represent their understanding primarily through writing. This is the dominant cultural tool in the culture of these schools. It is apparent that there is a cultural and historical pattern built into cognition. One of Vygotsky's colleagues, Luria, studied what was happening in the 1930s in agricultural regions in central Asia. He was looking for evidence that there were differences between the cognitive processes used by literate people in the cities and generally illiterate and uneducated peasants. The analysis of what he found was criticised for being pejorative about peasant society. He suggested that the ways in which peasants classified and sorted objects in their lives was inferior to the sorting into clear categories more evident in educated societies. Later consideration, however, suggested that functional sorting of artefacts was culturally relevant (e.g. sorting out clothes so that they would not be eaten by moths, putting food into sealed jars to keep out insects, keeping tools on a high shelf out of the reach of children) rather than cognitively significant for development. It is worth thinking about how many of the ways in which we sort and categorise objects are determined by the demands of education rather than of culture. Think about how many times you find children in nurseries and schools being asked to sort things by colour or shape or size for no obvious or useful reason.

Vygotsky believed in socially meaningful *activity*. As a Marxist he was concerned with activity that would offer some benefits to the group, the culture or the society. Early childhood educators often talk about meaningful activities and by this they mean activities that make *'human sense'* to children. Human sense was a term used by Donaldson (1978), who believed that much of what young children are asked to do in schools is *decontextualised* and abstract: the purpose of many activities is not clear to the learner. Think about asking children to complete a worksheet that requires them to colour in all the triangles red and all the squares blue. The teacher's goal is apparent to us. She wants to check that the child can identify two different shapes and colours (and, perhaps, can colour in neatly). For the child this cannot be described as a meaningful activity. Contrast it with the child, at play, setting the table and spontaneously looking for another red saucer to match those she has put on the table. Here the purpose, defined by the child, makes human sense to her. There is a purpose to it.

Intersubjectivity

So far we have looked at the child as constructor of the world with help from others – i.e. making sense of things in social contexts. Our focus has been on how the child comes to understand the physical world. Let us now turn our attention to how the child begins to make sense of the *social world* itself. In other words, let's begin to look at how the child comes to see herself as distinct from others, but in relation to them. One of the key themes here is that of *intersubjectivity*.

It is apparent that the human infant is interested in and responsive to the emotions and the behaviour of others. Colwyn Trevarthen (1977) showed that infants as young as 2 months of age show a different response to someone who speaks to them than to someone else in the room who remains silent. Johnson (1990) showed that newborn infants pay closer attention to an object with a face-like arrangement of blobs on it (eyes and mouth) than to an identical object with abstract patterns on it. It seems that human development is almost naturally social, in the sense that humans are inclined to react socially in cultural contexts and to both make and share meaning. Those who adopt this view of development see relationships and communications with others as the most significant feature of the child's environment.

Trevarthen (1998) went further and looked at how children come to learn the culture into which they have been born. He asked why it is that very young children are so keen to learn the language and all the other habits, customs, rituals and beliefs of the community around them. He said that a 3-year-old child is a socially aware person who can make and keep friends and negotiate and cooperate with many different people in many different situations. For Trevarthen young children primarily make sense by sharing. They use their emotions and the emotions of others to categorise experiences that will help them cooperate. For many years Trevarthen has been analysing, in minute detail, videos of infants and their mothers and in doing this he has been made aware of some things that made him turn to a concept first introduced by the philosopher Jürgen Habermas. The concept is that of intersubjectivity and a common-sense definition of intersubjectivity is having a shared understanding. This definition makes clear how important it is for both partners to come to a shared understanding of both the issue (or the event) and the intention (or the purpose).

Did you know that, in order to discuss an idea with another person, you have to be able to almost be that other person in the sense of knowing what they are thinking? This is the very essence of intersubjectivity. If you are interested in this there is a book called The Intersubjective Mirror in Infant Learning and Evolution of Speech, *written by Stein Bråten (2009). The book has been well reviewed by Trevarthen.*

Like many theorists in the developed world, Trevarthen was interested in the early interactions and bonds between mother (or primary caregiver) and infant. Before infants acquire language, interactions take place around objects or events and are very much to do with what is happening in the here and now between the mother (or caregiver) and the infant. Each is responding to the other and commenting on what is happening, sometimes verbally but always showing affect or emotion.

The mother tickles the baby: the baby chuckles: the mother smiles and tickles the baby again.

Trevarthen believed that what happens in these dance-like exchanges is a growing awareness in the infant of the feelings or the emotions of the mother. He called this *primary intersubjectivity.*

Some suggest that this simple exploration of the feelings of others begins to develop at around 9 months of age. It is then, Tomasello (1997) noted, that the mother follows the child's gaze to determine what the child is interested in or paying attention to (or vice versa with the child following the mother's gaze or actions). Attention becomes shared around what is being focused on and it is this shared focus of attention that now moves beyond the here-and-now interaction into the world of objects – perhaps toys, or food or other people. This is a really important point.

Uri looks at his mother and sees her looking out of the window. He sees the car out of the window and points to it. 'Yes,' says the mother, interpreting the question he cannot yet ask through following the child's gaze. 'Your daddy's home.'

Trevarthen called this *secondary intersubjectivity* and believed that its importance was that it allowed the infant to develop a realisation that the events, objects and people in the world and the actions made on or with these, can be experienced by more than one person. Göncü (1998) stated that the importance of this is that it prepares the child to share meanings with peers and it is through their new symbolic competence that children can construct and develop intersubjectivity in peer interactions. This involves them in discussion, negotiation, sharing meaning and collaborating. You will find examples of this in Chapter 7.

This brings us – for the first time – to considering the importance of *play*, particularly of *social pretend play*. What children do when they pretend is that they use physical, psychological or symbolic ways of representing the meaning of something else. There is a well-known video sequence produced many years ago by the Open University that shows a little girl called Helen playing being the 'manager' of a canteen. This 4-year-old was not the manager of anything, but in her play she demonstrates that she has incorporated some of the language, the gestures, the intonation patterns and the ways of interacting that sum up for her someone with an important role to play. Where she has gained these ideas from is open to debate. Perhaps her mum is a manager; perhaps she has watched how the nursery teacher behaves; perhaps she endures her older sister being bossy. But she has clearly worked out some behaviours that define for her what it means to be in charge and she uses the words and actions to represent her understanding of the role. When two or more children join together in collaborative pretend play they have to identify many issues: what the place will be about who will take which part and more. Göncü tells us that when trying to analyse what happens in pretend play we can turn, again, to Trevarthen. For the play to be successful the children have to have a shared focus of attention. As we have said, they have to agree on certain things relating to what the play will be about and what parts need to be played. Are they are both going to be fairies? Is one going to be the doctor and the other a patient? Who should be the mother and who the baby? They need to coordinate and share intentions and these are cognitively complex issues to resolve.

There is something else that happens at around 9 months of age and that is the beginning of self-awareness. When the child is able to follow the gaze of the mother there is the suggestion that the child is realising that the mother can look independently just as the child can. This leads on to imitation and more complex behaviours and action. Between about 15 months and 2 years of age most infants will recognise themselves in a mirror. Some theorists (e.g. Meltzoff and Gopnick, 1993) suggest that this indicates the beginning of self-consciousness and this may be illustrated by a child perhaps hiding behind the mother because of feeling shy or awkward. This may be the first indication of the infant having a sense of herself living in a social environment alongside other selves who can both see and interact with her.

In this social world of ours children are constantly involved in acting and communicating in exchanges with others. This is where meaning is shared. Rogoff (1990) suggests that what happens in these exchanges is a blend of internal and external. Whatever is the focus of shared attention (let's take a book as an example) we cannot say that the book belongs to the mother or to the child. Where the mother reads to the child and points to the book, the meaning of a concept (perhaps there is a dog eating a bone, or a baby crying, or wild things swinging from trees) must be negotiated if there is to be shared understanding. Rogoff thinks that what happens is that the child appropriates something from the shared activity and is able to use this in later activities – alone or in participation. It is her belief that social exchanges themselves are the medium for social activities to be transformed and used by individuals according to their understanding and their involvement. Wertsch and Stone (1979) tell us that the process actually becomes the product. Communication and shared solving of problems may bridge the gap between what is already known and what is to be learned.

This might suggest that this learning will lead to a mere repetition of what is already known, but Rogoff argues that the child is actively constructing meaning and is thus engaged in a *creative process*. So we are back to some of the ideas discussed in the previous chapter as we examine children's increasing ability to use analogy as a tool of thinking. There are many examples in the literature of children engaged in discussion or dialogue, where they demonstrate a striking ability to make connections between ideas. Rogoff offers a startling example of two sisters, aged 4 and 7, with their mother. It all starts over a pizza at the kitchen table when the 4-year-old asks her mother where they all came from and how they came to be alive. The answer is, 'from your mother and father who came from their mother and father' which leads to the 7-year-old volunteering that long ago there were no people, only apes, and that all people were descended from apes. The discussion then moved on to talking about where apes came from, and where dinosaurs came from, right down to one-celled creatures. When the mother then asked the girls where these one-celled creatures came from the older girl volunteered the response 'From ENERGY.' The mother was stunned to learn that this response arose from a conversation the girls had had with their grandfather two weeks before. Here is 7-year-old Luisa's explanation (note that doodle-doodles was the term used by Grandpa for electrons and neutrons and doodle-doodle-doodles the term for quarks and neutrinos):

> Well, Grandpa told me that molecules . . . were made up of atoms, and atoms were made up of doodle-doodles . . . and those were made up of doodle-doodle-doodles . . . and *they* were made from ENERGY, just energy. So, I just figure that energy is what the one-celled animals came from.
>
> (Rogoff, 1990: 200)

Constructing the social world: what children need to know and do

In order to build a picture of a world made up of other people children need to begin to construct representations to explain to themselves how others feel, what they want and need, what rules operate to hold their society together and what other people may be thinking. One of the most significant contributors to our understanding of this is Judy Dunn, whose seminal book *The Beginnings of Social Understanding* (1988) is still a key reference text. Dunn spent time observing young children (a recognised and valued way of studying children and their development). Much of her work involved looking at young children in the settings of their home. She found some very interesting things, many of which are in direct contrast to what had been thought by Piaget who, as you may remember, believed that young children were unable to decentre or take on the point of view of others.

Dunn tells us that children are not just passive partners in interactions with others, but are active participants. This means that when they engage in relationships and interactions with parents, family members, other children and teachers or doctors or neighbours, they work hard at making sense of the feelings, the needs, the intentions and the goals of these others. This is to allow them to be able to function as members of their social group. So our mythical twenty-first century child, as a player in her society, needs to explore the various systems with which she is involved – the nursery or setting, the home, the neighbourhood, the local clinic and so on. From early on she is actively making sense of the rules that make these systems viable.

In her book Dunn carefully illustrates how this takes place. We know that from birth the human infant is predisposed to learn about the characteristics of people, as we have seen through their attention to human faces and voices over other stimuli. At the age of only 2 months the baby can already differentiate between someone who wants to communicate with her from someone who is talking to another person. By the age of 7 or 8 months babies seem really attuned to different emotional expressions in adults and they begin to play cooperative games like 'peekaboo'. This is a game with built-in routines and patterns and we examine the functions of these with regard to intersubjectivity later in this book. At this age babies share in the daily routines of feeding, changing, dressing and soon begin to demonstrate that they share a communicative framework with others – for example, by waving goodbye, eye-pointing to what they want, or smiling with pleasure. They are highly social and sociable beings, intent on communicating with others. From the age of roughly 18 months old children are able to understand how to hurt and how to comfort others; the consequences of their own actions on others and something of what is allowed or not in the world of their family. They are also able to anticipate the responses of adults to their own misdeeds or those of siblings and peers.

Dunn found that children's *understanding of the feelings of others* develops early in their second year of life. They start to respond empathetically to the distress of others and are interested in the way others feel, exploring the causes of pain or distress, anger and pleasure, comfort and fear. They joke and play with and tell stories about these feelings and, Dunn believes, the foundations for kindness are well established by the age of 3. The examples below are drawn on those given by Dunn but also on personal observation notes.

> Eighteen-month-old Sarah hands her bottle of milk to the baby beside her on the bus who is crying inconsolably.

> Ben, aged 2, seeing that his mother is distressed, asks, 'Mummy crying?' To which his older sister replies, 'No, mummies only cry when their daddies die.'

In terms of *understanding the goals of others*, Dunn illustrates how sensitivity to the goals of others emerged in the play of 2- and 3-year-olds and entered into the stories they tell, the pretend games they play and the questions they ask.

> Three-year-old Emily is shocked when her mother screams and jumps on a chair when a mouse runs across the kitchen floor. 'Mummy, did you jump on the chair 'cos of the mouse? Are you scared, mummy?'

Playing shops at home, 3-year-old Rashida picks up a block and hands it to Ade to pay for the goods she is buying.

Ade: 'Is this your money?'
Rashida: 'It's my credit card.'
Ade: 'Oh, plastic money. You must be buying lots of things.'

As very young children raise questions and make hypotheses about all they see in their everyday lives they begin to explore what makes some types of behaviour acceptable and others not. This implies that a set of social rules (specific to particular families and groups and societies and cultures) apply and children work hard in the early years to *understand these social rules*. Dunn's observations showed that between the ages of 2½ and 3 children demonstrated some understanding of responsibility, of excuses and explanations for why they have done things. Embedded in her observations is the evidence that children do notice and attend to the distress of others – a clear indication that young children can, indeed, decentre.

Two 3-year-olds are playing together in the bedroom of one of them. The visiting child, Leon, picks up a crayon and starts to draw on the walls. Mustafa shrieks in dismay. 'No, no! You are not allowed to do that in my house. My mummy doesn't let me draw on the walls. We use paper.'

Finally, Dunn talks about how, in the course of their third year, children begin to talk about things like knowing and remembering and forgetting. They are talking about their own cognition and show that they are aware of their own minds and of the *minds of others*. She suggests that as children's thinking about the minds of others develops this becomes more important to them than the simpler examinations of the feelings and goals of others.

Jacob (aged 3): 'When we came to visit you in London you lived in a big house and we slept upstairs and you slept downstairs. And your car was red. And my daddy watched the television because he was missing Sydney and we played with those blocks you've got.'

A 9-year-old child watched the interactions between a boy of about 7 and the man sitting beside him on the train. 'I don't think he was his father because he asked him questions to things he would have known if he was his father. And I think the little boy was really sad. I wondered if something had happened to his mother.'

Did you know that to become cooperative members of their cultural groups, developing children must follow the social norms that apply to their group? In a recent paper Schmidt, Rakoczy and Tomasello (2012) found that young children are not just blind norm followers, but are active norm enforcers, for example protesting and correcting when someone plays a conventional game the 'wrong' way. In two studies they asked whether young children enforce social norms on all people equally, or only on ingroup members who presumably know and respect the norm. They looked at both moral norms involving harm and conventional game norms involving rule violations. Three-year-old children actively protested violation of moral norms equally for ingroup and outgroup individuals, but they enforced conventional game norms for ingroup members only. Despite their ingroup favouritism, young children nevertheless hold ingroup members to standards whose violation they tolerate from outsiders. For more information read Schmidt et al. *(2012).*

Development viewed in the contexts of place, time and culture

We have focused throughout this book on how development must always be viewed in the contexts of history, society and culture. Important too are things like climate and geography. In these examples we examine how children begin to construct the social world that is particular to them. Many of the world's children grow up in societies that adopt a collectivist approach where the focus is not on the individual, but on the individual in relation to others. A case study in point is that of the Nso children who live in the Bamenda Grassfields of Northwest Cameroon. Nsamenang and Lamb (1994) studied the socialisation of these children through interviews with volunteer parents and grandparents, carried out in the language of the Nso people, Lamnso. They found that Nso children, together with their families, are active participants in their own socialisation. The principles and values of their families include obedience and social responsibility, not individuality and the ability to express ideas verbally. They are still deeply rooted in their ancestral traditions, despite the impact of Westernisation on them. Much of the learning of the children comes about through guided participations, as described by Rogoff. You will remember that this is where children learn alongside adults or more experienced others, almost like apprentices. Nso children do play and they make their own playthings and the process of making these things is thought to help them develop an image of themselves as creators or producers. Segall *et al.* note that 'The process of making these toys teaches the children how to plan work, organize tools and materials, to make measurements and to conceive of objects in three-dimensional space' (1990: 123). The example of cultural traditions like weaving, sculpture, embroidery, leather working and pottery is evident in what the children produce. You can see how the children use their cultural tools in order to make toys.

Nso children live in communities where the peer culture is powerful and this allows for *peer mentoring* and *perspective taking*, allowing children to develop their sensitivity to the needs and feelings of others, particularly of younger children. The children play together and in this play they need to agree what their agenda is, to allocate and accept roles, and to understand the feelings of others and anticipate the impact of their actions or words on others. Older children have authority over their younger siblings and they are allowed to correct and reprimand them. So parents do not have sole responsibility for the *affective and cognitive development* of the children; children themselves are co-contributors to the socialisation of other children. It is suggested that Nso children learn to speak more from other children than from their parents. Stories and proverbs (other cultural tools) play an important role in educating the children into understanding the morality of the community – what is seen as right and wrong, for example. This is true of many cultures, as illustrated by the many stories with morals in them to be found throughout the world.

The families of the Nso children are extended families, as we have seen. Whatever families look like – and they vary enormously in their composition and structure – as you will know, there can be little doubt that they contribute enormously to child development. Barbarin and Richter (2001) examined what children need most from families in order to thrive and develop. They were looking at children in South Africa and the questions they asked included:

* Do families provide essential socialisation in terms of the values children need?
* Does the wealth of the family contribute significantly to the ability of the family to keep children safe and have their primary physical needs met?
* Is it the links and relationships and support within and between families that allow children to have a sense of belonging?

In this detailed study four separate analyses were carried out and the researchers themselves add a note of caution about over-interpreting the results. Nonetheless, some of the findings give food for thought. In terms of children's social competence their findings suggest that where, within families, there were prosocial ways of resolving disputes, children's social competence developed. This means that in families where difficulties were dealt with positively and calmly, without anger or aggression, children were more likely to become socially competent. They also found that in smaller families, with fewer dependent children, children became more independent and socially competent.

Summing up

In this chapter we have looked both at how children learn more about their world through their interactions with others and at how they make sense of these others who inhabit their world. The key theorists mentioned in this chapter are Vygotsky, Bruner, Trevarthen, Dunn, Rogoff, Nsamenang and Lamb. So now our portrait of the twenty-first century child has an added social and cultural dimension. She is learning through her interactions with family members, peers and others she encounters and she is also beginning to think about what it is that makes her distinct from but part of others. Through her interactions with others she is able to know that other people have needs and desires, likes and dislikes, minds and thoughts. She knows that within her culture some things are accepted and others not. She can empathise with others and share meaning with them.

Things to think about

* What do you understand about how others, children and adults, mediate cultures and enable children to gain knowledge and make it their own?
* How is intersubjectivity important in enabling young children to share meanings, develop awareness of self and begin to understand the feelings, goals and rules of others?
* Are you able to interpret young children's actions and words in terms of how they are making sense of both the physical and the social worlds?

Chapter 4

The child at play becoming a creative thinker

In this chapter we start to look at how the child, having constructed some views of the physical and social worlds, starts to represent and re-represent these in order to be able to remember them, build on them and transform them to become more complex understandings. In doing this we look at play, which is something children seem impelled to do and analyse its importance in becoming a creative thinker.

> When Ola was 10 weeks old she spent hours watching the leaves moving above her basket. She watched the movements with intense concentration. Some months later she started to enjoy some simple games that she played with her big sister, who would hide a favourite spoon and say 'all gone!' and then make it pop up again.
>
> When Ade was 13 months old he started to push any button he saw in the house to see what happened. If he liked what happened he pressed the button again. And again and again! His parents bought a new DVD player and he immediately went up to it and pushed the button and was delighted when lights came on.
>
> Poppy, at 18 months old, has become a problem solver and an imitator. When her childminder, Grace, is cleaning she follows her around with her own cloth and is desperate to have a go with the broom and the dustpan. Grace reported that when she wanted something out of reach she dragged her chair across the floor and then attempted to climb up on it.
>
> Ahmed has few toys yet spends hours sorting out the things he finds. He makes collections of things that are, in some way, the same for him. His mother noted that yesterday he put lots of dark coloured objects together and light coloured objects in a different place. Today she saw him putting lots of stones in one place, sticks in another and dry leaves in a third.
>
> Malika seems to be exploring the way in which some things will dissolve and others won't. She spends time putting water into some sand and stirring it. Then she tries putting water into gravel and stirring that to see what happens.
>
> Tahiba is now starting to pretend. She takes an empty tin and pretends to have a drink out of it. Or she makes dolls out of scraps of fabric and carries them round, singing to them.
>
> (Personal observation notes)

All these children are deeply engrossed in what they are doing. They are not engaged in trivial events, nor are they unable to concentrate over long periods of time. They are very busily engaged in trying to understand their world and as they do what they are doing they are, in all probability, asking questions in their minds and seeking to find answers. This, for some of the children, is before they have spoken language so for them the whole process is about exploration through their senses and physical exploration of the objects they encounter. Here is my analysis of what some of the children are interested in, trying to find out or questioning:

> Ola uses her eyes to track the movements of the leaves. What questions might she be asking? 'Why are they moving? What makes them move? Can I make them move? Will they stop moving? Why?' As Ola does these things it is apparent that some questions are being raised in her mind and it is these that impel her to keep on exploring. Only she knows what she is seeking to discover.

> Ade is behaving like a small scientist. He does something – makes a movement – and what he does creates some effect. If he likes what happened he tries again. He is exploring cause and effect.

> Poppy is acting as an imitator and problem solver. She watches what her childminder does and then tries out that role for herself. Perhaps she wants to know what it feels like to be big and to be able to use a cloth to remove dust. Perhaps she wants to feel the soft cloth in her hands. She is certainly exploring how one thing (a chair) can be used for different purposes (to sit on but also to stand on to reach something high up).

Any observation of children engaged in following their own interests will reveal the extremely serious and persistent nature of what they are doing and raise the question of what it is they are trying to make meaning of. You might be tempted to think that what they are doing is just fun, that it is nothing important or serious. But in effect what they are doing is trying to make sense of their world. All infants seem driven to explore what they encounter and to use whatever means possible to do so. These children are playing.

Since there are two main and linked themes in this chapter, play and creativity, it makes sense to start by defining both terms.

Defining creative thinking

The word creativity, like the word play, is often used loosely. For our purposes we need to be careful to define it so that we can see its role in the learning and development of young children.

Someone who is being creative often looks at a problem from *more than one perspective*, and in doing this arrives at an unorthodox solution. Here is a wonderful and true example that comes from children at the Diana preschool in Reggio Emilia, where a group of children were designing a new curtain for the theatre.

> The painting is almost finished when Leonardo asks, 'Why don't we put in some cells that come from outer space. And then they can decide what shape they want to be.' How in the spirit of the whole project this idea is: some natural form that can choose its own shape and, presumably, its own transformation. There is a lot of discussion about what a cell looks like and one child suggests looking in a book, another says he does not want to do that because he has a picture of cells in his

mind. At this point a little girl called Mimi gets up and starts moving around in a spontaneous dance whilst the others draw their ideas of cells.

(Smidt, 2013: 89)

All the children cited in the above example are being creative in the sense of being able to *imagine, invent* and *make something new*, something never seen before. Creativity is the ability to use existing materials or events and, by *transforming* or *adapting* or *combining* them, produce something new. Gunther Kress (1997) has written about how children throughout the world use what is at hand to make things that interest them. Think about the example he gives of two 6-year-olds who made a car out of two wire-mesh drawers, a pillow, a tool box and other bits and bobs. The finished product has all the things that these children decided are essential to cars – seats to sit on, doors to get into it and a small bonnet at the front. You may be intrigued by the fact that wheels don't feature in what is essential for them.

Creativity also involves the *willingness to accept change and novelty and to play with materials and ideas and possibilities*.

One of the examples of children at the beginning of this chapter referred to Malika. You will remember how she put water into sand and then water into gravel. She must have noticed that the grains of sand seemed to disappear or change when mixed with water and may have extrapolated from that to see what would happen to gravel in water.

Defining play

Piaget, Vygotsky and Bruner all saw play as being a significant feature of development. Piaget saw play – like learning – as being developmental and moving from what he called practice play, through symbolic play and into play of games with rules. He believed that what children do is to use play as the way of unifying what they have experienced and learned (and they do this through assimilation), rather than adjusting to what they do not yet know through *equilibration*. This equilibration is always changing and this explains why play is a process and not a steady state. He was particularly interested in how play allowed children to explore rules and norms.

Vygotsky accorded play a more vital role in his belief that children, in pretend play, show more about what they already know and can do than they do in any other activity. The zone of proximal development is created through play. He said that, in play, children stand a 'head taller' than themselves. Like Piaget, he was interested in play as developing into games with rules, but with his emphasis on the social nature of development and learning he focused on how every play sequence includes rules that the children must agree through negotiation. He noted that every game with rules contains imaginary aspects.

Bruner shared with Vygotsky an interest in play and he saw it as a way (or a mode) of learning, describing it as *an approach to doing something* and not an activity in its own right. This echoes the idea that *play is a process*. This is an important and interesting point. What it means for us is that we should not see play as an activity in its own right but realise that children can learn about aspects of language or mathematics or the physical world or the scientific world or anything else through play. Bruner, interested in the fact that the young of almost all mammalian species engage in play, regarded it as being 'non-serious' in the sense that the long period of human childhood relative to that of other species was precisely to allow the young human time for safe and playful exploration. He went on to suggest that without such playful exploration the development and use of tools would not have taken place. You will realise here that when he talks of tools he is doing so in the same way that Vygotsky did – talking about cultural tools like pencils and paintbrushes and scissors and books and computers as well as more traditional tools. This evolutionary approach to play is interesting, but not universally accepted. Bruner also believed that the 'in pretend' nature of play allows children to create alternatives to reality and in doing this they create symbols. In essence, in pretend play, the child simulates an action in play 'as if' it were real, or the child tries out new combinations and sequences in a 'what if' fashion. The vignettes below illustrate this.

> Martha is setting the table for a tea party in the home corner of her daycare centre. She is behaving 'as if' she is having a real tea party and drawing on her previous experiences of seeing people set the table, or being at a tea party or seeing what a tea party might look like in a book or on a video or film.

> Hamish is climbing to the top of the climbing frame in the playground and looking out to see if he can spot the pirates whom he believes are just beyond the sandpit. He is behaving as though he is a sailor and acting out what he thinks a sailor would do.

Bretherton (1984) believed that pretend play was significant to learning and development. She stated that mental trial and error (thinking of different ways of doing things) and the ability to imagine (to engage in make-believe) were two facets of the same ability to represent the world. In other words, children need both in order to do things and to think about things symbolically. In the first example above Martha is setting the table and imagining a tea party. In doing this she is using metaphor in the sense that she is acting like someone who has a tea party. Hamish is climbing to the top and looking out and imagining a group of pirates. He, too, is using metaphor as he plays 'like a pirate'.

Play, said Bruner, is *memory in action*. This is a wonderful way of thinking about play and it is worth spending time reflecting on it.

Tina Bruce has written widely and influentially on play in early childhood education. In most of her work she doesn't simply talk about play but about what she calls *free-flow play*, which can be defined as spontaneous play. Bruce (1991) discusses two contrasting views of play. The first is what she calls the play as a *preparation for life* approach and the second is play as an *integrating mechanism*. In the first approach, play as a preparation for life, Bruce argues that the play is very much suggested and controlled by the adult. This can be illustrated by comments like 'Go and play in the home corner, Georgia', or 'Why don't you play with your blocks now?' In this approach, play may be described by the words 'fun' and 'happy'. Children are released from the drudgery of work in order to enjoy the perceived triviality of play. This question of play being pleasurable is a vexed one and we will return to it.

Moyles (1998), in her writing about play, does not limit her discussions to young children. Play is something important to all children and sometimes to adults. One of her themes is the importance of the child having ownership of play. What she means is that, in play, where children choose what to do and thus *control the agenda* they can become *deeply engrossed* in what they are doing and are able to change the direction should things not go according to their original plan. In this way they cannot fail. She cites the work of Corinne and John Hutt (1989) whose model focused on what children appeared to be doing as they played. Their work helps us recognise that children's play is extremely complex. They drew a distinction between what they called *epistemic play* (play based around knowledge acquisition and involving an adult or more expert learner) and *ludic play*, which was their term for what we are calling pretend play or symbolic play or imaginative play. In their thesis children, in the earliest stages, seems to ask 'What is this thing?' and then move on to asking 'What does this thing do?' and finally 'What can I do with this thing?' so moving from exploring objects and their properties through to exploring the functions of objects and then using objects to meet their own purposes. Where the player has ownership the implication is that whatever it is that the player is doing is important to her.

Here is an example:

> Rasheeda (3:9) wanders into the home corner and picks up a pencil that is lying next to a notepad beside the telephone. She picks up the phone and begins to talk as though she is taking a message. 'Just wait. I'll write it down.' She 'writes' some parallel squiggles on the notepad and says, 'Now I won't forget. Bye bye.'
> She then pretends to speak on the phone again, this time ordering a pizza. 'Hello. We want three pizzas – one for me and one for my brother and a big one for my mum.' She pauses and writes some lines on the pad, but this time adds the numerals 1 and 7. 'Our house is number 171.'

Rasheeda has chosen what to do so this is clearly an example of play. She has chosen to use the materials provided by the teacher in order to follow up her own interest in what 'taking a message' means. In the simplest terms we can say that she is exploring the uses of the telephone and how one records things on paper. She then moves on in her play to ordering a pizza and in her writing she includes two numerals – the numbers 1 and 7. On the next day Rasheeda was again observed:

> Rasheeda is playing with her friend Aaron in the writing area and they are getting very noisy. The teacher becomes irritated and tells her to play with a jigsaw puzzle. Rasheeda grumbles about this, but being as helpful and malleable as many young children are, she complies and quickly completes a very simple puzzle. 'Done, miss,' she announces, and returns to giggling with Aaron.
>
> (Both sets of observation notes on Rasheeda
> from personal observation, 2001)

This is an example of the child doing what she was told to do by a teacher. Despite the teacher telling her to play, this was not something that was either interesting or relevant to her. The consequence was that she was not engaged in the task.

We can summarise what play means like this:

*   It is something the child has chosen to do. The child initiates the activity and in doing this is in control of her own agenda. The adult may play a role in the play. The teacher resourced the home corner and Rasheeda then chose what to do and how to do it with what was available.
*   It is often pleasurable and we often see children enjoying their chosen activity. Rasheeda was clearly enjoying acting like an adult, taking messages and writing them down as she may have seen adults do. She was highly motivated to keep playing. But play can be frustrating and complex and may not always be pleasurable.

- It is likely to always be deeply engrossing. The child may spend long periods of time following up her concerns. Children who have experienced war, homelessness, cruelty and trauma still play, and often it is a way of acting out symbolically the terrible things they have experienced. In cases like this play is certainly neither fun nor pleasurable.
- In play there is no risk of failure. Since the child has chosen what to do and how to do it, if something goes wrong she can just change her agenda and do something else or differently.
- The emphasis is on the process rather than on the product.

Play as an integrating mechanism

It is interesting that, despite the fact that play is such an important concept in Western views of child development, in English we have only one word to cover all aspects. In Italian there are several words – one relating to playing musical instruments, one relating to children's play and one relating to joking.

Tina Bruce described play as an *integrating mechanism* by which she meant that, in play, children draw on all their experiences and understanding in order to both consolidate what they have already learned and create new learning. She talked about children using their understanding of *rule formats* and of *scripts*. This refers to the work of Bruner (1982) and Nelson (2000). Both these writers focused on interaction and the rule-bound nature of interactions between adults and children as useful sources for the child to draw on. So a child, in play, draws on all the available scripts or formats to explore a concern or answer a question.

To make this clear let's go back to Rasheeda at play in the first example and try and identify the scripts and formats she is integrating.

- Rasheeda has almost certainly seen and heard people on the telephone, so she has a 'script' in her head for how this is done. This is what enables to use conventional English greetings like 'Hello' and 'Bye bye'.
- She has also heard people using the telephone for different purposes and worked out that there are different formats or patterns for how this is done. She has worked out that the tone and intonation you use to speak to your mother is different from that you would use for talking to an unknown person taking your phone order.

What we see is a child revealing her competence in 'acting like an adult' and in doing this she is integrating many of her previous observations, analyses, hypotheses and experiences.

Now let's go back to the example of little Colin who, you may remember, used a ball to be a baby and the mop bucket to be the baby's pram. We examined this earlier as an example of symbolic play. This is part of a long description of what took place.

> Anabel, aged 4½, came over to Colin.
> 'Can I have the ball, Colin?'
> Colin looked at her. He seemed puzzled. She picked the ball up and kicked it away from her.
> 'Nooo!' Colin cried and ran after the ball . . .

Colin picked up the ball. 'Don't run away, baby. It's all right,' he said lovingly. He then put the ball under his arm and pulled the bucket over to a small chair. He sat down on the chair and put the ball in the bucket. 'Going shops in a minute, baby, shops and sweets, baby, yeah?' he said.

(Allery, 1998: 30)

Later Colin went over to pick leaves from a bush in the corner and threw them into the pram for the 'baby', calling out, 'Dinner baby.' Then when he had to go indoors to get his own dinner he was told to leave the ball outdoors. He wheeled the bucket with the ball in it into the shade, patted the ball and went in for lunch.

The scripts and formats here are very different from those used by Rasheeda, but you will notice that Colin talks to the baby in the ways in which he has heard adults (and very possibly mothers) speak to babies. He has also noticed something about how to care for and show love for a baby. This is demonstrated by his putting the 'pram' in the shade and explaining to the baby what is happening, reassuring the baby that she is not being abandoned.

A significant factor about play that we have not yet mentioned is that it is very often in what we might call *'pretend'* mode. Children know that what they are doing is not 'the real thing'. Rasheeda knows that no pizzas will arrive and that the message she has written down cannot be read by anyone. Colin knows the baby is a ball, the pram is a bucket and that he is not the baby's parent. The pretend nature of the play allows it to be pressure-free and this lack of pressure is extremely significant.

Imaginative/symbolic play

The young constructor of meaning uses play as a tool, just as she uses physical exploration, stories, observation of expert others, interaction and other means to make sense of all aspects of her world. Bruner believed that the thing that makes humans so distinctive as a species is that they create and use culture. Symbols are the building blocks of culture. Different cultures use different symbols: these symbols define aspects of that culture. The particular language, music, food, art, artefacts and beliefs are some of the symbols that define Turkish culture, for example, and they will be different from those defining Nigerian or any other culture.

In pretend play the child turns one thing into something else and thus, in some senses, transforms reality. The child is being a creative thinker. Bruner believed that pretend play or imaginative play must be seen as a form of *representation*. The child simulates an action in play as if it were real. Think of the child using a block as a telephone and speaking into it as if it were real or Colin treating his ball-baby so lovingly. Here we are considering children playing *'as if'*. Now, if we turn our attention to children playing *'what if'* we see them trying out new patterns of action, and combining elements in order to create something new. They are being creative thinkers. Go back to Hamish on the look-out for pirates and notice how he combines sequences of action with his image of what pirates might be like, where they might be hiding and what he, as an explorer or an adventurer, might need to do about it.

We have touched on how, after the earlier play with objects through sensorimotor manipulation, children begin to represent experience and become generative, as they play out activities they have experienced or seen others experience. Observing children engaged in symbolic play you will see them using simple pretence about themselves (like using the block for a telephone), simple pretence about others (like putting the doll to sleep) and then sequences of pretence (like setting the table, cooking a meal, serving the meal). Some believe that pretend play moves from playing out *domestic roles* and sequences (those involving mum, dad, baby, sister, brother, grandpa) to playing out *functional roles* (those involving the teacher, doctor, nurse, train driver) to playing out *fantasy or imaginary roles* (fairy, vampire, dinosaur, witch). Children will sometimes engage in *solitary play* (and this is almost always the case with the youngest children) and perhaps then move on to playing alongside others but not interacting with them (called *parallel play*), to playing with others (called *collaborative or cooperative play*).

You will easily be able to say whether you think the play is fantasy or domestic, solitary or parallel, for example:

> Three-year-old Simnikiwe has made a doll out of scraps of fabric. She wraps the doll in some large banana leaves and carries her round, singing to her.

She is clearly playing the domestic role of mother. She is playing alone.

> A group of Guatemalan children of different ages are playing at cooking and serving a meal, using leaves to make tortillas and mud for the meat.

They are playing domestic roles but moving towards functional roles of cooks and servers of food. They are playing together, sometimes collaboratively.

> Four children in a playgroup in East London are acting out a scenario where there has been a traffic accident. The play involves making the noises of ambulances. Two children become doctors and treat the other two who are told to lie on the ground and 'act dead'.

This is collaborative role play where the script is agreed through negotiation. The roles played again include domestic and functional aspects.

> Four little girls in the hills above a small Italian town are collecting seeds in order to make 'medicines' so that they can make the dolls better. The dolls have been laid out on the path.

Functional roles are also explored through social play.

> Jio has a long length of fabric and he is using it first to represent a river he has to cross, then a magic cloak to keep him safe and then a bandage for his foot, which he pretends has been bitten by a tiger. This child's solitary play does not depend on toys, but allows him to draw on his knowledge of traditional and new stories in order to explore things that interest him – how to be strong in the face of terrible danger.

This is total fantasy play where the roles he plays are neither domestic nor functional, but imagined.

Claims have been made about the links between children's competence in imaginary play and their cognitive abilities (e.g. Hughes, 1995). In the developed world play has been elevated to a high status amongst early childhood experts and in the UK was regarded as being the primary mode of learning in the original Foundation Stage curriculum. It is important to note that this is not the case in all cultures or even in all groups within a culture. In her book *Starting School: Young Children Learning Cultures* (2002) Liz Brooker looked at the views of play as a mode of learning held by two different groups of parents: white working-class parents and Bangladeshi parents. She focused on a reception class in a primary school that was described as having a child-centred approach to learning, emphasising the importance of children being able to learn largely through play. Hers was a small sample and the research was limited, but her findings are interesting and raise some important questions. She found that the English parents had taken on at least some of the rhetoric about children learning best through play, which they saw as quite distinct from teaching. Their children had many toys and were encouraged to play with them and to get dirty and to talk a lot. The Bangladeshi children had fewer toys and their parents saw play as something children did after they had learned. It seems essential then to include in any discussion of play and learning a range of cultural dimensions.

Some years ago, in the developed world, there was much talk of what is known as Developmentally Appropriate Practice (DAP), which claims to draw on research and is often presented as the manual of current knowledge about young children. The research it draws on is almost entirely from the USA and DAP makes no attempt to examine values or cultural perceptions in relation to children. It takes an age and stage stance, very much influenced by Piaget, and is prescriptive, telling parents as well as educators what to do. The second edition, produced in 1997, did take some account of difference and recognised the terrible effects of poverty, but the approach taken was still essentially consumerist in nature.

DAP promotes self-initiated and self-directed play, which are described as being the most effective ways of learning and are upheld by a rich resource base of materials, activities and the support of trained educators. This all presumes that there are universal and predictable sequences of growth and play. It totally ignores different patterns of child-rearing, cultural expectations and practices, lifestyles and, most significantly, economic bases. There are several serious issues that arise from this.

The first issue is that through advocating a play-based approach to learning and development, play itself is often misrepresented as being dependent on a level and quantity of resourcing that is not possible for the majority of the world's children. We mentioned Viruru's (2001) description of nurseries in Southern India and you will remember that their decision not to offer a wide range of toys was a philosophical and not an economic one.

The second issue is the notion that parents can be taught to be 'good parents', which implies the adoption of a model of parenting that is universalist. Do you think it would be fair to say that this implies *'everyparent'*, the adult equivalent of 'everybaby'? Many in the developing world struggle to deal with the imposition this makes as educators, knowing little or nothing about particular cultures, routines and rituals, ways of child-rearing and interaction, seek to teach parents what to do and how to be.

For children to learn through play they must have chosen what to do in response to what interests, excites, surprises, engages them. Assumptions continue to be made about how far educators can trust children to be in charge of their own learning. Amazing is the example of the work of Sugata Mitra in India (reported in 2010) who was concerned with the huge numbers of children unable to attend nurseries or schools in India. He had the innovative idea of placing computers in walls of some slum buildings in New Delhi and then wider and wider afield throughout rural India. Cameras then filmed what groups of children said and did. Remember that these children had had no prior access to computers, knew no English, had never encountered the internet. What they did was to explore the computers just as all learners explore what they encounter, and as they did so began to show and explain to others what they could do with the computer. Mitra concluded that children will learn to do what they want to do and will teach one another. To see for yourself go to http://www.ted.com/talks/sugata_mitra_the_child_driven_education.html and watch the amazing video you will find there.

Imaginative play in diverse cultural settings

It seems evident that children's play, like every aspect of their development, varies according to their culture. Play is common in virtually all cultures but the way in which children play and the themes they adopt may be culture-specific. Roopnarine *et al.* (1994) found there were few detailed studies of imaginative play across cultures but since then studies are showing some interesting but not entirely surprising findings. Some studies have looked at how mothers play and found that the ways in which they play and view play vary enormously. Rogoff *et al.* (1993) report that Guatemalan mothers will laugh with embarrassment if asked to play with their children as they see this as the role of other children or sometimes of grandparents. In Italy mothers see play as inevitable but not requiring any adult intervention. In Turkey, as in the United States, Göncü and Mosier (1991) report that middle-class parents think of themselves as play-partners for their children. And this is the model being promoted by many of those involved with DAP, as we have seen.

Marc *et al.* (1999) looked at the exploratory and symbolic play of children under the age of 2 with their mothers from two cultures – Argentina and North America. They found that there were both similarities and differences in the play patterns they observed. In both groups boys engaged in more exploratory play than girls and girls in more symbolic play than boys. This was mirrored in the play of their mothers. In both there were individual variations in children's play and in each case this was closely related to the play patterns of the mothers. American children and their mothers engaged in more exploratory play than their Argentinian peers, but Argentinian mothers engaged more in social play with their children and gave more verbal praise to them.

One of the most frequently cited studies of cultural difference in symbolic play is that of Smilansky (1968) who looked at the play of two groups of Israeli children aged 3 to 6. One group was described as of European descent and middle class, the other as of North African descent and lower working class. Smilansky found significantly less dramatic play in the group of lower-class children. By dramatic play she was talking about imitative play, pretend play with objects, social interaction and verbal communication. She suggested that this was due to the fact that the parents of these children knew less about play (you will notice value-judgements about parents, again!), valued it less and had child-rearing techniques that did not promote the verbal and cognitive skills needed to develop imaginative play. No recognition was given to the pressures of the reality of life on the poorer families, the impact of poverty, the importance of different norms and so on. Negative findings like these have since been challenged.

More recent studies move away from such a deficit view to a more analytical one and find that children use pretend play in diverse contexts. In studies of observed play across India, Taiwan, Sierra Leone, Senegal and Guyana the following facts emerged:

- Children across these cultures (and certainly many others) can and do engage in elaborate role play during which they demonstrate that they sequence actions and adopt roles. It was findings like this that led Ebbeck as long ago as 1972 to suggest that accounts of imaginative play need to avoid making global assumptions and statements.
- Rates of symbolic play vary from culture to culture. Presumably this will be dependent on many factors, not least the economic position of the children and their families and communities. Children contributing to the economic life of their family will have less time for symbolic play than those from more privileged homes.
- Play themes in the countries being studied are more likely to involve roles and scripts related to family practices and the everyday activities of cooking, working, cleaning, marketing, preparing feasts and weddings rather than fantasy, although there is evidence of some fantasy play.

What do children play about?

We have seen that pretend play is a representational activity and that when children play in this mode they may use physical means (like objects) or psychological means (such as intonation patterns and gesture) to represent meaning. Do you remember the example cited earlier in this book of Helen who, when playing at being a manager, acted and spoke as she imagined a manager would? Once pretend play becomes social (by which we mean involves more than one child) it is essential that children agree on the reference of pretence: they have to agree what it is they are playing about and what they will do in their adopted or assigned roles. We have seen how this sharing of focus comes about through intersubjectivity. Here is an example to illustrate this:

> Three 4-year-olds are playing outdoors on the climbing frame. One shouts, 'Be careful! There are crocodiles in the river'. The others look down. They are on the top bar of the climbing frame and immediately 'see' the crocodile. This becomes the signal for how the play will progress.
>
> (Personal observation notes)

Here the children clearly have a shared frame of reference. When one 'sees' crocodiles the others know where to look and they also 'see' crocodiles. These imagined crocodiles become the focus of the play for the children. This is an extremely complex cognitive act of shared meaning making.

The play scripts and scenarios children follow are often culturally or emotionally determined. Many children use play as the vehicle for acting out – in safety – their deepest fears and concerns. Sometimes this is solitary play and sometimes it is done in collaboration. Sometimes the root of the play is evident: often it is not. Here are some vignettes to read, all based on personal observations of peers or colleagues. As you read them see if you can work out what the theme or issue of the play is.

Three-year-old Maria was playing with the miniature figures in the doll's house in her nursery. She took the adult male doll figure and put it repeatedly on top of the baby figure, moving the male doll up and down and crying out as if in pain as she did this.

It will surely help you to understand this seemingly random play when you know that her family was going through a grave crisis involving the abuse of several young children in the family.

Sarita is 5 years old and she and her best friend Ollie are playing in the garden. Sarita goes over to Jojo and holds up her hand, saying 'You are not to play here. We are in the palace and you are too poor to play with us.' Jojo protests 'I am not poor. I am just a boy'. 'Well,' says Sarita, 'This is a game just for girls.' 'I can be a girl,' says Jojo, 'if I put on this dress.' 'OK,' says Sarita. 'Now I am in charge and you are my servants.'

This was part of a wonderful set of observation notes given to me by a student. The play went on for a long time and even extended over several days. During the play the themes changed and included gender and what it means, bullying and power, money and status.

Like the examples above, many children's play themes relate to difficult and sometimes taboo areas. Vygotsky believed that pretend play develops when children begin to explore some unrealisable desires and tendencies. Imaginary play allows them to explore these within the safety net of the rules developed within the play. You may see here the link to fairy-tales and folk tales, which seem to develop in all cultures, and where difficult themes are explored (having a step-mother, being orphaned, overcoming evil and so on). In play, the child moves from exploring objects that dictate what she might do with them, to using objects to help examine threatening themes, feelings or questions. So a block of wood suddenly becomes a doll that can be sick or frightened or abused or bullied; a stick becomes a wand or a mobile phone or a magic weapon. Through symbolic play the child is learning that language and ideas and objects are not fixed but flexible. Ideas thus allow for *what could be* as well as *what is* and *what has been*. The imagination itself becomes a key feature of development – a central mechanism in communication; something that allows human beings to explore and respect diversity and to conceive of and create change. This is essentially the creative process in action.

Freud conceived of play as something cathartic for children. He believed that play allowed them to go in and out of reality in order to experience their own mastery and control. Children can then deal with their own anxieties, fears and conflicts in a safe way. This is the root of many of the play therapies that have developed since.

Penny Holland (2003) examined the difficult issue of aggressive behaviour in very young children and looked at what might happen if nursery classes and settings abandoned their 'no tolerance to gun-play' policies. What she observed was that the children, particularly the boys, did not abandon their aggressive play; in the absence of guns there were always sticks, stickle-bricks and a host of objects that could be used to symbolise guns. Moreover, she found that the children instantly picked up the message that aggressive play is unacceptable and this made it difficult for many since they need some way of expressing their strong negative feelings. All that happened was that the aggressive play went underground. Holland's contention was that banning play with guns was ineffective at best and damaging at worst. A close examination of what the children are actually playing about and exploring is worth doing.

Vivian Gussin Paley, who is known for her work in involving herself in children's dramatic play in her classrooms, has always been aware of the fact that many boys in the USA are engaged in aggressive behaviour using guns if they are available or making them where they are not. She neither promoted nor banned such play but also invited the children to make up and act out stories around issues that concern them. In her inimitable fashion she took detailed notes of what happened and analysed them. Take careful note of what she says:

> [B]oys' play is serious drama, not morbid mischief. Its rhythms and images are often discordant to me, but I must try and make sense of a style that, after all, belongs to half the population of the classroom.
>
> (Paley, 1984: 12)

Play and creative thinking

All those who pay attention to young children, wherever they are, recognise the importance of play to the quality of their lives. Play is important because it is the way in which children are able to use and reflect on their experiences, to represent their ideas and to ask and answer the questions that preoccupy them. Rinaldi describes children as 'the most avid seekers of meaning and significance' (2006: 113) and goes on to consider how, through the things they do and say, they show us their *developing theories*. For her and other educators in Reggio Emilia, the underpinning philosophy is a pedagogy of relationships and listening. It is also and essentially a pedagogy of watching. Children give evidence of their theories through their actions and words. In order to really know and understand children, adults have to pay close and sensitive attention to what they are saying or doing. When you do this you will notice that children are being creative in bringing together what they know and what they have experienced in order to create new understanding. You will remember this from Bruce's notion of play as an integrating mechanism.

Two small vignettes, drawn from Rinaldi's work, illustrate this:

> Federica, aged 3 years and 2 months, wanted to show a running horse in her drawing. She knew that horses have four legs and her solution to the problem she had set herself was to draw a figure of a horse with two legs on one side of the piece of paper and then turn the piece of paper over to draw two legs alone on the other side. She managed to find a solution – her own unique solution – to a problem she has set herself. Here is a child being essentially creative.

> A 3-year-old boy was playing with a piece of wire. First he made a bracelet and then put the wire on the back of a chair and let the wire become a horseman riding his horse (the chair). Finally, in the play sequence, the child turned the wire into a horse's ear.

Rinaldi's analysis of what is happening here is that, in each case, the child is demonstrating what she describes as *divergent thinking*. What Rinaldi means by this is that the children are bringing together things that don't normally go together and can do this because they have no theoretical framework to determine what is correct. The responses of adults to divergent thinking are often negative, giving children the dangerous message that thinking like that is not acceptable. Go back to Federica's horse and consider the response made to this by two adults, A and J:

> *A:*   Federica, don't you know that a horse has four legs?
> *J:*   What a brilliant idea to draw two legs on one side of the paper and two legs on the other side of the paper. Just like the legs on a real horse.

There is tremendous emphasis on offering children in the nursery schools of Reggio Emilia as many different ways as possible of *representing and re-representing their ideas*. Much talk has taken place about the so-called *'hundred languages' of children* – a phrase coined to describe the different ways in which children explore ideas, concepts and feelings. Educators in Reggio Emilia feel that in talking of languages they build on Vygotsky's work around language, signs and semiotics. There is, of course, much to be said in favour of children having access to many different ways of expressing their thoughts and ideas, but there is also the very real danger that, once again, a view of the ideal childhood, the ideal learner, is rooted in a Western and capitalist tradition where 'opportunities' and access to resources are vital ingredients in successful learning. We repeat that play is a mode of learning but not the sole mode of learning. It is certainly one most children discover for themselves and one that appears in most cultures and times. But it is not dependent on access to resources and is as possible in developing societies as it is in consumerist societies. Children play with what is to hand and children learn from all their experiences.

Moyles (1998) tells us that play can act as a scaffold for other basic learning. What she means by this is that it allows children to cope with not knowing for long enough to enable them to get to know. This frees them from worrying about 'getting it wrong' and gives them time to build their confidence to try new things. Here is an example:

> Adi is having trouble learning to read. He is only 5 years old and is a child brimming over with theories of his own. He can remember, in detail, things from years before and has a rich internal life where he plays diverse roles in contexts he delights in inventing. Sometimes in his play he 'pretends' to read – always making clear that he knows that this is not 'real' reading, but that it does not matter because it is all in his invented world. He is dealing with what he cannot yet do by trying it out in pretend mode – safely.

Some theorists are interested in the role of emotion in children's play and creativity. We have already agreed that imagination is vital in pretend play. It allows for one thing to be treated as though it is something else. Russ and Kaugars (1999) believe that emotion or affect (or feeling) is also important. Current thinking suggests that two types of affective processes may operate in play. One is *affect states*, which are described as moods or feelings. When children play aggressively their feelings or moods may be dictating what and how they play. The other is *affect-laden fantasy*, which refers to the ideas and images and themes that are imbued with emotion. When children play out things that cause them to feel emotions (death or loneliness or fear or separation) they have selected themes or scripts that are imbued with emotion for them. In much pretend play both of these creative affective processes may occur and develop.

Play and younger children

Earlier in this chapter we mentioned the work of Hutt *et al.* (1989). You may be interested in knowing more of what they said about the earliest stages of play. They urged people to take play more seriously than they had done before, arguing that it is not just something that all children do, but that it is something extremely complex and significant in the development of children. They said that epistemic play behaviour is primarily the search for meaning, involving skill and knowledge acquisition. They believed that this kind of play requires the presence of adults in order to support, encourage and question the children. Ludic play was characterised as being more playful and requiring adult involvement only in the sense of adults recognising children's needs. So an adult might notice that the child needs something in her play.

Elinor Goldschmied (1994) studied the play of very young children and introduced the term *'heuristic play'* to describe what she observed. She said that children's early play was dominated by the need to put things in and take them out – in other words, to fill and empty containers. For her, the child (and could this be 'anychild'?) appears to have an urge to repeatedly do this. Goldschmied believed that there must be some pleasure and satisfaction from these repeated actions. Possibly the actions raise questions in the minds of the children and the children notice what happens and either repeat or change their actions. Goldschmied suggested that the role of adults involved with young children was solely to provide resources to match observed needs. She was stern in insisting that what the children should play with should be objects made of anything other than plastic. Her lists included things like collections of corks of different sizes, lengths of chain from fine to medium-sized links; large buttons made of bone; empty tins and jars, baskets of different sizes; wooden clothes pegs and so on. She is famous for having introduced what she called 'treasure baskets' and, in her book, linked her thoughts to the words of Bruce Chatwin who wrote, in *The Songlines*:

> When an Aboriginal mother notices the first stirrings of speech in her child, she lets it handle the 'things' of that particular country: leaves, fruit, insects and so forth. The child, at its mother's breast, will toy with the 'thing', talk to it, test its teeth on it, learn its name, repeat its name.

Goldschmied suggested that educators should provide babies with the kinds of everyday objects found in their homes. The way in which treasure baskets developed become rather far from this model, with people vying to produce the most unusual, innovative, natural collection of objects. Treasure baskets are a fine idea. What concerns me more is her advice that adults should stay attentive, but, crucially, silent. You will realise that this is a model far removed from one taking heed of culture, context, language and interaction.

Summing up

Now our twenty-first century child is seen as being able to make meanings from all the events and experiences she encounters and to make her own personal maps – social, emotional, cognitive and symbolic. She makes meaning and shares this through representations. One of the ways in which she brings together her thoughts and questions and experiences is through play where she is able to explore deeply and over time the things that fascinate, frighten, interest or enchant her. As she plays – free of the risk of 'getting it wrong' – she can both consolidate her ideas and thoughts and sometimes transform them. Her play is based around what is available in her culture. She is making culture and beginning to construct metaphors (thinking about how something is like something else). Situated in a community she is learning through interaction, playing, watching, listening, being apprenticed and sometimes through teaching her peers. A competent and creative child, indeed.

Things to think about

- How would you explain the links between creative thought and play?
- What are your feelings about the importance of children playing in order to be creative?
- Do you think you could find examples through your own experience of children constructing metaphors and making culture?
- Have you ever encountered a child who does not play?

Chapter 5

The child as symbol user and symbol weaver

In this chapter we look at how the child, having started to use symbols in play, moves on to understanding the many complex abstract symbolic systems in her world. The abstract symbolic systems we pay most attention to in this chapter are speech, writing, reading and number. We explore other abstract systems in the chapters that follow. We revisit the idea of intersubjectivity to find out more about how children are able to work with others, making and sharing meaning.

> Louis has been learning the multiplication tables. His teacher taught him a trick to work out when the nine times table was correct. He spent an inordinate amount of time trying to find other tricks. This is one of the sums he invented. He showed it to an adult working with him and followed it with a detailed explanation.
>
> $5 \times 4 = ?$
>
> $4/2 = 2$
>
> 2 add a 0 = 20 and then explained it like this.
>
> Imagine you are doing 5×4. Now 4 is an even number, so for even numbers you break them into half and then add a zero to the number. See?
>
> Now listen carefully because the odd numbers are harder. Imagine we are doing 5×3. Three is the number you are going to work on, so this time you go for the number before 3 which is 2. Then break it into half which is 1 and add a 5 to it, which makes it 15!
>
> (Figueiredo, 1998: 30)

What it means to be human

Human beings are the only known species to have developed and used cultural tools and appreciated why these are important. You will remember that cultural tools refer to both physical and symbolic systems. So when we talk of cultural tools we could be referring to objects like hammers, computers, magnetic resonance imagers; or to languages, mathematical symbols; or to graphic representations, drawings, maps, paintings and sculptures; or even to governments and religions. None of these is the result of the work of one or two individuals. They are the collective products of culture created by many individuals and groups over time. Great apes, although genetically close to us, have not developed anything resembling cultural tools. And it is likely that a child born and placed immediately on a desert island with no other people to interact with would almost certainly not be able to invent for herself music, algebra or an alphabetic system. What makes

Figure 5.1 A letter to Sandra from Chloe – an example of the child as symbol user

humans unique then, is our ability to create culture and the main thing that enables us to do this is something we have already addressed – the ability to understand other people's intentions, interact with them and learn from them.

But how does this happen? Tomasello and Rakoczy (2003) suggest the following:

- At the age of about 1 year children understand that other people are *intentional agents* (which means they act with some purpose or goal in mind). They are able to interact with and learn from other people. This is called intersubjectivity. At this very young age children are able to participate in and master some cultural activities, including spoken language. By the age of 2 children understand the relationships between self and other and are able to take different perspectives on things. They can reflect on and make some judgements of their own thinking. This is *shared intentionality*.
- At the age of about 4 children are able to understand other people's thoughts (sometimes called '*theory of mind*'). This means that very young children are able to understand others as mental agents, which implies that they can appreciate that others have thoughts and beliefs and these are not necessarily always right or correct. Through their interactions with others their understanding becomes more nuanced and complex and they begin to comprehend some of the cultural institutions rooted in the collective beliefs and values of the culture. These might include money systems,

conventions surrounding births, naming, marriage and death and so on. These activities arise out of *collective intentionality*.

• Human beings appear to be unique in being able to understand, consider and reflect on the psychological states of people (or how others feel) as demonstrated by 1-year-old children understanding such things as intentions and attention. You will remember some of Judy Dunn's findings with regard to this. Tomasello and Rakoczy (2003) argue that this is a *biological imperative* (which means that human beings are impelled to do this) and that what follows – the ability to comprehend communicative systems – requires that children engage with others in social and linguistic interactions with no particular biological underpinnings. Their argument is that the key event, intersubjectivity (what they call the *'real thing'*) takes place when the child is possibly only 1 year old.

Perhaps this is difficult to understand, so here are some examples illustrating the real thing:

Babatunde's mother hums as she chops the vegetables. Babatunde imitates her by making humming sounds.

In order for this to be possible the child must understand that there are two people involved in this wordless interaction – Babatunde and her mother – and she must understand something of her mother's intention in order to mimic her. When very young children begin to use words to label objects they demonstrate that they understand what words like 'pig' or 'horse' or 'David Beckham' mean. (The choice of nouns here is entirely arbitrary.) Later children start being selective in the words they use to describe things and they do this to be more precise so that they are more likely to be understood.

Charlie (4:1):   That man . . . that policeman . . . is in his car.

You can see how Charlie takes care to be precise about the nature of the particular man he is talking about. What is happening is that children work out that sometimes a word is not enough to accurately portray meaning and they refine what they are saying. Through intersubjectivity they have started to realise that sharing meaning requires paying attention to whether the listener or the partner in dialogue has understood exactly.

David, talking to his grandmother, was trying to explain a recent experience and he wanted his grandmother to understand exactly what he was trying to say. In a sense he wanted them to have a shared image of what he was describing:

'I saw that thingy – you know, that boat . . . the blue one . . . the canoe.'
(David, aged 4: personal observation, 2001)

Entering the world of linguistic symbols: beginning to talk

From very early on human infants show a unique communicative pattern of behaviour. They begin to indicate the need to have things *labelled or named for them*. They do this by looking or *eye-pointing*, *finger-pointing* or holding up objects, all aimed at inviting others to share attention and provide the label. Tomasello *et al.* (1999) argue that in this way the child develops the *linguistic symbols* of her culture and moves on to being able to adopt different perspectives at the same time. In doing this they reveal an appreciation of the fact that one person can be an unknown woman or mum or grandma or my teacher, as illustrated by David's explanation:

> That lady over there . . . she is my mum and she is my sister's mum too.
>
> (David, aged 4: personal observation, 2001)

Children begin using linguistic symbols (sounds and words, for example) in order to communicate. There is almost certainly some *imitation* involved as the child repeats words used by adults, *internalises* the sounds heard and then makes those same sounds in order to *make and share meaning*. Imitation may be part of the story but there are questions to be asked and answered in order to know whether it, alone, can explain how children acquire their first languages.

The first question is what makes spoken language a symbolic act. Often people think of symbols as things that can be seen or touched or held or moved. Talk consists of sounds and these are not random or haphazard but combined in particular ways in order to represent things. Names or nouns represent or stand for objects or people and these are the first linguistic symbols children use. Nouns are then combined with other words in order to create strings of words, then phrases and sentences. Language is rule-bound so that the ways in which words can be combined in order to create meaning are both clear and clearly understood by language users. But language is not fixed and static. New words come into languages and some words drop out of languages. The TV documentary *49Up* showed a 7-year-old in the year 1963 saying 'My heart's desire is to see my father.' This is a phrase almost unknown in the spoken language of today. Language is not only fluid and changing but also creative. Children play with language just as they play with objects.

> Sammy, at the age of 5, looked at her sister sitting across from her at the table and commented 'She is oppositting me.' She created a new verb by combining words and concepts – sitting and opposite.

> Two-year-old Zac invented the word 'whatbody' from hearing the word somebody. He asked 'Whatbody gave you that T-shirt?' Perfectly logical with a very clear meaning.

> 'Twas brillig, and the slithy toves
> Did gyre and gimble in the wabe
> All mimsy were the borogroves,
> And the mome raths outgrabe.

The first two examples are of children making up words according to the ways in which they perceive words to work. The third is from that master of playful language, Lewis Carroll from one of the poems in *Through the Looking-Glass*.

The Russian linguist Chukovsky (1925/1963) wrote a fascinating little book called *From Two to Five*, which is full of the funny, perceptive and inventive things that Russian children said, revealing their abilities to use language creatively. If you can find a copy it is really interesting to read.

The second question relating to how infants learn to communicate is whether what they do when they engage with objects can truly be called symbolic acts. Think about these questions:

- When a young child puts a doll in a box is the child putting the doll to bed or just putting an object in a container?
- When the child pushes a block along the ground is the child using the block to represent a car or merely pushing a block along the ground?

Tomasello *et al.* (1999) believe that many of the examples of symbolic play recorded in very young children take place in the presence of adults who scaffold the child's actions. For example, where adults say to the child 'Give the dolly a drink' with a cup and a doll present – objects that are familiar to the child and whose purposes are clear through experience – the child is likely to act out that verbal script. But consider the example cited by Harris and Kavanaugh (1993), who gave a child a yellow block and a teddy and told the child that the teddy was in the bath and asked the child to show them what the teddy did with the soap. It was only children over the age of 2 who were able to do this. They suggest this is because the adults did not model the washing action using the yellow block and the children were extremely unlikely to have ever seen anyone washing with a yellow block. Much of the research suggests that true symbolic representation only takes place much later than some of the writings suggest.

The third question arises through considering the role of imitation in *language acquisition*. Language acquisition is a fascinating, tendentious and complex subject and theorists who disagree with one another do so with a passion. The notion that children acquire language largely through imitation dates back to the work of Skinner, some of whose work was touched on earlier in this book. Put very simply, he believed that much of language acquisition came about through imitation and through *reinforcement*. So the child makes a sound; the adult interprets the sound as meaningful and praises the child; the child repeats the sound. Put crudely, the model looks like this:

> The child babbles and within the string of sounds comes something that sounds like 'mama'.
> The mother thinks the child has learned to say the word for mother and kisses the child.
> The praise – the positive reinforcement – makes the child say the word again, hoping for another kiss (or hug or banana).
> The child has learned to say 'mama'.

Using language in order to communicate is a milestone in development. What is fascinating is that this remarkable intellectual feat, which usually takes place within the first year of life, occurs without anyone giving the child lessons. No one sets out to teach the child to talk. Rather, children begin to communicate with other beings through *gesture, eye-pointing, expression, intonation* and eventually through *talk*. In this social world children are surrounded by people who use talk in many, many different situations and use talk in order to communicate. The talk children encounter in their homes and communities is talk for real purposes and between people who want to share meaning.

There are no tests to fail or trick questions to answer. So the human infant, working hard to understand communication, does so in the supportive company of people who want to communicate with her.

The work of Noam Chomsky and his critics

Noam Chomsky, an American thinker and writer who is still alive, was the first to suggest that language acquisition is genetically determined. He believed that the human infant was born pre-programmed to work out the rules of speech. If you think about it you will realise that speech – in any language – must be rule-governed if people are to be able to understand it, use it and be understood. In English, for example, there are rules about the order of words. We can say 'the dog jumped over the fence' but if we say 'the fence jumped over the dog' it makes no sense because a fence cannot jump. If we say 'the jumped fence the over dog' we are uttering a string of exactly the same words but in an order that prevents it from being meaningful. The same rule does not necessarily apply to other languages. In English we have rules about how we use verbs when we talk about the past tense. So we say 'we walked' and 'we talked', the rule being that we add 'ed' to the end of the verb. We have rules about how to talk about more than one object. So we talk about shoes and socks and pens and pencils. The rule here is that we add the letter 's' to the end of a noun to make that noun plural. You, as a fluent speaker of the language, will know that there are exceptions to the rules. We say 'went' instead of 'goed' and 'flew' instead of 'flied': we talk of sheep instead of sheeps. Chomsky noticed that young children, having started out by saying things correctly through imitating what they heard adults and fluent speakers say, move on to making mistakes by applying the rules to all situations. The way in which he described this was that the children were *over-generalising* the rules. He used this as evidence that children are brilliant thinkers, working out the patterns they hear to make up the rules and then, logically, applying them to all situations.

It was these errors that suggested to Chomsky that children must have something that allows them to use the patterns they hear to work out the rules. What he proposed was that the structure of language, by which he meant the rules that bind it together to make it meaningful, depend on what he called a *Language Acquisition Device* (LAD). You will remember that language has to be rule-bound and the rules known to all for it to be used for sharing meaning. The rules that bind language together are its grammar. The LAD had, as its foundation, what Chomsky called a *'universal grammar'* or a linguistic *'deep structure'*, which he believed all humans are born with. The LAD is programmed to recognise, in the *surface structure* of any natural language (i.e. the words and other features), how the deep structure will operate. So the surface features that are particular to that language (to English or to Urdu or to Zulu, for example) allow it to be operated by the universal blueprint. This is what accounts for the fact any human being is born capable of learning to communicate in any language. These are difficult ideas to comprehend and his is an extreme but very plausible view.

Children are seen as potentially competent users of language from birth. By competence Chomsky was talking about the underlying and unconscious knowledge of the rule system for generating language that they are born with. The errors, or the mistakes, children make show us the efforts they are making to find the patterns in the particular language, to work out the rules and apply them. Here are some examples to make this more clear:

Fifteen-month-old Antonio points to the plastic farm animals he is playing with and labels them – 'cows, horses, sheep'.

Here you can see that this very young child is imitating the correct form of plurals he has heard the fluent speakers in his world use. He has not yet worked out the pattern that operates in English for making plurals. One might say that he is 'just copying'.

At 3 years Antonio points to the plastic sheep and labels them 'sheeps'.

Now the child has moved on from making a grammatically correct response to making an error or a mistake. Chomsky believed that this is because a child like Antonio has been paying attention to what he hears. He has worked out that adults have a pattern for making plurals: they add an 's' at the end of the word. Antonio, uses this pattern or rule to form all plurals he says. He hasn't yet learned what we know: that there are often exceptions to the rules. The consequence is that he applies the rule to all situations. A reminder: in the language of Chomsky he over-generalises the rule. No amount of correction at this stage will enable him to rectify his errors. It is only when he has discovered that there are rules and exceptions to rules that he will be able to use both forms. In other words, only with experience of listening to experienced others will he self-correct.

Steven Pinker is a linguist who was very influenced by the work of Chomsky and went on to write about the work of Chomsky in his 1994 book *The Language Instinct*. This is a very readable and chatty book, full of amusing games with language combined with some intricate explanations. The use of the word 'instinct' in the very title of the book points to the view of language acquisition he shared with Chomsky – that it was genetically determined. Pinker tells us that from Chomsky we learn two things:

1   That language cannot be merely a repertoire or a range of responses since everything anyone utters or understands is a novel or new combination of words. When a child says 'The birds flied off' or 'I seed it and I feeled it and it's not a dog' each of these is a unique set of words, making meaning, but never before uttered by any human being. So the brain must hold a recipe or a programme or a blueprint that can build an infinite number of sentences out of a finite list of words. These are known as *mental grammars*.
2   That children develop these mental grammars, which are very complex, extremely rapidly and without formal teaching.

Bruner was also influenced by the work of Chomsky and saw it as taking thinking about how children acquire language a leap forward from previous theories. He was very interested in language and particularly in talk. However, he saw a gap in Chomsky's theory and that gap was the lack of any reference to other people, which means a lack of reference to interaction, culture or context. For Bruner the development of language requires at least two people involved in negotiation. The purpose of language is communication and it is through communication that meaning is made and shared and fine-tuned. So, building on Chomsky's LAD, Bruner proposed a more sociocultural model which he called the *Language Acquisition Support System* (LASS). He conceived of this as a kind of adult scaffolding system. What happens is that children learn their language through their interactions with others, who cue the children's responses and share meanings with them in particular contexts and within cultures. So Bruner adds a sociocultural dimension to Chomsky's model.

Bruner was very interested in the linguistic games and routines that occur between caregivers, particularly mothers, and infants in the early years. He noted that interactions like these were evident in all cultures and believed that they laid the essential foundations for the development of communicative systems. He identified several ways in which the LASS helps the child move from *prelinguistic* (before spoken language) to *linguistic* communication. His focus is on what he calls *formats*.

The first formats are the routine and familiar formats where the adult highlights the features of the world that are meaningful to the child and have a basic or simple grammatical form. The features refer to the context or the situation. The interactions are often between mother and child and the formats are built around simple games. One of the formats he analysed was the simple 'peekaboo' type of game with which you may be familiar.

In the game something or someone is present, then made to disappear and then reappear. This is usually accompanied by a verbal noise like 'boo!' The game has been made up by people and it follows a set pattern so that it is tied together by simple rules which can only vary slightly.

Bruner argues that games like these offer the first occasions for the child to use language systematically with the adult and the first opportunity for the child to get something done with words. He describes the games as being idealised and self-contained formats. You can think about these game formats as having a deep structure and a set of rules and it is these rules that allow the surface of the game to be managed. Let's analyse a peekaboo game where something is hidden and then reappears:

- The deep structure is the controlled disappearance and reappearance of the object or the person.
- The surface structure refers to all or any of the following: the screens or cloths or whatever is used to make the thing or person disappear and reappear; the timing of each act; the actual words or sounds used and the choice of what it is that is to disappear.
- The game is described as being 'nonnatural' – it is invented or made up and it is tied together by the rules, which can be negotiated.
- The game is like language in that it involves turn-taking roles that are not fixed but can be changed. It does not matter who hides: there is always a hider and a hidden, an actor and an experiencer. Bruner calls these games little protoconversations.
- The game provides opportunities for spreading attention over an ordered sequence of events. So the game itself is the topic or the theme about which each of the moves can be seen as a comment.
- Games like this do not occur in the animal world: they occur only in the human world, perhaps because they are dependent on some use and exchange of language.

The second formats move into spoken language and are where the adult encourages and models lexical (or word) and phrasal substitutes for familiar gestural and vocal means in order to effect different communicative competence. So instead of hiding something and going 'boo!' the adult might hint, verbally, at a surprise to come, perhaps by saying 'One, two, three . . . look!' Or during the game the adult might ask leading questions, give hints or find things out. If you find this a little confusing just think of the familiar game 'I spy with my little eye'. As adults play these word games with children they model the different ways in which spoken language is used for different purposes. By the use of body language and gesture they give the child a hint of what the answer is. 'I spy with my little eye something that looks good enough to eat' whilst looking at an apple. Formats like this help the child learn to *ask for or request* something. One of the things young linguists have to do in order to request something is to share the focus of attention with the adult. Here are two examples to illustrate what children do to share the focus of attention. In each see if you can say just what it is that the child does to ensure the adult shares her focus of attention:

> Six-month-old Julie looks intently at her doll which is on a shelf in her room. Her mother follows her gaze and gives her the doll.

> Nine-month-old Giulio points to the apple in the fruit bowl and shakes his head when his grandma hands him the banana.

Adults involved with young children are very skilled at showing babies how to do this and use a range of tones of voice, gestures, eye-pointing and other means to share their focus of attention with the child. The child then adopts similar ways of focusing the adult's attention.

The third format is the play format, which allows the child to enter a pretend or an imaginary world in which she can adopt different roles and speech forms, address different audiences and try out new linguistic forms. Here is an example where a group of children are playing hospitals and move in and out of role, changing tone of voice, intonation pattern and style of speaking as they do so:

> Sacha, Stanley, and Holly are playing hospitals in the home corner. They are all 5 years old.

> *Sacha:*   Right, now what seems to be the matter?
> *Holly:*   My baby was sick this morning. She went blue in the face and she started crying in a very loud voice. I was worried and so we have brought her here.
> *Sacha:*   Stanley, you be the nurse.
> *Stanley:* I can't be a nurse. I am a boy,
> *Holly:*   Boys can be nurses, you silly. Be the nurse. Put on that costume.

> Stanley obeys and puts on a high-pitched voice.

> *Stanley:* Here baby. What's the matter? (He takes the doll and pokes its stomach.) This baby is very, very, very sick. This baby is going to die. You will be very sad, won't you mommy?
> *Holly:*   Oh no! I don't want my baby to die. You are a nurse. Make her better.
> *Stanley:* I am the boss here and I will make her better and then, Mrs Holly, you can take her home and look after her better.

> (Personal observation notes)

Notice how, when the children come out of role, their language changes. They are adapting their language to the context and to the roles they are playing. Out of role Holly becomes very bossy.

The work of Michael Halliday: thinking about semiotics

Michael Halliday also looked at language acquisition but from a very different perspective from that of Chomsky. He was influenced by both Eastern European linguists and British and American anthropological linguists, and spoke of *language development* rather than language acquisition. This was because he saw language as being an infinite, variable and dynamic resource for making and sharing meaning being constructed and maintained through interaction. Chomsky spoke of language acquisition, which may conjure an image of language as a commodity – something that one can acquire which is finite, unitary, monolithic and fixed. Talking of 'acquiring language' suggests that it is something an individual either 'has' or 'lacks'.

Linguists refer to Halliday's view of language as *'systemic-functional linguistics'* (SLF). Halliday stated that the interactions between infant and caregiver in the first six months of life are crucial. During these interactions there is what he called an 'exchange of attention' which he saw as the beginning of language. There may be no content to this exchange: it is about feelings and has meaning. Halliday emphasised two things: that language is a system for making meaning and meaning is created in the process of mutual exchange. The communication that develops as the child uses these shared attention contexts for engaging with the real world in these early months is known as *protolanguage*.

Did you know that the dictionary definition of protolanguage is a hypothetical lost parent language from which actual languages are derived? In an attempt to understand how humans develop language, Michael Halliday spent 21 months studying every detail of his son Nigel's language learning. He took copious notes from when Nigel was 9 months old until he was 2½ years old. He developed a three-stage model in which he argued that humans develop language because they are creatures who need to mean, and language, above all else, is our primary resource for meaning. Even the infant who cannot talk is developing language, and thereby learning how to mean. Just as the infant can't walk, but is learning how to use her body, she cannot talk either – at least not in the language of her home. But what the child does is use all means of communication available. So this protolanguage (sometimes referred to as protoconversation and protosemiosis) is made up of tones of voice, sounds, gesture, expression, eye-pointing, finger-pointing, crying, laughing, all in order to express meaning, all in communication with others, before she has words in her communicative repertoire. Her protolanguage, or child tongue, is created through interactions with native speakers of her mother tongue (i.e., caregivers, siblings, etc.).

Halliday's work is difficult to understand partly because of his use of very specific language. He suggested that the move from protolanguage to language itself involves the development of a *semiotic system*. Semiotics is often defined as the study of *signs* and *symbols*, what they mean and how they are used. You will have encountered signs and symbols and we have already talked about the importance of children developing an understanding of how one thing can stand for or represent another. In language the words we use, the words we say, the words we read are all symbols: they represent aspects of the real world. Marion Whitehead tells us that 'Human verbal language is a systematic and symbolic means of communication' (Whitehead, 1997: 13).

Semiotics is made up of the following three strands:

- *semantics* (which is meaning in language);
- *syntactics* (which refers to the formal properties of signs and symbols – i.e. grammar); and
- *pragmatics* (which is the study of language in social contexts).

In order for any child to use language effectively the child has to deal with both interpersonal meaning and representation. Halliday calls representation ideational meaning. So the child becomes not only able to share meanings but also to reflect on or think about them. Halliday calls both interpersonal meaning and ideational meaning *metafunctions*. They are 'functions' because they comprise the basic uses of language (to interact with another and to make sense of experience). They are 'meta' because they are not within the child but outside of the child and are the way in which meaning has become embedded in the sign or symbol. This is very interesting but really beyond the scope of this book.

Vygotsky and language

Vygotsky was interested in the development of *'higher psychological functions'* such as *attention and memory*. A key feature of these higher functions is that they are mediated by the use of signs. You may want to go back to page 33 to remind yourself of this.

Some years ago it was common to tell someone to tie a knot in their handkerchief in order to remember something. The knot acted as a sign or symbol, allowing the person to remember something. It stood for or represented the thing to be remembered. This is important because it transforms remembering from a process dependent on direct stimulation from the environment to a process that can be voluntarily regulated and reflected on. The learner no longer has to be in the presence of the thing to be remembered but has made an internal representation to allow her to remember the thing. Nowadays fewer people carry handkerchiefs and people have developed different (and sometimes very personal) ways of creating signs or symbols to enable them to have a mental representation of something. This is what allows us not only to remember, but also to think about the things we remember. So we reflect on what we recall.

Here is an example to illustrate this:

> Four-year-old Joe could remember in detail some of the things that had happened on a visit to his cousin's house in Manchester a year before this conversation took place. He said, 'We had a blue car and we stayed in a big house. I was in one room right at the top and my sister was in the room with me. There was a cat and I was scared that the cat would bite me . . . or scratch me (giggles). I was only little then.

You can see how a return visit to his cousin's house prompted Joe not only to remember some of the physical details of an event long past, but also to think back and reflect on his own behaviour. He could remember being scared that the cat would bite or scratch him and analysed that as justifiable because he had been 'only little then'. Talking and thinking about an event and being able to reflect on it through language are complex *higher-order cognitive skills*.

According to Vygotsky, not only were higher psychological functions mediated by the use of signs, but they arose out of social interaction. Vygotsky believed that, in human development, these higher mental functions appear twice: first as *inter-mental functions* that arise through interactions and are mediated by speech and second as *intra-mental functions*, mediated by internalised semiotic processes. Inter-mental means between mind and mind; in other words, by sharing ideas or concepts. Intra-mental means only in the mind of the individual. So through sharing experiences, bathed in language, a concept or idea or experience once shared becomes available internally to the child. The child has made some sort of *mental map* or image or thought of what was shared and this is now available to her without mediation.

The terminology used by Vygotsky is difficult to deconstruct and it is important to remember that his writing was in Russian so what we have are always translations. What he was saying here is that learning first takes place through interactions between people (and specifically in interactions where talk is involved). The child who is a participant in the interaction becomes able to reflect on what has happened and to internalise this, drawing on previous experience and understandings. In other words, infants are conscious and mentally active beings from birth, and their consciousness is later shaped by language. Language, however, can only function in this way as a feature of the individual's intra-mental cognition on the basis of having first been initially experienced inter-mentally in communicative exchanges with others (Painter 1999: 26).

Vygotsky's strong focus on the importance of interaction has influenced educators over many years. We have examined whether children learn best alone, collaboratively in groups or pairs; how adults can scaffold learning; that a child's performance can provide a window into her potential; and gained a recognition of the importance of language for learning. Vygotsky was deeply interested in the links between speech and thought. He drew a distinction between *pre-intellectual speech* (which is speech before the emergence of thought) and *pre-verbal thought* (which is thought before the emergence of talk). It is astounding to remember that children under the age of about 2 use vocal activity in interaction to communicate not only their ideas but also their feelings and emotions. More than that, they use speech to establish and maintain social contact. They are also capable of goal-directed or purposeful activity that does not require speech. Here are some examples:

> Amina, involved in a peekaboo game with her carer, joins in with the 'boo' by laughing aloud to show her pleasure.

Remembering the game and its outcome, she is using vocal activity to join in and show the emotion of pleasure.

> Amina drags a chair over to the shelf near the window of her room and climbs onto it to reach her favourite toy duck.

Wanting to reach her toy duck enables her to engage in a goal-directed activity without speech. This stage – sometimes described as 'primitive' – is followed by a stage of so-called 'practical intelligence' where the child uses syntax and logical forms of language that have parallels in her problem-solving activities but may not be linked to them in any particularly useful way. Here is an example to clarify this:

> Liam is drawing on a piece of paper, using a thick blue felt-pen. As he draws he chants 'Ooh, a thick blue line. Very nice. Thick and blue. I like blue. It's my best colour. Except for red (changes pen), which is also my best. And gold. I love gold.'

Liam is using spoken language to parallel what he is doing but not really to reflect on what he is doing or solve any problems he has set himself.

In the third stage the child starts to use external symbolic means – speech or other cultural tools – to assist internal problem-solving. It is at this stage that we often overhear children talking aloud as they solve problems or describe their actions.

> Mohammed arrives in the nursery and announces that he is going to build a tower from the top down. The teacher is very interested in what he does and watches and records what happens.
> (Goes to fetch small ladder. Gets Avril to help him set it up.)
>
> M: Please put it here, Avril. Just on the carpet so the tower will be right in the middle. Now I need to get some blocks to start the tower. I am going to take two of these big flat ones because they will look really nice at the top. They could be like a helipad.
>
> (Picks up two flat blocks, holds them in one hand and climbs up the ladder.)
>
> M: Nearly ready now.
>
> (Reaches the top – stretches out his hand and stops.)
>
> M: Oh, no! It isn't going to work, is it? Because when I let go the blocks won't stay where I want them. They are going to fall. Oh no!

Some authors call this *monologuing*: and once it becomes internalised Vygotsky called it *inner speech*. The internalisation marks the point when the thinking required for problem-solving has been established. So language becomes something that is used to reflect on action and develop thought rather than as a pre-requisite of problem solving. In other words, children become able to use speech and language as tools in their problem solving because speech allows them to reflect on and consider what they are doing.

The social dimensions of this are apparent as they are in all of Vygotsky's work. The child first expresses emotions and establishes contacts with others and then uses language itself to communicate and to represent thoughts and ideas and this moves on not only to making meaning but also to sharing meaning with others. So inner speech moves on to social speech. The child's private monologues in the head may be the precursors of thought.

Narrative: language as a dialogic process

The Russian philosopher and linguist Mikhail Bakhtin wrote widely about language and had what is often called a *dialogic* view of language. It is not difficult to understand what is meant by dialogic because it is so close to the word dialogue. For him, learning to use language meant leaning to interact with others in particular social situations or contexts. Within any context the child learns to be part of an appropriate or dominant 'truth' available within that context. A child coming into a new class, for example, has to learn to be part of the language and the culture of the new class and this involves complex makings of meaning relating to power, control, rules and so on. These are complex ideas, couched in difficult language, but keep reading – what Bakhtin said is both interesting and relevant. Let's look at some examples:

> Helena enters a new class in the infants school and finds she is the only black child in the class.

> Dominique wants to join the football team but it is made up entirely of boys.

> Marlena has just arrived from Poland and has to start school. She is the only Polish speaker in the whole school.

Think about how each of these children's *social positioning* might affect what happens. Children's scripts are formed where their social interactions meet their inner meanings and the cultural symbols available to them. The cultural meanings available to a small child may be different from those of an older child; the meanings available to a black child may be different to those of a white child which, again, may be different to those of a speaker of another language. This means that children learn to talk (and act) differently in different contexts and with different people. To make this clear you only have to think about how you speak differently at work from the way you do at home; or to your grandparents as opposed to your children; or to friends as compared with powerful others like doctors or lawyers.

According to Bakhtin each individual has a unique point of view. But we live in a world of others and we experience our own perspective – our own understanding of the world – in dialogue with these others. They, in turn, see us as situated in a context. Bakhtin goes on to say that these others become the central figures – the heroes, if you like – of our lives and in the stories we make to explain our lives.

> It is about the others that all the stories have been composed, all the books have been written, all the tears have been shed . . . so that my own memory of objects, of the world, and of life could also become an artistic memory.
>
> (Bakhtin, 1981: 111–112)

Bakhtin, with his sociocultural approach to learning, offers us a useful framework when we turn our attention to children as *story makers*, *storytellers* and *narrators*.

Stories form one of the cultural tools that are found in every culture we can think of. The members of cultural groups make up and tell and re-tell stories about their lives and their feelings, their experiences and fears, their past and their imagined future. In some cultures – often described as having an oral tradition – stories are passed on through routines and rituals and become changed in the hearing and in the telling. You may well have come across some of the devices storytellers in some cultures have for indicating a story is about to begin: 'Cric-Crac' or 'Are you sitting comfortably? Then I'll begin' are signals to the listeners that a story is to be told. They are *cultural narrative markers*. In many cultures children hear and see stories on television and videos and in film or in cartoons and books. Children throughout the world begin, from very early on, to structure their own narratives. In order to make meaning and to share meaning children begin to sequence and structure the things they have done or experienced, first into simple proto-narratives, but later into more and more complex sequences.

Here is a simple proto-narrative told by 22-month-old Hannah when she came across a huge jacaranda tree in the park:

I could climb up and up and up . . . and then down and down and down.

This small child drew on her experience, which included knowing the story of *Jack and the Beanstalk* really well. Whitehead (1997) cites examples of some simple narratives created by children as young as 2 years old. Here is a wonderful example of what a black 2-year-old in the USA contributed after a first visit to church:

It's a church bell
Ringin'
Dey singin'
Ringin'
You hear it?
I hear it
Far
Now
                (Heath, 1983: 170)

This child is using poetic language (the arrangement of the words on the page is that of an adult, of course). What is significant is the act of composing or making up a story, which appears to be an essential ingredient of development. It involves selecting and structuring experience and feelings into something that can be told and listened to and reflected on. Harold Rosen (1984), in a pamphlet produced for the National Association for the Teaching of English and called *Stories and Meanings*, tells us that there may well be a disposition or a tendency to *narrative* that is as universal (or more so) than Chomsky's *Universal Grammar*. Barbara Hardy (1968) calls storying a *primary act of mind*. Most significantly, Bruner regarded narrative as a primary meaning-making tool. It appears that there may be a universal desire to create stories and the making of stories requires exposure to the cultural ways of storying we encounter. There is no correct way of making stories: we learn the story grammars and discourses and patterns from our society and our culture.

Rosen reminds us that it is important, however, to remember that narrative is fiction. Story makers – children and adults – draw on their own experience but also use their imagination – the worlds in their heads. So we are back to the words of Bakhtin about using others as our heroes. As story composers we cannot remember everything. We have to select the salient features of the story we want to tell and we use language to order experiences and memories. Rosen tells us that the story is out there, somewhere, awaiting a crucial step. The creator of the story must seek for and make meaning. To give order, then, to all the possible ways of telling that story *a sequence must be plotted* – we must invent *beginnings* and *endings*. In each story there must be a resolution or an outcome. Contradictions must be resolved. A tale must be told.

There is a long tradition in Jewish literature . . . of bearing witness through telling stories . . . In this way, history is preserved as personal history; history is given shape and meaning through the interpretation of individual lives. And just as history is made up of personal histories so too are personal identities formed in relation to a larger ethical and cultural context.

(Aarons, 1996: 60)

The symbols children use in their spontaneous writing

Much has been written about how children come to understand the written world in which they live. Researchers have looked at how very young children attempt to write and in doing so invent or re-create the symbols of their culture and language. At the beginning of this chapter (Figure 5.1) is an example of a very early piece of writing. The child used coloured felt pens and made zigzag marks across the page – one line for each colour. As she made the marks she related a simple 'story' to her mother. As she did this she revealed some of her thinking about what it is that writers do.

One of the most significant early pieces of work was a study of how children come to construct their own hypotheses about print and the alphabetic system. Ferreiro and Teberosky's seminal work *Literacy Before Schooling* (1979/1982) described a project examining the hypotheses of 4- to 6-year-old Spanish-speaking children from different socioeconomic backgrounds. The children were asked to produce disconnected fragments of writing in somewhat formal conditions, in a one-to-one relationship with an adult rather than in their peer groups. Tasks tended to focus on the *orthographic features* of the words. These are the marks that children make in their attempts to write. Their findings are interesting and sometimes moving. They are often surprising. They found, amongst other things, that 4-year-old children know what makes a picture and what makes 'writing': they know that writing is more than just squiggles, lines and dots, but symbols representing something else; they do not know that writing is 'speech written down'. They represent something that is large in life (an elephant, perhaps) by a symbol or group of symbols of proportionate size. Names of objects or people are the only linguistic forms to appear in the writing of these children. Ferreiro and Teberosky arrived at a stage theory of development in writing based on their observation that children move on from a hypothesis when something occurs to cause some cognitive dissonance. Here is an example:

> Sukvinder wrote a series of parallel straight lines and said it was writing. Two days later she did the same thing, but this time included some dots and curly lines. A week later she said 'I've got too many of these all the same ones'.

Ferreiro and Teberosky proposed that children naturally, over time, go through a predictable sequence from early *mark-making* to more recognisable *letter-like forms*, to *alphabetic letters* that are finally linked to sounds. There are studies that show that children make a similar journey in whatever language they are attempting to write.

Significant as this study was at the time, there was little opportunity for children to display a repertoire of skills in terms of the kinds of symbols they might use in varying contexts. Sulzby (1986) showed that the requests of adults affected the symbols children used. Children who were asked to write everything they could tended to write lists of words using conventional spelling, but when asked to write like grown-ups they produced scribble – showing an awareness of the shapes of cursive scripts.

Marie Clay, working in New Zealand in 1973, observed 5-year-old children in classrooms and she found something different. Rather than a clear linear progression she found that children, once they started to write, used a mix of principles. For example, they began to realise that a limited number of signs is required (Sukvinder in the example above shows a dawning realisation that too much repetition is not acceptable as 'writing'); that a limited number of signs when used in different combinations will result in different words (for example rat, tar, art are all made up of the same three letters). This is a clear focus on signs: Clay's approach is semiotically based. The children pay attention to writing as a system of signs in which how the features are arranged is vital. The features they pay attention to are how the marks are aligned on the page, the direction in which they are written and read and the specific aspects of the written language they see in their homes and cultures. Bengali children sometimes include horizontal lines in their early writing and Urdu or Arabic early writers used many curls and dots.

Vygotsky focused, too, on semiotics and did not see the development of writing as linear, but rather as a complex and dialectical process where children go backwards and forwards, using changes and *transformations*. Early writing, characterised by simple mark-making, seems to disappear, only to re-appear later on in a different form. So he saw children's development as writers as social, dynamic and continuous. The child's understanding of signs is interwoven with sociocultural experience. There is constant interplay between the interpersonal (what happens inside the child's thinking) and the intrapersonal (what happens between the child and others).

The child, as a symbol user, relates the forms of the signs and symbols to the various discourses (or genres) they encounter. You will be familiar with the concept of *genres* and may find it interesting that Harste *et al.* (1984) found that children as young as 5 were able to use different types of symbols to depict different genres: their maps and lists and personal letters all look distinctive and different from one another. Some children in nursery classes have been seen to write 'a song' using musical notation. Kress (1997) observed that children use whatever is to hand to make representations of things:

> Abdul, aged 7, made a model of a moving creature based on something he had seen on television: then he drew the creature and then made one out of Meccano. Finally he produced a small collection of drawings with labels on which he called a 'Meccano catalogue'.
>
> (Personal observation, 2004)

In this way children develop a social semiotic way of representation and communication as they choose signs and symbols that are best suited to their intentions. Kress identified two principles to explain the choices children make. One is *interest*, which arises from where the child is and what she finds of interest and allows her to make her own individual representation. The other principle is *metaphor*, which suggests the most appropriate things to use for the representation. The question the child appears to ask here, in the choice of resources, is, 'What is most like this thing I want to represent?' You can see how *analogy* comes into play here.

When children come to use symbols to create text they are trying to represent ideas that are important to them. Barrs (1998) cited the wonderful example of a 5-year-old boy who made a map to be used in a complex play sequence where a hero figure had to overcome physical obstacles. The child placed symbols on his map to give instructions to an adult, who had to play the role of the hero.

Figure 5.2 is an example of a very young child's early attempts at writing her name, Chloe. Her mother, Andy, put circles around each of the three attempts and added an explanation to help us know what the child was doing. In the first attempt the child made marks from right to left and said that it was her name. In the second attempt she used letter-like shapes and included five of these to match the five letters of her name.

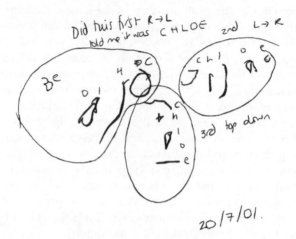

Figure 5.2 A very young child's early attempts at writing her name, Chloe

In the final attempt she wrote from top to bottom. The explanation for this is beyond me. What is clear is that she knew that her name included one letter that looks like a vertical line and one that looks like a circle and she included the letter C in one attempt. How hard she was working to 'write like a writer'. She was not yet 3 years old.

Into the world of reading

We clearly do not have room in this book to discuss in any great detail how children become *readers*. As you will know, this is an area even more contentious than some of the other issues we have looked at. However, in light of our contention that children actively seek to make and share meaning, we can focus on how children, in their encounters with the written world, seek to make sense of it and of what the others in their world do with it. Children seek to understand what it is that readers do when they see marks on a page, on an advert, on a road sign and so on. So becoming a reader also becomes a sociocultural event with expert readers mediating what happens between the child and the symbols on the page (or on the hoarding or on the sign or wherever).

Infants explore books just as they do other objects they encounter. Many books encourage exploration through the use of colour, picture, and devices like flaps to be lifted, holes to be peeked through and so on. Books designed like this operate on the assumption that children will be encouraged to explore the books alone, or with others, and will use some of the routines built into games like the peekaboo games discussed earlier. Just think how well 'lift the flap' books do this. Children who are fortunate enough to be able to engage with books together with adults may have their introduction to book reading take place in positive exchanges. Since books read to a child sometimes allow the child to explore some painful issues safely, this emotional support can be very helpful. This is not to imply that those who come to books later or on their own will not become and remain readers.

When children start to read they may start by re-telling the story, first from the pictures or from their memory of what the story is about. From there they move on to paying attention to the actual marks on the page, realising that it is these marks that make the story remain the same on each re-reading. In the ideal case, children are seeking to find the meaning, to lift the writer's tune from the page, as Myra Barrs (1998) tells us. Sometimes these attempts are frustrated when children are taught at a very young age to pay attention to the individual units – the letters – that make up the words that make up the sentences that make up the meaning. In the current climate there is a concerted attempt to insist that most early reading focuses on these smallest units of meaning rather than on the meaning per se. This is the *synthetic phonics approach* to reading. It is obvious that at some stage early readers do need to learn about the sounds and letters that make up words, and about the rules that make written language readable. But many – particularly those of us who focus on the meaningful nature of reading, its function as a way of making and sharing meaning – believe that young readers need to acquire as many strategies or tools as possible to enable them to both decode and to remain engaged in the meaning of what they are reading.

Did you know that the new phonics test administered to Year 1 children in England for the first time in 2012 is assessing their abilities to 'read' real words and nonsense words? This phonics screening check is described as being a short, light-touch assessment to confirm whether individual pupils have learnt phonic decoding to an appropriate standard. It is aimed at identifying the children who need extra help so they are may be given support by their school to improve their reading skills. Here comes the best part. The screening check contains 40 words divided into two sections, each of 20 words. Both sections contain a mixture of real words and pseudo-words. The pseudo-words are shown to children alongside pictures of imaginary creatures. According to the Department for Education this allows teachers to explain to the child that the pseudo-word is the name of a type of creature they haven't seen before. This, they insist, will help children to understand they should not try to match the pseudo-word to their vocabulary. In light of all you have learned so far about young children as makers of meaning, how do you think a test which asks them to 'read' non-words helps them make meaning? Have you considered whether children already able to read might do less well on this test than non-readers, precisely because they are looking for meaning that they will never find? And have you asked how good it might be for a 6-year-old to already fail?

And what are these symbols? Into the language of counting

Marks representing *numeric symbols* are found in almost all known cultures. Young children encounter these symbols in many places and begin to consider what they represent. Obvious examples are numbers on the doors of houses, buses, price labels, car number plates and more. In many cultures children are taught to chant the number sequence often before they have any clear understanding of what it is they are saying. Parents and carers count as children climb up the stairs, or as a child is tossed in the air or as the spoon approaches the open mouth. The question arises as to how the child knows that the words 'one, two, three . . .' and so on are words specifically relating to counting. Gelman (1990) suggests that very young children keep the set of count words separate from their set of labels. This, again, is complicated. Let us take the example of cars. The child, when acquiring speech, learns to attach the label 'car' to vehicles with wheels. Cars may be blue or green, big or small, but they share some key features. But when the child is presented with four cars and asked to count them the child will not get far simply chanting 'car, car, car, car'.

Figure 5.3 Drawing made by a child to illustrate four objects in a box

The child needs different labels to do this and these are the labels the language uses for counting – in English, for example, one, two, three, four.

When children come to exploring symbols they will sometimes invent their own symbols to represent a number of objects. One of the most famous studies of this was carried out by Bialystok (1992) who presented children with boxes, each filled with a different number of small objects. She asked the children to stick something on the lid of each box so that they would know how many were in the box without having to lift the lid. Children produced either traditional number symbols or analogical representations (e.g. six dots or six lines or drawings). Analogical notations were less help to the children when it came to recognising and decoding their meaning.

Figure 5.3 shows four small drawings made by a child to illustrate the four objects in one box. The child had more difficulty in remembering the number and had to count the drawings each time. She was perfectly able to recognise the symbol 4 and to state immediately that there were four objects on the box with this drawing on the lid. Karmiloff-Smith(1992) suggests that this occurs later in development than more simple symbol memory or pictorial representation.

You will realise that numerals are only a small part of coming to understand the world of mathematics, which is in itself an abstract and largely symbolic world. We will talk more about this in the chapter on the child as investigator.

Summing up

In this chapter we have looked at the child as a symbol user and examined the whole concept of symbolic representation, looking at how the child begins to use one thing to represent another and then moves on to more abstract symbolic systems – specifically talk, mark-making, reading and using numerals. The work of Chomsky was introduced and critiqued in light of the views of people like Bruner, Vygotsky, Halliday and Bakhtin. Our twenty-first century child is now seen to be able to use one thing to represent another and in doing this enters the worlds of signs and symbols to make and share meaning.

Thing to think about

- Do you think that cultural tools are of importance to the development of young children? In what ways?
- Do you agree with the musician Daniel Barenboim, who said that our culture pays more attention to the eye and what is seen than to the ear and what is heard? What are the implications of this for those of us involved with young children and their learning?

Chapter 6

The child in culture

Having spent some time thinking about the child in society and the child beginning to use symbols we now turn our attention to the child in culture and exploring it. So we look at how children are inducted into their culture and how they define themselves and are defined by others. This introduces the theme of self-identity, which we explore in more depth in Chapter 7. We also touch on a consideration of the capacities children have to make informed choices within their cultural contexts.

> Luigi is 7 years old. He lives in a small village in a relatively unspoiled region of Italy where his mother is part of a group of people who cook together and then set up tables in the streets where friends, neighbours and the odd visitors can come and eat delicious food. He is described by his family as 'the best pasta maker' in the village and they say this is because when he comes home from school he joins the cooks and spends all his time making pasta. They call it his job. At school his teacher describes him as a 'very pleasant but rather slow child with no particular aptitude'.

> Abdul is 9 years old. He lives in Balkur, Iran. He was asked about what work he does to help his family income and he said that he felt that he could be involved in watering the plants. He said, 'Now that I am 9 I am strong enough to carry the water from the well. Last year I was too small and weak. Now I have strong hands and good legs. I water our rice field and our garden for two hours every day. I would like to work in the hotel because you get more money but my parents say I am too young. I go to school in the mornings and when I come home I help with the rice fields and the garden.

How would you define Luigi's culture? Do you see it as one culture or more than one? Might there be a culture of the home, of the school, of the streets and community, or the village itself? And perhaps there is a culture of the country that in some ways touches little Luigi. And how about Iranian Abdul?

We have talked about culture throughout this book without stopping to define it. This is partly because everyone holds a common-sense definition of culture in their heads. This relates to the beliefs, artefacts, values and other things that bind people together. It might refer to the dance, music, food, language(s), religions, rituals, values, celebrations, customs and everything else that make members of a group feel a sense of belonging to that group. This is rather a superficial definition and ignores the role played by the players in making culture and passing it on and changing it. It makes it seem that culture is something fixed and 'given' to those born into it, rather than seeing its dynamic nature.

Culture, like language, changes with usage and over time. Pinker (2002: 60) offers an interesting definition of culture:

> The phenomena we call 'culture' arise as people pool and accumulate their discoveries and as they institute conventions to coordinate their labours and adjudicate their conflicts. When groups of people separated by time and geography accumulate different discoveries and conventions we use the plural and call them cultures.

Cultural tools, as you know, are the artefacts, symbols and systems developed by people within groups and used to make, share and transform meanings. They are often specific to cultures and used to define culture. You have only to think about how we talk about Chinese food, Italian cars, French style, Yiddish chutzpah or English sense of fair play to see how we take single aspects of one culture and use these to create stereotypes. It does not take much imagination to make the next link to 'Muslim fundamentalism', 'black athletic prowess' or the 'superiority of the English language' to see how dangerous this is. You will not be surprised that all three of these phrases occurred in the English press during one week in September 2005.

Did you know about, and are you amused as well as horrified by, the Mapping Stereotypes *project, which is the work of Yanko Tsvetkov, a graphic artist who also goes by the name Alphadesigner? His first map presented a Europe made up of competing interests and reductive presumptions. For example Russia was simply labelled 'Paranoid Oil Empire' and most of the EU came under the heading 'Union of Subsidised Farming'. He later made a map of 'The World According to Americans', with Kazakhstan renamed 'Borat' and the Falklands marked 'British Riviera'. Tim Dowling, reviewing this work in the* Guardian *in February 2012, said he was certain that there was potential for every person in the world to take offence at something in his map.*

The cultural theorist Stuart Hall (1992) said that

> People who are in any way different from the majority – 'them' rather than 'us' – are frequently exposed to [a] binary form of representation. They seem to be represented through sharply opposed, polarized, binary extremes – good/bad, civilized/primitive, ugly/excessively attractive, repelling-because- different/compelling because strange and exotic. And they are often required to be both things at the same time!
>
> (Hall, 1992: 17)

He suggested that children can be defined by others – often negatively – on the basis of their class, their gender, their physical features, their race or their language. So we hear children talk about others as 'specky four-eyes' or 'pakis' or 'tub of lard' or 'poof'. As children begin to work out who they are (their self-identity) they also try to work out who they are similar to and different from in some ways. So when we identify ourselves as one thing we, at the same time, differentiate ourselves from others who are different in some way. When we say we are women, we indicate that we are not men, for example. There are also within-group variations. A person who has been an immigrant in this country for a long time will have had different experiences and hence a different identity from a newer arrival although we often tend to talk of them as 'immigrants' as if that were a sufficient description of them and their experiences.

Children *construct their identities* from their experiences and through their interactions. This includes seeing themselves as part of a group sharing a culture. The ways in which they and other members of their group are represented will be crucial in doing this. So children construct their identities partially from how they (the group) are represented. It will feel very different being the only black child in an all-white class, or being the only girl on the football team, for example. How children define and identify themselves is a complex process and one that essentially involves their *self-esteem*. The reactions of others to them or to their group impact on self-image and hence on self-identity. Children who encounter few images or predominantly negative images of themselves and their group will suffer damage to their self-esteem and the whole process of identity construction will be difficult.

In their remarkable book, *Minority Education: From Shame to Struggle* (1988), which is now regarded as something of a classic text, Skutnabb-Kangas and Cummins include a moving piece by Antti Jalava called 'Nobody could see that I was a Finn'. In this disturbing autobiographical piece Jalava wrote about his experiences after his family moved from Finland to Stockholm in Sweden when he was 9 years old. On the first day at school the principal did not know what to do with this little stranger: all she could do was hold the child's hand as they walked to the classroom: 'Holding hands was the only language we had in common.'

In class the child was called names and teased. He tried to adjust:

> Adjusting was not, however, at all simple. To what did one have to adjust and how? There was nobody to explain things, there were no interpreters, no Finnish teachers and no kind of teaching of the Swedish language. And I was no chameleon, either, for I only wanted to be myself, out of habit and instinct. *When the others wrote in Swedish, I wrote in Finnish* [emphasis added by Smidt]. But that was something that just couldn't be. The teacher grabbed my pencil and angrily shook his finger at me. In spite of everything I continued to fall back on my mother tongue.
>
> (Skutnabb-Kangas and Cummins, 1988: 162)

You get a really strong sense of the child's struggle to both become part of the new host culture (Sweden and school) but also to retain part of his self-identity (his language). In the italicised sentence this is powerfully illustrated. As the children in the class wrote in Swedish Antii did the only thing that was possible for him as a child who clearly had the capacity to understand the task together with the implied rules and conventions, but was not equipped with the essential tool of knowing the Swedish language.

Antii ended up in the principal's office. That night he threw a stone through the window of the office, and never again wrote in Finnish. He bonded with a band of 'brothers' and said that violence became the only language understood by all of them. By the time he moved up to the junior grades he had learned some Stockholm slang and said that the language of the classroom, which he described as middle-class Swedish, was as impenetrable to the working-class Swedish boys as it was to him. He was fiercely homesick and went down to the docks to watch the boats from Finland come and go. He wept in private. But with time the idea grew within him that it was shameful to be a Finn. The way in which he writes about this is both powerful and painful:

> Everything I had held dear and self-evident had to be destroyed. An inner struggle began, a state of crisis of long duration. I had trouble sleeping. I could not look

people in the eye, my voice broke down into a whisper, I could no longer trust anybody. My mother tongue was worthless – this I realised at last; on the contrary it made me the butt of abuse and ridicule.

So down with the Finnish language! I spat on myself, gradually committed *internal suicide* [emphasis added by Smidt] . . . I resolved to learn Swedish letter perfect so nobody could guess who I was or where I came from.

(Skutnabb-Kangas and Cummins, 1988: 164)

You can see how difference and prejudice can operate against groups and also within groups. This child made the terrible decision to give up his language and become as perfect in Swedish as it was possible to be, precisely in order to disguise his true identity as an individual and his identity as part of a group. The italicised words in the above excerpt illustrate the depths of his despair.

Throughout this book we have been looking at the developing child as more than a constructor of meaning: we have been looking at the child as active, strong, competent and in interaction with others in a range of contexts and settings. Each of these contexts has its own sets of beliefs and values – its own sets of cultural tools. Children, from their first explorations of the world, interact with, contribute to, adopt and change these beliefs and values as they become members of different cultural groups.

Children's capacities

Writers and theorists are beginning to think in more depth about *children's capacities*, which is, in effect, thinking about their competence to make decisions about issues that affect their lives. There is a general acceptance, particularly in the developed world, that adults are competent but children lack competence. In much of the Western world children are generally excluded from the responsibilities of the adult world, keeping them apart from participation in activities that might confer social status. They are still perceived of as physically, socially, emotionally and economically dependent and spend longer and longer time at school. It is as though they live in this protected cocoon of 'being a child'.

Yet children in many countries are critical of the fact that adults do not acknowledge the responsibilities they take and they recognise that adults often fear that children might become a more vocal and powerful group. Mayall (2002) talked to children between the ages of 9 and 12, some of whom talked of teachers who offered double standards by expecting much responsibility and a lot of work at school, whilst treating the children as unreliable, and lacking in a sense of moral agency. It was felt that teachers often accused them of being deceitful or dishonest. Some of the children also noted that the independence and respect they sometimes gained at home through being responsible and helpful did not transfer to how they were viewed by teachers. Children throughout the world may be concerned with the levels of respect accorded them in their different cultures. For example, adolescent boys often feel that they receive no respect at school but can earn respect on the streets through their adoption of the culture of the streets.

Bissell (2002) carried out a piece of research in Bangladesh examining the perceptions children had of themselves and she found that they described themselves as either big or small, not on the basis of their physical stature or the wealth of their families but in terms of their own autonomy. One example was of an 11-year-old girl who described herself as small. When the interviewer asked her why she did this she explained that it was because she could not make decisions or do any work. It emerged that she did, in fact, work in the garment factory, but her self-esteem remained low because she earned less than her parents. In her terms that made her remain 'small'. Another girl talked about how her image varied from medium to small according to whether her mother was away from home or present at home. When her mother was away she was expected to make decisions and carry some of the responsibility for the family. This made her medium, but when her mother returned she reverted to being small. In school she saw herself as small because, she said, 'I don't know anything' (Lansdown, 2005).

Social and cultural *expectations* play a vital role in the demands made of all children. This clearly affects their capacities to exercise responsibility. In Nepal girls take on the adult work roles at the age of 12, whilst boys do not do this until two years later. Indian girls are perceived to reach adulthood at the age of 14 years whilst boys do not attain this until they are 16. In Bangladesh children are perceived to cross a threshold that separates out a stage of innocence (shishu) to an age of knowing. This transition is not associated with specific ages. Tonga children of both sexes in Zimbabwe participate fully in the money-earning enterprises of the family from the age of 10.

It is clear from this that children make sense of how they are perceived by others in their cultural contexts and often recognise that they are sometimes perceived as not being capable when, in essence and in reality, they clearly are.

Some interesting work demonstrating the capacities of children with disabilities is being carried out through the auspices of Save the Children UK, which set up a project in Nepal where 22 children with disabilities who had been successful in getting some education in mainstream schools were being encouraged to tell their stories about their successes to other children with disabilities. A famous Nepali writer worked with the children and helped them get published in local newspapers. This raised the profile of disability, offered role models and allowed children to raise their expectations of what they can achieve.

Did you know that since the first edition of this book there has been a considerable body of work examining issues relating to children's rights and capabilities in terms of being able to be active and heard participants in issues affecting them and their families? Read on . . .

Some of the work is included in a new and valuable book called *A Handbook of Children and Young People's Participation: Perspectives From Theory and Practice*, edited by Barry Percy-Smith and Nigel Thomas (2010). In this book activists like Gerrison Lansdown and Berry Mayall discuss issues that affect children and young people being able to have a voice, to understand some complex issues and to be heard. If this is an area of interest to you I suggest you read the book. You will find that much of it relates to older children but there is a section written by Priscilla Alderson where she looks at how younger children can start to be heard and taken account of within their homes. She notes the work of Mayall (2007), who found that parents – particularly more advantaged people in the developed world – tend to respect their very young children, seeing them as individuals who are good at interaction and interesting to listen to. Within the context of everyday life very young children can come to take on the views of others and consider issues like fairness, equity, rights and wrongs. My ex-colleague Helen Penn (2004), with a focus on parents in the developing world, found that although they perhaps do not engage in so much dialogue with young children, they do allow them autonomy.

Many young children in these families do engage in some work like herding goats and thus contribute in cash or kind to the family. It is salutary to consider that poverty seems to allow children to be given more respect by their parents when they work independently rather than alongside the parents (Invernizzi and Williams, 2008). Alderson herself noted how some young children involved themselves or were drawn into aspects of repeated health issues in the family and thus developed clear opinions on what is right in terms of treatment or maintenance. For example, 3-year-old Maisie always told her mother when she was feeling 'hypo', and 5-year-old Ruby could test her own blood sugar level and decide how much cake she could eat at a birthday party.

Did you know that involving children and young people in participating in the wider society is difficult but there are some relatively recent examples worth reading about?

The first example is drawn from a piece by Renate Kränzl-Nagl and Ulrike Zartler (2010).

Stop Child Labour in Albania
A nationwide programme was set up to offer non-formal education and psychosocial help to children aged 6 to 16. A major activity was to set up children's clubs to try and increase the number of children and young people participating and talking about the effects of child labour, sex work, child trafficking and other negative features of the lives of street children like themselves.

The second example comes from a piece by Lucy Jamieson and Wanjiru Mukoma (2010).

Dikwankwetla: Children in Action
In South Africa, since the beginning of democracy, attempts have been made to establish and protect the rights of children and a Children's Bill was made law in 2003. Soon after this the Dikwankwetla project was set up aimed at facilitating the participation in decision-making processes of children who had been made vulnerable through the death or infection of significant adults throughout the AIDS/HIV pandemic. Twelve children aged 11 to 17 were involved, all either orphaned, living in child-headed households or suffering some abuse or deprivation. A number of NGOs was involved and there followed a series of workshops aimed at enabling children to make sense of legal language, rights and legislation. Interestingly, the approach involved what is called narrative therapy methodology where each child produced a 'Hero Book' to illustrate a particular problem and solution. For me this makes a great deal of sense and is something that those working with very young children and wanting to take their thoughts seriously will be familiar with.

The intersecting cultures of childhood

Uri Bronfenbrenner (1979) was one of the first theorists to examine the intersecting worlds of children through his *'ecological'* model. The classic version consists of four concentric circles; Figure 6.1 is a revised version that refers also to time and is called the *chronosystem*.

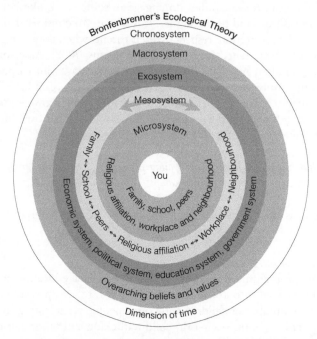

Figure 6.1 The intersecting cultures of childhood (adapted from Bronfenbrenner's Ecological Theory, http://geopolicraticus.wordpress.com/2011/03/23/ecological-temporality/)

You will see how this model works with the individual child at its centre and then the concentric circles, one within the other, to show the movement from the most intimate contexts of the home to the more remote contexts beyond. So the innermost circle, the *microsystem*, represents the everyday context of the life of young children, which is usually the home but may move beyond into the extended family, the neighbourhood and perhaps the crèche or the nursery setting. The next circle represents what is known as the *mesosystem* and these are seen to be the links between home and clinic, home and church or mosque or synagogue, between home and nursery or school and so on. More remote yet are things that affect the child more indirectly and these are called the *exosystem* and include things like community networks and the workplace of the parents, perhaps. Finally, and most remote from the child but still impacting on her life, is the *macrosystem* which is where social systems like laws and economics and the media and the education system make decisions that affect the child and his or her family. You can see how the child's cultures come together through this model.

Within each of their cultural groups children set about defining themselves as members of that group, using the cultural tools available to them to define their family roles, gender roles, images, languages, in their complex worlds. This, the *construction of identity*, is one of the earliest tasks for the human infant. Neither identity nor culture are fixed but are dynamic and fluid, and can be considered as relational and relative concepts. So the identity of the child at home is not one thing but might be baby or sibling or competent or difficult according to circumstance and context. Here are some examples:

Masha is very quiet and withdrawn when her Uncle Leo visits. He is a big and noisy man and he terrifies her. But when he leaves she returns to being her cheerful and outgoing self.

Henry is the older sibling and is expected to be grownup and sensible and responsible. Usually he is but every so often he loses his temper and resorts to stamping his feet and shrieking like a 2-year-old.

The identity of the child away from home requires further construction and elaboration. We know that in order to construct self-images in new contexts the child has to come to know which cultural tools are available and use these in order to become part of that context. So children need to make sense of a wide range of things including language or languages, together with relevant *dialects* and *registers*; *discourse* or discourses, which are ways of speaking and acting; religious practices and belief systems; values and norms including knowing what is acceptable and what not; and customs, which can include ways of eating, dressing, speaking, gazing, interacting and learning. So within their separate and their intersecting cultures children learn the relevant tools and sometimes encounter conflicts and dichotomies.

Cultural capital: the ideas of Bourdieu

Bourdieu was a Marxist sociologist who examined aspects of society in terms of things like power and class. In Marxist theory *capital* is power, which is acquired through labour or work. If you work and earn a salary that salary is your capital and you can use it to acquire more capital in terms of a place to live, possessions and so on. It is capital that forms the foundation of the class system and social structure in many societies. Bourdieu believed that capital should also have a symbolic component – so that it went beyond the economic definition. By *symbolic capital* he meant things like cultural, social and linguistic facts, which can either benefit individuals or hold them back. Like many theorists his writing is difficult to understand because of the dense language he used. We will take time to define some of the terms he used:

- *Cultural capital* can be loosely defined as being *'what people know'*. Perhaps you are studying for a qualification and when you have completed your studies part of your cultural capital will be what you have learned.
- *Fields* are thing like 'from home to school' or places where things take place, or exchanges are held.
- *Social capital* can loosely be defined as *'who people know'*. You will be familiar with name-dropping – the habit of inserting the names of famous people or current celebrities into conversation in order to impress people. The people you know may well contribute to your social capital.
- *Habitus* is a system of *dispositions*, habits or attitudes that explain the differences we see in all societies between and within groups. Put crudely, children with a disposition to enjoy formal education and learning are more likely to succeed in schooling. Habitus is acquired by individuals and by groups through experience and is the product of the history of the family or individual and of their class and cultural context. Within the concept of habitus there is the concept of family habitus. The *family habitus* of

middle-class children in the United Kingdom is likely to be closer to the habitus valued and recognised by teachers.

You will realise that Bourdieu's use of the concept of cultural capital was a social and cultural analysis of the reasons for the failure of individuals and groups. It situated the reasons within an *economic and power framework* and specifically stated that failure was not the result of lack of natural aptitude. In other words, certain groups of children may struggle at school because of the effects of poverty or the impact of prejudice, not because of lack of ability. Aspects of the notion of cultural capital have been criticised as offering a rather passive view of the child in her acquisition of capital and some of this relates to the emphasis in some of the studies on how mothers and other caregivers are viewed as being able to 'give' their children the necessary cultural capital to allow them to succeed as learners. This is an attempt to explain why in many places poor children fail to thrive in the educational systems. Bourdieu is an important thinker and writer who has contributed much to our understanding of children and culture. Prout (2005), however, reminds us that his theories do not fully allow for children being *active agents* not only in their *acquisition of capital* but also in their abilities to *appropriate and transform culture*.

Children inhabit *complex cultural worlds* and to each new field or context they bring a store of cultural capital. Where the cultural capital they bring is close to that valued and held by an institution (for example the classroom), they are likely to be advantaged. Their cultural capital is accessible to their educators. Where children bring cultural capital that is divergent from that of their educators, the educators do not know what to recognise and value. For every child the habitus of 'now' is the sum total of the culture and class history of the child herself and her family. The case study that follows is that of two of my own grandchildren and how they were active in adapting to and transforming their own habitus in order to become accepted members of the wider community.

> In the school attended by Hannah and Ben the family habitus they bring is different from that of many of their peers. Since many of the pupils are members of dominated groups by virtue of poverty, immigration, ethnic origin, or low occupational classification, they may share common characteristics in terms of both their responses to their present situations and also to their hopes and aspirations. It is evident, however, that individuals from dominated groups have become extremely creative and successful in their learning, their lives and their relations. This is an illustration of the fact that there is a difference in how members of these groups are able to exercise agency and change the aspirations of the family or group. Each child coming into the classroom brings with her or him the family habitus but also the potential to develop their own, unique primary habitus. They do this through the strategies they develop to deal with their own experiences in the context of both the family habitus and the school habitus. For the novice to schooling whole new sets of rules and roles and identities need to be mastered in order to become a member of the new cultures of the classroom, of the dinner hall, of the playground.
>
> Children in the classroom and in the playground start to use their own habitus and their cultural capital to create new cultures with new rules, roles and identities. When Hannah first started school the cultural capital she brought included an intimate knowledge of stories in books and from videos. One of the ways in which she worked to use this cultural capital to become part of a new culture was to 'play' the stories

that she knew. This seemingly simple act is, in fact, an extremely complex exploration of cultural meanings. In a group of children, each with a unique habitus, some agreement must be reached in order that the children can inhabit a shared imaginary world. Each child has to have an identity and a place within the story and in order to do that the children need to explore their own understandings, many of which will be drawn from their personal exposure to culture – popular and other. Hannah, now aged 7, still takes in the stories she reads at home and sometimes becomes what might be called a 'cultural leader 'in that she offers the stories to her group for them to play. Most recently she has taken in a story she has been reading with her mother called *Parvana's Journey* by Deborah Ellis, which is a harrowing account of the experiences of a young girl in Afghanistan under the Taliban regime. When talking about the play Hannah commented that one of the children in the group had 'loved the bit where the hands were cut off'. This exploration of extreme physical aggression and unfamiliar notions of justice falls into what Dyson calls 'unpopular play' – play that is or contains elements that might be considered unsuitable by adults, or that they might not approve of. As in the children described in Dyson's study, the children in Hannah's peer group, creating their playground culture, are exploring complex issues relating to the real world in which they live and where they hear, daily, talk of war and weapons. In London in 2003 there is little possibility for these children, in Year 2, to build on this intense exploration of serious and deeply frightening concerns within the classroom. They spend their days practising for the coming SATS tests. The children demonstrate their skills as creators of culture by doing so in the playground.

(Smidt, 2004: 81–82)

As these children play the roles they have agreed on, using their own attitudes and dispositions, they begin to create a new culture – a *shared culture* brought about by the mixing of their languages, their ideas, their feelings and their experiences.

Did you know that the political jazz trumpeter and singer, Hugh Masakela, exiled from apartheid South Africa, has recently gathered together songs of migration. The chants and songs people who had to migrate from one place to another to seek work, earn money, escape torture or war or death, wrote, sang and passed on to their children? Listening to these in the Hackney Empire I was overwhelmed by how many of the sounds encapsulated in the languages, rhythms, words, feelings and pain were somehow embedded in my brain from my own childhood in apartheid South Africa. Although the songs were often in languages I could not understand this music of my complicated cultures (white, privileged, Jewish, atheist, from a politically aware family) was clearly part of my cultural capital.

Languages and culture

Millions of children throughout the world are speakers of more than one language and many of them have to come to understand and use the symbolic systems of these different languages. Some recent studies fall into a paradigm based on *syncretism*, which was a term used by anthropologists studying how African and European Christian religious traditions overlap and intersect in some Caribbean cultures. Gregory *et al.* (2004) say the term has taken on broader and more positive connotations and has now come to mean *the creative transformation of culture*. To elaborate this we need to examine how syncretic studies see development as a creative process wherein people, including children, reinvent culture, drawing on their resources, old and new. And since it refers to cross-cultural exchanges the issue of *power* is one that has to be considered in the contradictions and sometimes the conflicts that arise. We spoke of the possible conflicts children encounter where there are collisions of culture. Speakers of languages other than English going to school in England clearly have to learn to speak, understand and deal with the host and dominant language (which is also the language of power, education, government and the media) and find ways of being able to maintain and use their home languages. As we saw earlier in the story of Antii, this is one potential area for dissonance.

In summary, the principles of a syncretic approach include the following:

1   Children are active members of different cultural and linguistic groups and appropriating membership to a group is not a static or linear process.
2   Children do not remain in separate worlds, but acquire membership of different groups simultaneously, i.e. they live in *'simultaneous' worlds* (Kenner, 2004: 107–126).
3   Simultaneous membership means that children *syncretise* the languages, literacies, narrative styles and role relationships appropriate to each group and then go on to transform the languages and cultures they use to create new forms relevant to the purpose needed.
4   Young children who participate in cross-linguistic and cross-cultural practices call upon a greater wealth of metacognitive and metalinguistic strategies. These strategies are further enhanced when they are able to *play out different roles and events*.
5   Play is a crucial feature of children's language and literacy practice with siblings, grandparents and peers.
6   The mediators, often bicultural and/or bilingual, play an essential role in early language and literacy learning. Studies investigate different forms of 'scaffolding', 'guided participation' or 'synergy' as young and older children or adults work and play together.

(Gregory *et al.*, 2004: 5)

Did you know that metacognitive means the ability to think about thinking itself: metalinguistic means knowing about language itself?

We know that children learn to decode and interpret the particular *graphic sign systems* used by the cultures in which they live. We know too that these signs are socially constructed and that children make meaning from these through their interactions. Recent research looked at how, when children were able to play the role of 'teacher' they began to re-interpret their own understanding in order to explain it to their peers.

Kenner looked at what some 6-year-old bilingual children were doing at a Community Saturday School where they were learning to write in their family language whilst continuing to learn literacy in English at their primary school. *Peer teaching* sessions were set up so that the children could teach one another how to write in Chinese or Arabic or Spanish – three languages with very different graphic systems. Here is an extract from what happened when Tala tried to teach Emily to write a word in Arabic – a language with which Emily was not familiar. Tala wanted to teach Emily to write her brother's name, Khalid. This is written in two parts, 'Kha' and 'lid' because, according to the rules of Arabic writing, the letters 'alif' (which represent the 'a' sound) cannot join to any following letter. Tala wrote the word herself, in front of Emily, telling her what she was doing:

Do that – it's like a triangle, but it's got a line like here . . . go 'wheee' like this [as she finished with an upward stroke]. Emily tried to follow this lead, saying as she wrote 'It looks like an "L" . . . it looks like steps.' As Amina had done with Chinese, Emily was interpreting an unfamiliar script from the basis of English and of visual images. However, Tala realized that Emily had over-interpreted her instructions, with the result being too stylized and she commented 'It's not exactly like that – she's done steps'. Indeed, Emily's version looked like steps in a staircase rather than the fluid curves typical of Arabic writing. This difficulty continued during the lesson and to help her friend produce more appropriate writing, Tala resorted to a technique used by her own Arabic teacher. She provided a 'join-the-dots' version of the words required.'

(Kenner, 2004a: 113)

You will see how in this small exchange the children demonstrate a desire to learn from and teach one another, share their skills as experts about their own languages and cultures and learn from their peers. This desire to share meaning across languages and literacies has been well documented by Datta (2000) and by D'Arcy (2002).

Learning styles and culture

In an earlier chapter we looked at play as a learning style and recognised its importance, but realised, too, that it is not the only way in which children and others learn. Romero (2004) looked at the different styles of learning she observed amongst Pueblo children of New Mexico. In North America and in the United Kingdom and through much of Europe there is a strong emphasis on school readiness, with parents being encouraged to 'educate' their children in the skills and knowledge that will allow them to succeed in school. In this way parents are being urged to build their children's cultural capital. In other countries preparation for success at school is less important than preparation for living in their community. In such communities there are things that children need to learn and these are directly related to the cultural beliefs, principles and values, which themselves are linked to the economic survival of the group. Romero's writing is full of fascinating details about the lives of Pueblo children that we do not have time to explore here. Our focus is on some of the ways in which children are expected to learn.

Pueblo children interact with primary caregivers on a daily basis and with secondary caregivers (those within the community) less regularly. Through all these interactions Pueblo children make and share meanings.

- *Learning by doing*: a key factor in the socialisation of Pueblo children is to allow the children to learn by doing. An example might be learning to bake bread in the large outdoor ovens where women work together and children are close at hand, first watching and then doing. This is analogous with what Rogoff called guided participation.
- *Silent learning*: silent learning is sometimes called legitimate peripheral participation (Lave and Wenger, 1991) and is where the child is on the periphery of some activity, silently observing and joining in at some level. The example cited by Romero is of a young child going with his father to the house where the older men smoke, drum and sing. The child intently watched what was happening and then silently imitated

the behaviours he observed – including smoking his crayons! In an inner London infant school a young boy with Down's Syndrome in a mainstream class sat and listened to the other children attempting to read, and watched intently what they did. After some months he was able to hold a book and mimic the reading behaviours he had observed.

- *Role modelling*: as in all cultures children spend time watching their family and community members in interactions in the home and beyond. As they do this children begin to understand what behaviours, intonations patterns, and gestures define which roles. We have had examples of behaviours like this throughout this book, including the one of Luigi at the start of this chapter. For the Pueblo children there is some evidence that the roles they observe are the roles they aspire to – for example, to be a traditional leader.
- *Mentoring*: very close to all of the above, mentoring implies that the child will learn from an expert other – perhaps an older sibling or a parent or grandparent or a community member. The example cited by Romero is that of pottery making. At home the children observe the women potters and are exposed to the whole process. They may also go into the mountains with the potter to collect clay and other materials, or they may be given pieces of clay to play with. Sometimes simple instructions are given. Mainly, however, the child is an onlooker and not expected to be a potter until adolescence, which is when specific teaching will be offered.

The family: transmission of beliefs and values

In coming to understand development as a cultural process, theorists have come up with the idea of the *developmental niche*. This is defined as being made up of three elements within the environments of the children that influence their development. Lansdown (2005) refers to these as:

- *The physical and social settings of the child*, which refer primarily to the child's family and the ways in which daily and social life are organised.
- *The culturally regulated customs and practices*, which relate to how children are reared, how the relationship between care and education is perceived and what the attitudes to play, discipline or training are.
- *The beliefs or ethno-theories of the parents*, which mean the goals and priorities of the parents for their children together with their views on how their children can best be 'prepared' to achieve these goals.

Remember that children do not live *monocultural lives* but are active players in making and transforming culture. However, there are circumstances that have a daily impact on the lives of children – particularly within the family – which impact on this. In some cultures the passing on of values and beliefs is seen as a way of handing a legacy to the children. It may help children make sense of life and death or develop a set of perspectives to organise their relationships with one another. So the passing on of values and beliefs helps young children understand their roles with regard to obligations, responsibility and rights. It is through the exploration of these concepts that they become able to find their place in the world and explore what it means to belong.

Let us take some examples drawn from the cultures of South Africa where much emphasis is laid on the role of the family in transmitting cultural values and norms. This family socialisation is seen as one way of protecting children and preparing them for life within that particular society. In poor families it may happen that the older family members, aware of the impact and effects of poverty, prepare their children for self-denial and self-regulation. An example is cited in Barbarin and Richter (2001) where a family may deny a child access to sugar in order to prepare her for future life so she will know not to request sugar as a guest. Implicit in African culture is the obligation to cater for the needs of guests. In many cultures, including those of South Africa, one of the tasks of the family is to pass on religious cultural norms and practices. One of these is respect for ancestors. This involves a series of rituals to mark rites of passage, and protect people from illness and harm from the supernatural world. You may have heard about how, in Mexico, the Day of the Dead is one of the most important cultural rituals. The Mexican attitude to death has sometimes been described as national fatalism. Death is feared but also made absurd through the images produced. Made of papier mâché or tin or fabric, skeletons and skulls are depicted riding horses, smoking cigars, dancing in the streets, wearing top hats. You can see clearly here how cultural tools are used to depict society, comment on aspects of it and sometimes transform it.

It is evident that there are many factors that impinge on how effectively families are able to nurture and socialise children. Included in these are family structure, income, health, mobility and so on. In Southern Africa the ability of the family to nurture children and socialise them into the culture is being deeply damaged by the HIV/Aids pandemic. When the first edition of this book was written 4.3 million children had died of the disease and in the worst affected countries of Southern Africa something like 20 per cent of households were child-headed. Other children were and still are being reared by grandparents. You can see from this how poverty itself can impinge on culture. It is pleasing to note that child deaths from AIDS are falling.

High culture: popular culture?

In the first chapter of this book we looked at how images of children have changed over time and considered some of the paintings of Paula Rego, the Portuguese-born artist. We saw how her own experiences of Portuguese imperialism affected her paintings, which are like visual fables, drawn from a range of sources. These include the surreal paintings of Luis Bunuel and the early work of Walt Disney, whom she described as 'a genius'. Rego's paintings cannot be described as 'popular culture' yet Disney's work certainly can. Rego is cited here precisely to illustrate tentative ideas of what makes some culture good and some not worthy of academic attention. Involved in some way in the lives of young children, you will know how important popular culture is to them.

For Vygotsky, learning was to do with the transmission of culture: the passing on of the things pooled and discovered, adapted and changed, from generation to generation. This is not a passive but is an essentially creative process. Paula Rego created something new out of her experiences, observations, feelings and exposure to artefacts and other things. In doing that she drew on a range of sources. The Mexican artist Frida Kahlo was someone else who melded popular culture into her art. In an attempt to recognise and celebrate the indigenous culture of Mexico as opposed to the imposed Spanish imperial culture, she included the colours, symbols, patterns and materials of this culture in her paintings. Cultures are never fixed, but change and develop. The art produced by Frida Kahlo, drawn from her unique experiences and the meanings she made from this, will be reflected in the work of others to come. Cultures change as innovations are made.

Both Bakhtin (1981) and Vygotsky (1978) recognised that children's *consciousness*, by which we mean their awareness of their world and those in it, exists only as part of the social and cultural worlds. Remember that it is others who induct children into the signs and symbols that exist in their world. So it is through their interactions with others in meaningful and relevant contexts that children become part of the world of reading, writing, mathematics, art, music and other symbolic systems. Vygotsky reminds us that children 'grow into the intellectual life of those around them' (1978: 88).

Stuart Hall and others at the Birmingham Centre for Cultural Studies in the 1960s and 1970s talked of *cultural relativity*, looking at the web of strands that link state, society and cultural forms. This model of cultural relativity illustrates powerfully just how multilayered and multifaceted culture is. It is made up of a myriad of discourses and subject to change as individuals appropriate aspects of it.

These are quite difficult ideas to come to terms with but, as is so often the case, looking at an example might help clarify. In our culture there is a divide between what is called popular culture (the culture of the streets or the day-to-day lives of people) and what is known as high culture. High culture is often used to describe things like literature or art or opera or classical music. In effect, however, what is now known as high culture has been elevated to this 'higher' status having started off as something for people in their everyday lives. For example, the opera *The Magic Flute*, originally written by Mozart as a popular opera because he needed the money it would make, was later taken over by the elite and became something performed by highly trained singers and musicians in costly specialist theatres and opera houses. We need now to think about how status and power affect our perceptions. Partly what accounts for the changing view of what is popular culture is the relationship between popular culture and power in society. By power we mean things like control of the media, education and production. Gramsci was an influential Marxist philosopher who looked at how the dominant classes manage to retain their control over those 'beneath' them in the social structures. He talked of *hegemony*, which he described as the process by which influential groups impose their power on others and maintain their hold once it has been established. The class holding power does not need to use coercion or brute force, but finds more subtle ways of imposing a set of ideas, values, principles, beliefs, objectives, cultural and political meanings. In other words, the people need to be persuaded of certain things in order to support them and the persuasion comes partially through popular culture. Think particularly about the American electoral process and how much importance is attached to celebrity support, image, dress, the adoption of key songs and so on.

But popular culture can equally act in the opposite direction. It can become the medium for helping those subject to powerful forces from above to resist. A famous case in point is what happened in Chile in South America, where a strong and popular music developed from folk songs and where the singers were strongly opposed to the forces being massed against the people. The songs they wrote and sang became popular and powerful forces against the government – so powerful, in fact, that some of the singers – like Victor Jara – were jailed and subsequently killed. In apartheid South Africa, too, music became an extremely powerful influence in the fight against apartheid.

The popular culture of children today is made up of a huge number of strands. Cartoon films offer images of violence but also of fantasy and gentleness and humour. Some children will watch Asian films. Some will listen and dance to popular music. Some will spend time dressing their dolls in doll-sized versions of adult clothes. Alongside that is the culture of the Harry Potter and Philip Pullman books and a proliferation of films and DVDs made, exclusively, for the consumption of children. It is a long way from the childhood of the Middle Ages discussed in the first chapter. As societies have changed and cultures become globalised and increasingly commercialised, a whole children's culture has developed. Lash and Urry (1994) talk of the dematerialisation of products. By this they mean the impact of mass media (like television, the cinema and, of course, the internet) on products. These are dematerialised because of the speed with which such images can be conveyed across the globe. The effects of this may be regarded as paradoxical because they have the potential to bring about global homogenisation (as in the dominance of English as a language; of American images of heroes and villains and so on) but also of global differences. The creation of images of difference may be regarded as one of the outcomes of what is often described as the relativism that global culture brings.

One of the impacts of this globalisation is to make more difficult the concept of society. Societies are less and less able to secure their cultural and defining boundaries. In Tuscany, for example, local people fear that the influx of English home-owners is diluting their culture and their traditions and resent the fact that children want to learn English because of all that is available to them through the internet, the cinema and videos. In the same area the Chinese are feared and hated for 'stealing' the designs and processes involved in the textile industry. Pistoia, once famed not only for its art works but also its textiles, feels it has lost an essential part of its culture.

Becoming integrated into a cultural group or niche involves understanding the rituals and rules and the language of that group and of being able to participate in those rules and rituals. Becoming a member of a group, then, means that the rules have to be worked out or inferred. Just as children new to any setting, for example a classroom, have to learn the language and rules of that setting in order to develop the new identity of 'member' or 'friend' or 'pupil', so they have to develop what we might call a repertoire of cultural registers in order to be admitted. Inevitably there are groups with a perceived higher status than others, and, just as in the adult world of work and institutions, aspects of 'gatekeeping' operate. Sarangi and Roberts argue that 'learning "how to be" and "how to act" involve developing an understanding of events, feelings, roles and statuses . . . as relative newcomers participate in new social practices' (2002: 200).

Although Sarangi and Roberts are looking at adult newcomers to professional institutions (medicine), their analysis can equally well apply to children. At the age of 8 Hannah wanted to be part of a particular group of girls who were perceived by her to be 'high status'. In order to do this she analysed what shared cultural capital they had and then set about working on her own cultural capital so that she would be able to use the languages (in the broadest sense) they used to allow her access to the group. The group she wanted to join were interested in pop music and dance. The children already in the group were effectively the 'gatekeepers' – the ones who decided who to admit and who to exclude. Hannah engaged in the intricate cognitive task of working out how to align her actions to those of the group. She had not, of course, had to sit down and read the works of Bourdieu to do this. She had to work out for herself what would allow her access to the chosen group. In other words she made herself develop *cultural competence* in an aspect of popular culture. Erickson and Schultz (1982) talk of *gatekeeping* encounters as being neither neutral nor objective but suggest that they are like a carefully rigged game in favour of those who are most like the members of the group in terms of both social background and communication styles.

Building on culture in play: symbol weaving

In looking at how children draw on culture – including popular culture – in their play, it is evident that children draw on different texts and influences, weaving them together into a new theme. Dyson (1993) described this process as 'symbol weaving', where children draw on myriad cultural influences and references as they play or write or draw or model. She reminded us that it is as children that we utilise all the materials we encounter in our lives to use in expressing our thoughts and ideas – unaware, as yet, of the barriers society erects between good and bad, *high culture* and *popular culture*. Kress (2000) used the term *'communicational webs'* to describe children's ability to draw on a huge range and variety of texts and artefacts in their own attempts at storying and meaning making.

As children move from one cultural space to another they are engaged in what is sometimes called *'border crossing'*. Pahl (1999) observed many examples of border or boundary crossing in the nursery she visited in order to do her research. Those working with children will want to be able to identify and understand the sources children draw on. As children are exposed to more and more influences on television, DVDs, the internet and other media, it becomes more and more difficult for adults to recognise what Geertz (1983) calls their *'local knowledge'*. This refers to the detailed knowledge they carry within them of their home and community plus local details and the detailed personal knowledge they have of worlds in their heads. The old adage of knowing what children know and recognising its relevance remains crucial. It is only by doing this that we are able to have a fair image of the child of the twenty-first century.

Summing up

In this chapter we have moved on to looking at the child in culture and seeing how the child works to use the cultural tools available to her and construct meaning. We have looked at how culture is dynamic and at how children do not live in one culture only, but inhabit the cultures that apply to them in a range of intersecting discourses, one of which involves what is known as 'popular culture'. Our twenty-first century child is now seen as able to operate differently in different contexts, using what is relevant from her culture to apply to another and able to share aspects of one culture with others.

Things to think about

- How would you define your culture? Would you include your rights in this? How does your culture affect the way in which you perceive yourself?
- Do you believe that cultural capital is inevitably linked to either success or failure?
- Why might you welcome popular culture in your setting?

Chapter 7

The child as role maker

In this chapter we start to think about how children position themselves in different contexts and play the roles assigned to them within these contexts. In order to play a role in society the child has to understand whether she does or does not fit into the group. So she will have to explore who she is in relation to others. Is she the youngest or the oldest in the family; an only child or one with siblings; a boy or a girl; black or white; sharing a language with the group?

We start with an extract from Jeanette Winterston's 1985 book *Oranges Are Not the Only Fruit*. In this semi-autobiographical novel Winterston drew on her own home life where she was an only child in a strange family dominated by God and the church, with clear-cut divides between enemies and friends. She knew she was special and was curious about school but her mother refused to send her until instructed to do so. She did not know what to expect: her mother always referred to school, negatively, as a Breeding Ground:

> At first I'd done my very best to fit in and be good. We had been set a project just before we started last autumn, we all had to write an essay called 'What I Did in my Summer Holidays'. I was anxious to do it well because I knew they thought I couldn't read or anything, not having been to school early enough. I did it slowly in my best handwriting, proud that some of the others could only print. We read them out one by one, then gave them to the teachers. It was all the same, fishing, swimming, picnics, Walt Disney. Thirty two essays about gardens and frog spawn. I was at the end of the alphabet, and I could hardly wait. The teacher was the kind of woman who wanted her class to be happy. She called us lambs, and had told me in particular not to worry if I found anything difficult.
> 'You'll soon fit in,' she soothed.
> I wanted to please her, and trembling with anticipation I started my essay . . . 'This holiday I went to Colwyn Bay with our church camp.'
> The teacher nodded and smiled.
> 'It was very hot, and Auntie Betty, whose leg was loose anyway, got sunstroke and we thought she might die.'
> The teacher began to look a bit worried, but the class perked up.
> 'But she got better, thanks to my mother who stayed up all night struggling mightily.'
> 'Is your mother a nurse?' asked the teacher, with quiet sympathy.
> 'No, she just heals the sick.'

. . .

> 'When we came back from Colwyn Bay Next Door had had another baby but there are so many of them Next Door we don't know whose it is. My mother gave them some potatoes from the yard but they said they weren't a charity and threw them back over the wall.'

You can see how little opportunity this child has had to develop the particular language, gestures and positions she needed in order to become an ordinary school pupil. Her cultural capital – rich in terms of her ability to use biblical language, write rather than print and understand much of life – clearly did not equip her to adapt easily to school. Playing the role of school pupil remained difficult. Her home experiences were so different from that of her schoolmates and so remote from what the school expected that adapting to school life was virtually impossible. And she was so immersed in the language and concerns of her home and church that she was, at first, unable to make the moves necessary to allow her admission to the role of school pupil.

Constructing identity: playing roles

Who are you? If asked this question you might tell us your name, age, and perhaps your address and position in the family. You might add something about your work and home and the things you enjoy. But defining yourself in terms of your identity is more difficult because it suggests defining yourself in relation to other people. Women may define themselves as 'someone's mum' or 'someone's wife' or 'someone's daughter'. Identities, like culture, are not simple or single, but complex and dynamic. Over the course of our lives, we come to define who we are according to where we are, with whom, what we are doing and how we are observed. Here is what a very old woman said when looking over the course of her life:

> When I was a child we lived in a lovely house near the sea. I was the oldest and the apple of my father's eye. Anything I wanted was mine. I didn't go to school but had a governess and we read romantic novels and listened to music and collected shells. I was pretty and privileged. Then my family had to emigrate. We were Jews living in Greece and life was becoming intolerable so we set off for South Africa where we had some distant relatives. Soon after arriving I went to the University. And there I found a different me. I was a good student and enjoyed studying and being different. Because I had come from Europe and spoke Greek I was admired. I was also pretty – which helped.
> After I graduated I married and had a child. Two more roles to add to my growing repertoire. But these were not roles that I excelled at. I didn't like the restrictions I felt were imposed on me by being someone's wife and I found motherhood deeply unsatisfying. I loved my child dearly but the thought of spending day after day with him drove me to despair.
> I decided to go out to work and employed another woman to look after my child. I managed to find work in a law office where I met interesting people and was thought to be efficient and organised. I enjoyed being in control. I played the role of manager well and enjoyed the recognition I got from colleagues and peers.
>
> (Personal communication, 2005)

You can see how the roles this woman played varied according to time, place, audience and circumstance. Her sense of her own identity changed alongside this and often in response to how she believed she was perceived by others.

The human infant begins to define her identity first by starting to see herself as unique but also as connected to others. For most infants these others are members of the immediate family and, for some, the more extended family and then, perhaps, the local community and neighbourhood. Here the child begins to interact with people and in doing this learns to see others as having feelings and intentions. Young children begin to pay attention to what others say and do: in part they *mimic* what they see and hear and they also internalise ways of acting, speaking and being. These build into a store of *memories* that can be drawn on in the complex scripts they will develop to play out the roles they need to play.

So the young child who starts to play at being different people is, in effect, trying out what it feels like to be in someone else's shoes.

> Lilliane is playing in the garden with her younger brother Thomas. She is being the mother and he is the baby. She holds his hand very tightly in hers and tells him to walk more quickly. 'Come on!' she says, in a loud and irritable voice. 'I am sick of telling you. Come on! We are going to be late.' And she pulls his arm to hurry him along.
>
> (Personal observation)

A very simple role play script, but what a lot is revealed. Here the child tries out what it feels like to be an adult – a mother, whose child is not walking fast enough. She is able to select the tone of voice and the speech patterns she must have heard adults (her mother and others) use when angry.

> Zwelethini is the older child. Busi is her younger brother. The children live with their mother and life is hard, particularly for Zwelethini, who must look after Busi, help her mother in the house, go to school and, in the afternoons, help out in the village. Zwelethini loves Busi but is envious of his status as both boy and younger child. Notice how this emerges in their play.
>
> *Zwelethini:* Now I am going to be the baby and you are my big brother and you have to look after me.
> *Busi:* Don't want to.
> *Zwelethini:* If you want me to play with you, you must do it. I am the baby and I am crying and you must bring me some food to eat.
>
> Busi scrabbles in a box and brings her a handful of leaves.
>
> *Zwelethini:* You must mash this for me and feed me. I love being the baby. I don't have to do anything and you have to do all the work.
> *Busi:* I want to be the baby now.
>
> (Personal observation notes, 1998)

Often the first role play children engage in is playing out their domestic roles within the setting of home and family. When they start moving beyond the immediate family their play evolves to enacting more functional roles. Here is an example of three children playing 'school'. It is taken from Ann Williams's piece called 'Playing school in multiethnic London' (2004). Wahida is 10 and Sayeda is 8 years old.

> *Wahida:*   Now we are going to do homophones. Who knows what a homophone is? No one? OK. I'll tell you one and then you're going to do some by yourselves. Like watch. One watch is your time watch, like 'What's the time' watch: and another watch is 'I'm watching you. I can see you . . .' So Sayeda, you wrote some in your books haven't you? Can you tell me some, please. Can you only give me three, please.
>
> *Sayeda:*   Oh, I wanted to give you five.
>
> *Wahida:*   No Sayeda, we haven't got enough time. We've only got five minutes to assembly.
>
> *Sayeda:*   Son is the opposite of daughter . . . And sun is . . . It shines on the sky so bright. . . .
>
> (Williams, 2004: 63)

In this wonderful example you see Wahida using the language of the classroom and the intonation patterns used by teachers. She is clearly in control and inducts her younger sister not only into the mysteries of homophones but into the practices and language of school. Later in the same chapter, Williams cites a pretend telephone conversation between 11-year-old Lee and 7-year-old Cathy.

> *Lee:*   (pretending to phone) Hello Miss Rhodes?
>
> *Cathy:*   (talking with an upper-class accent) Yees.
>
> *Lee:*   Your daughter's gone on a trip and she won't be back until about six o'clock tomorrow night.
>
> *Cathy:*   Has she now! Not again!!
>
> *Lee:*   I imagine she stayed overnight at school so I'm very sorry about that.
>
> *Cathy:*   She said she was writing a story.
>
> (Williams, 2004: 60)

Children are consummate players of this game of being other people. They are able to mimic the language patterns of people in authority and introduce into their role play an exploration of some of the issues that currently concern them – in this case possibly excuses, lies and explanations.

In their role play children sometimes use toys or objects to enact roles they have chosen for them. In this sense the objects become the living beings – puppets in the hands of their puppet-masters, the children. In doing this the children then adopt the voices and the language they have agreed on in designing and enacting their negotiated chosen scenario. Here are Hannah, aged 9, and Ben, aged 7, playing a complex game that went on over days. This is a very brief extract:

> *Ben [in a high-pitched voice, manipulating a Lego Knight he made]:*   You will do exactly as I do – exactly! If you do not do this you will die spectacularly.
>
> *Hannah [also in a high pitched voice, wielding a Groovy Girl doll]:*   Sir, sir, I beg you. Be kind to me. We were only practising our spells. We did not intend any harm. [Note the use of the language of books.]

Ben [high-pitched voice again]:   Practising? Well you weren't very good at it, were you. They would not want you in Hogwarts. *[Note the reference to the fictional world of Harry Potter.]*

Hannah [out of role – using her normal voice]:   Shall I get one of those [points to a Lego Bionicle] to be the chief?

Ben [in role, nods]:   Now, do as I say or you will . . .

Hannah [in role]:   . . . pay the price.

Ben [out of role]:   How much is the price?

Hannah [out of role]:   Not money, silly. It means you will have to pay for what you have done – get punished. We need to decide on a good punishment.

Ben [out of role]:   I know a good one. We could make them play a game of chess and then they could be stalemated.

Hannah [out of role]:   Or checkmated. Which is which? I never remember.

Ben [in role]:   I challenge you to a chess match. And if you don't win and I don't win we will be stalemated. And if we are stalemated then I will not play with you any more. You won't be my best friend any more.

(Personal notes, 2001)

Here the children are trying out voices, going in and out of role as they construct identities for the toys they are using to also play roles. They draw on strands from their normal lives, the books they read, the films they see and the games they play, to sort out issues that concern or interest them. Later in the play the toys are used in a more complex sequence relating to issues of friendship and power that were, at the time, issues that deeply concerned both.

In all these examples of role play we see children involved in answering the questions they have set themselves, all of which appear to be of the 'What if?' variety. What if my friend is nasty to me? What if I could be the younger child? What if I felt really angry? Engaging in the play, they must make decisions about who and what is involved in the play, where the action takes place and what the central themes are. This requires them to develop and use a range of complex cognitive and social skills including *skilful negotiation, logical sequencing of events, drawing on and combining experiences, symbolisation, speaking and listening.* As they move into more abstract play the same principles apply. The children create their own script, negotiate about who will play what part and use what is to hand to represent anything they agree.

Just playing?

The social construction of identity

Mindy Blaise (2005) is an early childhood teacher who moved away from the traditional influences of child development, largely because her interest in gender led her to believe that she needed to take a more *justice-based political stance*, examining what it means for children to be girls or Hispanic or of mixed race, for example. She contends that the concept of what is known as *Developmentally Appropriate Practice* (DAP), with its model of the 'naturally' developing child, conceals the ways in which gender (or race or other difference) influences a child's experiences and how the child interprets these experiences. Moreover, DAP fails to address the impact of how being a girl, for example, may affect the child's learning and development. Blaise adopted what she called a *feminist poststructural approach*, which looks at the issue of power in society. Poststructuralism will be feminist, she argued, when matters of gender become a central concern. She drew heavily on the work of Foucault (1979) who believed that power operates in all relationships and is expressed through discourse. Any consideration of how children construct gender or class or race or disability needs to take account of power. In a society like ours, power continues to be held largely by people who are white, educated, privileged, male and healthy. Those who are not may have little access to power and thus have to develop strategies in order to construct a positive identity for themselves.

Developing a cultural identity is a fundamental and complex task for all young children and one that takes place initially within the family and then broadens out into wider community and society. Children acquire a sense of 'belonging' within their own culture, which allows them to accept and coexist with individuals of other beliefs and cultures. The experiences children have will vary according to the values and traditions, customs and beliefs or their individual families and the culture of the family will shape identity in unique ways.

The image of identity development in many African cultures is that of *'polycropping'* where the shared and the social rather than the unique and individual aspects of identity are valued and emphasised. We in the developed West are used to the stance of Vygotsky that the development of identity is primarily sociocultural. Traditional African cultures accept this but go beyond it by sensitising children from an early age to seek out others and extract 'intelligences' and define self in order to 'gain significance from and through their relationships with others' (Ellis, 1978: 6). Zimba (2002) describes the South African Zulu style of nurturing as 'umuntu umuntu ngabantu', which literally means that 'a person is only a person with other people'. We may pay lip service to appreciating this view but in reality it is very far from our emphasis on the individual child within the tidy nuclear family.

By fostering children's close identification with the group, the traditional social values in many African cultures and found in ceremonies around naming, marriage and death, focus on social development and draw children into the rituals and convention associated with these. So each child, as part of the group, develops an identity as an individual but within a group. In a similar way, the peer cultures in many African societies tend to complement and extend the family's imprint on the developing individual. So the young child moving slightly away from the home and engaging with peers adds another aspect to her identity. Cohen (2001: 6) argues that the process of identity formation can be problematic for some African children because their families 'have been caught up in the web of cultural transition where there are no longer clearly defined values and moral *codes of behaviour* that should be instilled in children and young people'. This is not confined to African children: many children in many places face similar difficulties.

> The process of developing a sense of self is a process of connecting an individual's personal identity to their social identity. Individuality and connectedness are not dichotomous qualities; they develop together in the same child, within the same skin. In some traditional African cultures, children individuate by being inter-connected with others and 'transform' en route to adult identity through responsible participation in real life tasks (Nsamenang, 2004).

(Drawn from Brooker and Woodhead, 2008)

One could, of course, still adopt a sociocultural approach to considering how children construct gender and/or other images. The approach of the socioculturalists to gender, for example, would be that it is neither a product of biology nor simply of socialisation. It is a product of human meaning making. So the concept of gender that we construct makes the maleness or femaleness of people significant. We do it all the time, mostly subconsciously.

A famous piece of research cited in Lloyd and Duveen (1990) makes this clear. They asked those involved in the study to dress their baby boys in pink and baby girls in blue. You will know that blue and pink are still, in 2012, the colours often used to define gender in the USA and Europe. In their experiment they observed that people encountering the babies for the first time assumed those in blue were boys and those in pink were girls and treated them accordingly. The girls were called 'pretty' and were cuddled and treated gently if they were distressed or had hurt themselves. Boys were called 'big' and 'strong' and played with in a more boisterous way. The meaning of this is that the *socially constructed markers of gender* (in this case colours) affected the ways in which the children were treated. And it does not require a huge leap of logic to recognise that the way in which children are treated will affect their images of themselves. Gender, in this sense, operates in all cultures and powerfully affects the images children create of their own gender identity.

So gender becomes something that we 'do'. It runs so deeply through our society that we assume that it is genetic. But socioculturalists hold firm to their belief that gender, like culture, is a human construct. Look at the gender symbols built into this portrait:

> In Covent Garden in London a man was pushing his small child in a stroller. He was clearly enjoying the experience and chatting away to the child, and appreciating the smiles given to both of them by passers-by. These passers-by were 'doing gender' in the sense that they clearly liked the sight of this father caring so lovingly for his child and they gave him signs of approbation. Moreover the child was dressed in blue dungarees and had long curls. It was impossible to tell from the clothing what the sex of the child was. But when the father handed his child a doll the child's gender was being 'done'. Those who saw the child with the doll began to respond to the child as a 'girl'.
>
> (Personal observation, 2006)

What is it that happens when children construct their gender identity? Do they simply learn to adopt the roles that are assigned to them by society? If this was the case there would be no change and one role would be passed on from generation to generation. But we know that this is not the case. Francis (1998) believed that identity is not fixed, but fluid and that it is positioned by the different discourses (or contexts and interactions) that individuals engage in. This discursive positioning is something we have touched on earlier in this book when we look at the views of children and childhood and how these changed over time and place.

According to Foucault the role of power in discourse is complex. It is like a web or network in the sense that those involved in a discourse can both exercise power and be affected by others exercising power. It permeates all relationships from the most intimate and personal to the institutional. Jacques Derrida (1972), the French philosopher, was responsible for introducing the concept of *deconstruction* which involves examining the ways in which something – such as gender, for example – has been socially constructed and looking at what the consequences are. The word 'deconstruction' might make you think that Derrida is talking about destroying something: on the contrary, it is a very careful way of unpicking or unfolding to see what has been hidden or avoided or left out; for considering what different routes might have been taken and for examining the use of taken-for-granted concepts. Deconstruction is a really useful tool for examining something carefully.

Children actively construct identities through 'reading' and interpreting what they encounter. But in coming to make meaning, the interpretation open to the child is constrained by the accepted values and customs of the culture within which the child is operating. The child may construct many meanings but some are going to be limited according to the prevailing norms and principles, or by the values and the customs of the community or culture or society in which identity construction is taking place.

> Leroy is 4 years old. He lives in North London. He loves nothing more than to dress up in the clothes in the dressing up box in his nursery. And most of all he likes to dress up in a particular pink dress and drape a purple scarf over his shoulders and totter around in shoes that are too big for him. But he will not do this after lunch and when asked why he explained that he didn't want his mum to see him dressed like that because 'it's girly and I'm not a poof'. He seems to fear that his mum will tell his dad.
>
> (Personal observation notes, 2005)

Let us now try to deconstruct this small case study. This child appears to want to explore what it might feel like to be a girl and does this by dressing in girls' clothes. It is clear that this is something that is acceptable in the nursery. But Leroy has internalised something about the powerful discourse operating in his family and fears the disapproval of his father. The use of homophobic language gives an insight into the language accepted at home including the negative implications that some of it carries.

Very young children demonstrate strong opinions about their gender positioning. The social construction of gender operates in various ways. Children may encounter views on gender at home, like Leroy above, and/or in their community, hearing about what things are regarded as appropriate for boys and what for girls. Sex-role *stereotyping* becomes cemented by practices in society, which hardens the gender roles. But since we are suggesting that there is no one fixed self or identity and that identity is constructed and not imposed, children are able to fluctuate in their identity. There are, however, some situations in which children's freedom to construct their identity is limited by race, class, language or physical ability.

Gender continues to be an extremely significant factor in the childhood of millions of children throughout the world. Over generations there have been huge discrepancies in the numbers boys and girls being born, surviving and dying in different groups at different times. At the time of writing there are roughly 107 boys born to 100 girls, worldwide. The reasons for this are, like everything, complex and involve the fact that in some countries boys are more valued than girls, partly because they will provide the family with an heir. And there are, of course, variations according to where in the world the children are born.

Opportunities available to boys and girls vary according to economics, to philosophy, to values and to place. In many countries throughout the world girls still have fewer educational opportunities than boys. The reason for this might be the traditional expectation in many societies that the roles of girls are to be mothers and wives. And in these cultures early marriages sometimes put an end to schooling. The consequence is that literacy levels of women are often significantly lower than those of men and this has an impact on the women themselves and on their children. There is evidence that shows that educated girls are less likely to die in childbirth and that they give birth to fewer children. The children themselves are less likely to die in infancy, are better nourished and suffer less from illnesses (Bellamy, 1999: 52).

The good news is that, in 2009, 46 per cent of children worldwide had access to free primary education compared with 33 per cent a decade earlier. Significant gains were made in South and West Asia where the number of entrants doubled and in Sub Saharan Africa access to some form of preschool provision increased by 6.2 million children.

Language, identity and roles

There is a considerable body of research documenting how closely language is tied to identity. You will remember the sad story of Antii cited in the previous chapter. People who have been uprooted and moved to a country which uses another language, or people living in countries where their own language is marginalised and not given recognition, suffer loss of identity and some theorists describe this process in very emotive terms by talking of the *genocide of minority languages*. The example below is drawn from the true story of the Hasbudak family.

> More than 20 years ago two children, born in Britain to parents from mainland Turkey who had neglected to renew their permission to stay in Britain, were deported. The older child, Zeynep, was 8 when they left. English was her first language – her mother tongue – and she became the spokesperson for her entire family, talking to reporters and officials and others when the campaign to prevent the deportation, led by their Infants School, became public. When they got to Istanbul she found herself in a country where she did not know the language and where she was teased for speaking English. She quickly learned to speak Turkish but, in the process, lost every word of her English. On her return to the UK, 20 years later, her English was not that of a native speaker of the language and she had to go to English language classes to try and regain it. She said, 'When I couldn't communicate in English I felt like nobody. I didn't know who I was any more. And when I learned Turkish I didn't want to speak English in case I became different again. It was terrible.'

Zeynep, born in London was a fluent and articulate speaker of English and one of her key roles during her childhood had always been as spokesperson for her family in many situations – at school, at the local clinic, in dealing with officials and so on. When she had to go and live in Turkey she gave up her mother-tongue to protect herself and devoted her time to learning the language of her new home. In doing this she not only abandoned her first language but also managed to lose it almost entirely. And with it much of her identity.

Just how closely language is associated with identity, self-esteem and a sense of dignity is illustrated by Primo Levi in his 1989 book *The Drowned and the Saved*. As you may know, Levi was a survivor of Auschwitz, living for long enough to write poignant, powerful and bitter accounts of what he experienced and witnessed in the camp. Living with him in the camp were those whose first languages were Yiddish, Italian, Greek, Hungarian, French and German. The language of the camps themselves became something else – something unique – tied to the place and the time. And although the language of each camp differed in some respects, all denied the inmates respect for their language or identity. A German Jewish philosopher, Klemperer, labelled the camp language as the *Lingua Tertii Imperii* – the language of the Third Reich. Levi observed that where violence is inflicted on people, it is inflicted on language. For the Italians in the camps attacks on the some of their regional dialects did much to damage their self-esteem. In Auschwitz the word to eat was *fressen*, which is the word used almost exclusively to describe what animals do. In Ravensbruck, the only camp exclusively for women, two words were used to describe them: one was *schmutzstuck*, which means dirty, or garbage, and the other *schmuckstuck*, which means jewel. You may have heard the term *Muselmann*, which literally means Muslim, but was used to describe those worn-out ravaged prisoners close to death. The reasons for this are unclear although Levi suggests they could refer either to fatalism or to the head bandages which might have resembled 'a turban' (Levi, 1989: 77).

Levi pointed out that having a language of potential use within the camps, for example, German, was not a luxury but a life-saving necessity. He noted that those prisoners who did not understand German died within the first ten days after their arrival. The fact that they could not communicate meant that they could do nothing to ameliorate their conditions: they may almost certainly have perished in any case. This is complex stuff and requires careful reading and thought. What happened was that those in charge, those holding the power – the Nazi *kommandants* – did not denigrate their own language of German – that civilised, sophisticated and respected language of Schiller and Goethe – but used a bastardised version of it. This enabled them to retain an image of themselves as 'civilised'. In stark contrast, the prisoners, deprived of their liberty, families, hair, names and language descended into an impossible invisibility and anonymity.

In *The Truce*, Levi, looking at what happened when the camps were liberated, described the tragic story of a 3-year-old child, Hurbinek, who 'was a nobody, a child of death, a child of Auschwitz' (1979/1991: 197). He was alone, paralysed from the waist down, unable to speak at all. The name had been given to him and his eyes were full of anger and anguish. A 15-year-old boy in the camp tended to Hurbinek, brought him food to eat, cleaned him and talked to him slowly and carefully in Hungarian. After a week of doing this the older boy told the others that Hurbinek could say a word: what the word was no one knew, nor did they know what language it was in, but it was apparent the child was attempting to communicate. Levi tells us that the child experimented with making sounds – desperate to be understood – and despite the fact that around him in that abominable place there were speakers of nearly all the languages of Europe, no one could understand him.

> Hurbinek, who was 3 years old and perhaps had been born in Auschwitz and had never seen a tree; Hurbinek, who had fought like a man, the last breath, to gain his entry into the world of men, from which a bestial power had excluded him; Hurbinek; the nameless, whose tiny forearm – even his – bore the tattoo of Auschwitz; Hurbinek died in the first days of March 1945, free but not redeemed. Nothing remains of him: he bears witness through these words of mine.
>
> (Levi, 1979/1991: 198)

We, as a species, not only take on the roles of others but also use narrative or story to make sense of the world. In doing this we are able to explore what it feels like to be in someone else's shoes. We have considered how small children make up stories to allow them to explore the different roles that they – and others – play. In doing this they are free to explore every facet of their constructed identity and build inner and outer dialogues. You can find evidence of this in the autobiographies people write or the self-portraits they paint. Each self-portrait is an autobiographical narrative.

Did you know of the Mexican painter Frida Kahlo, whose whole life was marked by a traffic accident in 1925 that left her with severe injuries and pain throughout her life? During her lifetime she painted 66 self-portraits, each reflecting some aspect of her self-identity. One of the best known is The Broken Column, *painted in 1944, and showing her nude body divided into two by a broken classical column, representing her fractured spine. Numerous nails puncture her skin, acting as symbols of her intense pain, as well as the tight leather braces that hold her body together. These signify her entrapment as a result of the immobility that followed the accident.*

Bakhtin (1981) explored the ways in which we create images of ourselves and others and you may remember that these images can be verbal or visual. In doing this Bakhtin was concerned with analysing how we are able to construct a self-image both in life and through art. He suggested that there are three elements to doing this:

1   First, there is the construction of *how others appear to us*, which might include the representation of significant role models or influential people.
2   Second, there is the way in which the individual analyses how *she appears to others*, which might be called the social persona.
3   And finally, there is the question of how *the individual appears to the self* – in other words self-identity. Implicit in this is the mixture of the internal and the external.

All of these notions are constructed initially inside families and are hugely influenced by culture. Bakhtin believed that the stories we create in words, symbols, pictures or role play are what gives coherence to the constant re-writing of self. This is a useful reminder that self-identity is not fixed and forever, but fluid and dynamic.

Establishing identities: street children

In the first edition of this book the focus of this section about street children was solely on children from the streets of Lima, in Peru. But in the years since that first edition the numbers of street children throughout the world have increased and so this edition will take a less localised view and try to be more analytical. The very task of counting or estimating the number of young people who can be defined as street children is difficult and so numbers remain open to interpretation. Most of the current literature about street children accepts that there are something like 100 million children living on the streets throughout the world. This horrifying statistic is, of course, open to interpretation but some things are clear. With global warming and changes in the climate, together with widespread economic recession, more and more young people are finding it essential to move to the cities. The question arises as to who counts as a street child. UNICEF relies on a definition developed with Latin America in mind (UNCHS, 2000: 74). They define a street child as:

any girl or boy . . . for whom the street (in the widest sense of the word, including unoccupied dwellings, wasteland, etc.) has become his or her habitual abode and/or source of livelihood; and who is inadequately protected, supervised, or directed by responsible adults.

(Glasser, 1994: 54)

Until fairly recently experts were arguing as to whether street children should be described as living on the street or as being of the street. In the first definition children actually live, eat and sleep on the street: in the second they work on the street. What is clear is that both groups of children have to develop multiple relationships and identities. More recent thinking suggests that these children cannot be thought of as a clearly defined and homogeneous group but rather as children who are regarded by the public to be out of place (e.g. Raffaelli, 1999; Ennew, 2000) or as 'agents' or capable social actors – a perspective that brings children from the margins to focus on them as social actors in their own right, with varied lives and diverse experiences (as in the work of O'Kane, 2003; Ennew and Swart-Kruger, 2003; Prout, 2005; Ansell, 2008). This is my preferred view.

In the last decade stereotypes of street children as being drug-addicted, victims, thieves, beggars, deviants and more have been overturned as researchers have found evidence of substantive and dynamic diversity among characteristics and conditions. What seems to be taking place is the formation of street communities, where those living or working on the street learn to interact and negotiate with one another, set up rules about expectations and begin to focus on the aspects of their lives that please them. And there are some!

Some research has recently shown significant shifts in characteristics of street life over time in the same city. For example, two studies, eight years apart, of street children in Vietnam's Ho Chi Minh City found striking differences in drug use. In 1992 it was stated that none of the 200 children in a survey were drug users. Glue or lacquer sniffing, widely practised amongst street children in Thailand and in South American countries, was absent in Ho Chi Minh City. By the year 2000 at least one in six children living on the streets was said to use heroin: 'There is little doubt that heroin addiction is the biggest problem faced by street children in HCM City today. The children themselves say so, as do the service providers and other concerned agencies' (Bond, 2004: 155).

Whilst it is comforting to think of children living or working on the streets as being agents and not victims we must, nonetheless, keep in mind the enormous issues associated with poverty, alienation, lack of health facilities, family and other networks, lack of access to education and more. The issue is so widespread that solutions must be found.

Do you know anything about the many grassroots organisations mushrooming throughout the world, trying to do something about all of this? Here is what one such organisation, the Shack/Slum Dwellers International (SDI) are doing. They are an organisation where women play a prominent role as co-agents of change and is only one of a number of similar networks of street-vendors, home-based workers and waste pickers.

This is what they believe:

> *We believe that unless we band together, the challenges of urban poverty will not be addressed. By joining forces and pooling our knowledge, experience and creative solutions, we can achieve*

action on a meaningful scale. So it is that slum dwellers in such cities as Nairobi, Kenya, and Kampala, Uganda, are consulting counterparts in Mumbai, India, who persuaded government, railway authorities and international development lenders to relocate some 20,000 households as part of an effort to update the rail system. Ultimately, the Mumbai slum residents were able to design their own resettlement, moving from locations where many children had been killed by trains passing a mere nine metres from homes.

(UNICEF, 2012: 72)

So the organisation has hundreds of thousands of federated members in cities spread across 34 countries. They work for decent housing and infrastructure and try to ensure that they are able to collaborate with local government. They insist that they take the long view, have patience and spend time analysing each problem and working to find a solution. The system starts with the women forming a collective, and they then pool their resources so that they are able to make small loans – enough to put food on the table, buy essential medicines, pay for children's education and more. At the top of their list of essential needs are things involving safety. We all know that children need a decent place to live and play and feel safe. They need clean water and toilet facilities. They need homes where they can feel sure they can stay for a long time so that children don't have to live with the forever-present threat of having to move on again. The children's sense of self carries with it the responsibility for aspects of their own safety and that of their peers and families. They are the ones who have to keep a look out for demolition squads and when they spot them they become the road runners, bringing the news to the adults.

The SDIs perform the much needed task of recording who is living illegally on waste land, in shacks, on the streets thus ensuring that these people get to be counted in the census; have their children's births recorded and gain access to the voters rolls. They do this through settlement profiles and family identification papers. This documentation can help in the future in identifying more accurately real housing needs, immunisation programmes, who is in work and where, school places and more. For street children the possibilities of being more legal in the sense of having an existence on paper also implies that they will have access to seeing themselves as citizens.

Summary

This chapter has adopted a rather different approach to the previous chapters, incorporating the writing of novelists and others in trying to examine the complexities of children learning to play the many and different roles they need in their lives. We have touched on issues affecting how self-image is constructed through the playing of roles by boys and girls, children alienated in one way or another and street children. Our twenty-first century child may find herself playing some demanding roles in this increasingly tense and often hostile world.

Things to think about

* What have you learned from reading this chapter about using the image of 'everybaby' or 'everychild' to consider the realities of the lived lives of the world's children?

Chapter 8

The child as thinker
Questions and solutions

In this chapter we turn our attention to children everywhere working hard to understand everything in their worlds and doing this without the need of specialist resources. We examine how aspects of the worlds that children live in raise questions in their minds or pose problems for them to solve. We see how children develop a range of strategies as problem solvers and in doing this make hypotheses, try these out, analyse what happens, identify patterns, generate rules, use analogy, come to conclusions and move on. The problems children address range from very simple physical phenomena such as why things always fall downwards, to more complex things like why people fight, how people came to be living where they live, who makes up the rules, where the rain comes from, what it feels like to be powerful and so on.

Throughout this book we have come across children encountering things that interest or fascinate them and raise questions in their minds. In Ho Chi Minh City we met Hung who went to the airport after school every day to sell his postcards to help with the family finances. There he taught himself English and in the process found people asking him what the time was. As he watched the big clock on the wall questions arose in his mind. Why a big hand and a small hand? What did the little black marks around the edge mean? Why were the hands moving? The answers he arrived at helped him learn to tell the time. Eventually he could answer the questions asked (and sometimes get a tip for doing so). In Lake Atitlan in Guatemala we came across some children watching their mother and older siblings making tortillas on the fire. As the young children watched the process questions were raised in their minds. Why did the dough have to be rolled and then flattened? What happened to the tortillas on the fire? What made them taste so good? We came across Louis in a school in London learning the multiplication tables and being fascinated by a trick the teacher taught him to work out whether or not the nine times table was correct. He then used trial and error over and over again in order to check up on whether his answer was, indeed, correct or not and from this was able to generate his own conclusion that justified the rules he had generated.

In all of these examples and others throughout the book the problems raised are real ones in the sense that they matter to the child. They are not decontextualised school-based problems – not even Louis's maths problem. In all the situations the children set up finding an answer using their own developing capacities as thinkers. Hung used the situations he found himself in to analyse what he needed to learn in order to make money for his family. The children in Lake Atitlan were learning through watching an essential activity in their own culture. They watched, listened and sometimes they joined in.

Finding, using, making, evaluating

Kress (1997) saw children as being practised makers of signs in many semiotic modes. As children use the things they encounter to represent the world, they are exploring a rich world of meanings. For Kress the children's abilities to explore things in many different ways is an essential antecedent for moving into the unidimensional world of written language. All children make signs and these represent what they are interested in at the time. Ben encountered a problem when he wanted to make moving models like the 'zooks' he had seen on television. It was computer technology that allowed the zooks to move. When Ben found he could not succeed in making moving models he just looked for and found things lying around. These are the things that Kress describes as being 'at hand'. Ben's solution was not to abandon his interest but transform it. He made a series of static models. How fascinating that alongside this he wrote out the instructions for how the 'zooks' could be made to move (see Figure 8.1).

Like Kress, Pahl (1999) was interested in how very young children in nursery classes express complex ideas through making things out of materials found and given. She noticed how the making of models (and not necessarily realistic models) involved much more than mere cutting and sticking, but represented complex planning, making, trying, changing, elaborating and evaluating. Once the child has completed making a model the finished product itself offers the child much to think about. In other words, the act of making in itself is an engaging process that may challenge children's thinking and the

Figure 8.1 Ben's home-made 'zooks'

finished product, once examined, raises more questions to be answered. The process appears to be:

- asking a question;
- attempting to answer it by raising a hypothesis;
- doing something to test the hypothesis;
- noticing what happens;
- confirming the hypothesis or not;
- coming to a conclusion or returning to check out the hypothesis in a different way.

I would argue that this is very much the process engaged in by both scientists and artists. What is happening is a transition from one form of reality to another.

> Zethu made a necklace out of some seeds that she found and then threaded on some wire her dad had given her. Having the seeds and the wire she then needed to find a way to make holes in the seeds in order that they could be threaded on the wire. Her brother offered her a stick but it would not work. Her mother gave her a sewing needle, which she used successfully. [She tried the stick and the needle to find out which would work.] She then carefully threaded the beads on the wire and measured it against herself for a length that she liked. Her brother cut the wire for her and she twisted the two ends together as she had seen him do when making wire toys [learning from the model of her brother]. She then sat back and looked at the necklace and decided that it needed to 'look prettier'. She found some of the paste her aunt used to decorate the clay pots and applied that to the beads, carefully, using a feather and a thin stick. When she had finished she announced that next time she would paint the beads first because it would be easier. [A reflection on what she had made – the product – enabled her to consider what she might do differently, indicating some of the learning that had taken place.]
>
> (Personal observation notes, 2003)

Pahl spent time observing the children in the nursery and some of her observations powerfully illustrate the complexity of children's investigations into some idea that has arisen in their minds. Here are some examples:

> When I sat down at the modelling table, I was fascinated by Lydia making what she told me was to be a carpet, with pieces of felt. She then selected a container which she described as a basket. At the bottom of the basket she placed the collection of felt squares. The carpet had been transformed and was now a basket with a soft covering at the bottom.
>
> (Pahl, 1999: 19)

> I watched Lucy make a shopping basket out of an old tissue box. She carefully made a handle for it. She then wrote out a list which she attached to the basket with a piece of tape. When I asked her what the writing was she said that it was 'writing to show my mum'.
>
> (Pahl, 1999: 21)

You may remember that Halliday talked about signs and specifically about how we represent ourselves to the world when we communicate. He mentioned three functions of signs:

- The first was what he called *ideational* – by which he meant the way we say something about the world through an object.
- Then there is the *interpersonal function* where we say something about the object's relationship to the world.
- Finally there is a function that we have not mentioned before. This is the *textual function* where we say something about the sign's form and composition – in other words we say how it is made.

Pahl's analysis of Lucy's basket above is that the ideational aspects are the objects, the shopping basket and list, which both arose out of a shopping project in the nursery. The interpersonal aspect is the sign's relationship with the outside world and you will note that Lucy specifically did this in words when she talked of writing for her mum. The textual function is what the basket was made of. Lucy chose an empty tissue box and used masking tape and string. In the making of objects all three functions are at play.

In coming to understand children's representations it is important to remember that, for the child, there will be no distinction between the different ways of representation – drawing, writing, playing, constructing, making models, etc. For the child something – a question, a feeling, an idea – is the starting point for an exploration or investigation and one thing leads to another. For Ben it may well have been the mobility of the 'zooks' that he wanted to investigate and when he couldn't he chose to explore other aspects that had entered his mind during the making of the models. This is what we mean when we talk about the importance of children being able to represent and re-represent and it is important here to remind ourselves that this does not imply the necessity for expensive things. Ben's models are three-dimensional in form and he used a range of materials to make them: what he used was what he found in the house where he was staying.

For both Kress and Pahl the signs that the children produce as they make models are intimately linked to their culture and their society and are also a precursor to literacy. We find children painting and modelling as ways of communicating their complex ideas before they arrive at literacy. It is worth reiterating that when children draw, paint or make models they draw on their particular cultural tools and their individual or collaborative experiences. Children making things in South Africa use what is to hand and make wheeled toys out of pieces of wire, dolls out of cornhusks wrapped in scraps of fabric, necklaces out of seeds threaded together and furniture our of empty crates. Children in Mexico are influenced by the icons and images they see around them and use sheets of thin metal, brilliant colours, skeleton figures and, in some places, detailed miniature versions of people and animals sometimes set in empty nut cases.

John Matthews, who has written in detail about young children as early mark makers, has a passion for understanding what is happening when children draw. He was influenced by the work of Trevarthen who, you will remember, showed that even newborn babies are able to take part in shared meaning making with caregivers. Matthews drew parallels between language and drawing in the sense of incorporating Chomsky's notion that children generate rules and use language creatively. All children make novel utterances when they say things that they could not have heard from a fluent speaker. They could not have copied many of the things they say. So a child, having worked out the rule that all past tense verbs in English end in 'ed', say things they have never heard, such as 'I eated the cake.' In a fascinatingly similar fashion Matthews believed that in the process of making marks children *combine movements and sensations to produce new marks* – ones never seen before – in their search for meaning. In his book *Helping Children to Draw and Paint in Early Childhood* he looked at the development of his own child, Ben, and asked if, when Ben scribbled, he was 'babbling with paint' (1994: 18). Matthews was keen to point out that those who are intent on assessing children as 'artists' do so against some notion of what accurate representation should be and in doing this they are using a culturally restricted and narrow definition of art that is Western European in origin and doesn't allow for artistic representations from other cultures including the use of pattern, colour or specific symbols, like the dots in Aboriginal art.

Sue Cox (2005) looked at children's drawing within the same philosophical and pedagogic framework as Pahl, Kress and Matthews. She observed children in a nursery where they were able to initiate activities and follow through their own ideas and she did not limit her observations to drawing (defined as the making of marks on a two-dimensional surface), but also looked at them engaged in model making and painting. Her analysis of what the children were doing – the processes in which they were involved – is far from the traditional ways of looking at children's drawing in a Piagetian stage-type analysis. She is little interested in representation in the sense of the child being able to make something that accurately resembles or represents something else. There are a number of reasons for her criticisms of this approach to drawing; not least in that it is very culture specific and open to judgement as 'good' or not. Cox seeks to understand what the *purpose* of the drawing is for the child.

For Cox, then, drawing takes place – as do all other expressive activities – in specific cultural contexts and is imbued with personal significance. Here is one of the examples she cited to illustrate this:

> Three-year-old Leanne was drawing with felt pen on green paper, on her own, in the writing corner of the nursery classroom. She began by drawing an enclosed oval shape. She then proceeded to fill the shape with dots, some of which, as her arm descended with some force, became more extended marks. As she continued, she began to talk to herself, unaware that I was listening. [I was observing some other children at the time.] She identified the shape as a duck pond and the marks she was making as ducks. She then made a final dot within the shape, and declared it to be the plug where the water goes out. She moved to the corner of the page where she made some individual shapes working from left to right. Reaching the edge of the page she continued immediately beneath. As she did this she said slowly, as she was making the marks, 'To Auntie Bonny'.
>
> (Cox, 2005: 118)

In her analysis of these detailed observation notes Cox remarked on how the child was ascribing meaning to the marks she was making and that 'reading' the drawing through carefully following the child's processes allows the observer to guess at what her *intentions* were and how they changed as her movements and mark-making changed. Looking at a 'finished product' could not possibly have given anyone such an insight into this creative process. Cox also showed in her piece how the marks made by a child can be changed as external events affect the child's thinking. She illustrated this by talking of a child who produced three arched lines and called them, first a rainbow, but when a child close by sneezed, the child changed the label to 'a sneeze'.

Transformations occur on different levels and children play with the marks they make or the models they create just as they play with words. A mark made in what might be regarded as the 'wrong' place can be explained by the child as part of a joke, a story or a play on reality. Cox was interested in the monologues she heard the children use (as in the example of Leanne above) and felt that these do not reflect the child trying to justify a drawing that is not visually accurate or pleasing but just to explore the same idea or ideas through another mode, in this case spoken language. We are back to the idea of investigation or exploration involving different modes of representation.

Signs and symbols are not limited to the visual. And thinking about transformation, I urge you to read the account of the designing of a curtain for a theatre in Reggio Emilia by a group of young children, all of whom made conscious decisions about the transformations they wished to make to their own designs (Smidt, 2013).

All human infants are exposed to sounds before birth and there is evidence that infants start to respond to music very early in life. Ilari (2002) noted that infants start to produce 'musical babbling', consisting of sounds of varying length and pitch which seem to descend in melody but need not be imitations of anything heard. You will see here the links with mark making and spoken language. Moog (1968/1976) noted that babies a of about 1 year old showed likes and dislikes, by responding positively to songs, rhythmic words and instrumental music but negatively to sounds like those of traffic or vacuum cleaners. Older infants begin to beat or tap or clap hands to join in with musical games. They also move to music, spinning round, making stepping or dance movements. Hargreaves (1986) noticed that the songs children made up often contained a melodic phrase, sometimes made up of three notes of different pitch. Beetlestone (1998) offered the example of 5-year-old Fay who was fascinated by the sheet music that accompanied her toy piano. She asked endless questions about how the dots on the paper could be translated into sounds to be made on the piano and through this began to see the relationship between the visual symbols and the auditory sounds. After a while she started making up tunes for herself, sometimes attempting to 'write' them down.

Trevarthen (1998), in his examination of how children need to learn a culture, found that mothers in many cultures sang to their children, danced for and with them and exposed them to the popular music of their time and place. He believed that children have an innate sense of musicality that allows them to communicate with others before the acquisition of speech. Music, said Trevarthen, is a communal, cultural and communicative act. In the last chapter in this book, which examines what we are beginning to understand through developments in neuroscience, there is very interesting evidence on the significance of music for learning and development.

Music is just one of the potential languages available to us all for expressing our ideas, feelings and thoughts – a reminder of what Malaguzzi said about the significance of the hundred languages of children being able to represent and re-represent their findings.

Solving problems

Greco (1962, in Williams and Kamii, 1986: 23–26) told the wonderful story of how 5-year-old Jean-Pierre solved an ongoing problem relating to his daily life. He lived with his mother, father and a sibling in Paris. Each day his mother would ask him to put out the table napkins for the main meal of the day. On the first day Jean-Pierre started, logically enough, by taking one napkin at a time and putting it on a plate before returning to fetch the next napkin. He was depending on the concept of one-to-one correspondence in order to do this. He had to make four trips for each meal. He continued to make his daily four trips for about three months. And then, on one day, he decided to count the plates (he could count to 30) and then counted out four napkins – and lo and behold, he only had to make one trip. He repeated this new pattern for six days but on the seventh day there was a guest for dinner and Jean-Pierre found there was an additional plate on the table. He took his four napkins in one trip as before, but when he got to the table realised that there was a plate without a napkin. Dismayed by this he returned all four napkins to their place in the cupboard and then started all over again, this time making five trips to and from the table.

The following day the guest was no longer there, but Jean-Pierre made four trips to the table and continued to do this for five more days when he again reverted to his four-napkins-at-once method. Ten days later he was told there was, again, to be a guest for dinner. This time he counted out his four napkins and then returned to the table to collect one extra for the empty plate. And on the following day when lunch was for his family alone he reverted to four napkins in one go.

Jean-Pierre's mother, in the context of everyday life, had asked him to do something perfectly within his capabilities and as part of family life. His initial solution worked for about three months, but then he seemed to think that there might be a simpler and more efficient way of doing things. A question had been raised in his mind. His first solution was to rely on one-to-one correspondence. After some time he was able to remember and hold a number in his head. This was disrupted when there was an extra person for lunch. This new variable made him revert briefly to one-to-one correspondence. Remarkably he seems to have been left alone by the adults to find his own solutions.

You will remember Piaget's image of the child as tireless rational scientist, trying to make sense of the world without reference to context or other people. Is Jean-Pierre an example of this? Or is the context of home and the presence of others, however separate, still significant? Those who argue against this see the world in which children live as being both objective and subjective, meaning that there are always things to explore and questions in the world: each person's exploration will be unique. So the child raises questions, finds answers and creates knowledge of her own but does this within the context of her culture and its collective knowledge. The implication of this is that the child cannot make knowledge her own if she is required to integrate it into something of which she has no experience or understanding.

The same may be equally true for adults. Try this to see if you can understand it.

> The afferent function of the non-specific structures involves branches from fibers in the trunk-line specific projection systems. Conduction within the non-specific system is to widely separated points, pooling the excitation from different senses, and the rate of conduction is slow. The cortical bombardment from the non-specific system therefore derives from all the senses indiscriminately.
>
> (Hebb, 1958: 80)

Could you make sense of this? Here is a clue. It comes from a textbook about psychology. Did that help? Here is another clue. The chapter it comes from is called 'The nervous system' and the section of the chapter is subtitled 'Afferent, internuncial and efferent paths'. Did any of this help you? Presumably you struggled to make sense of this because it refers to things you have little or no experience of and hence have nothing to help you on your path to understanding.

Bruner said that learners beginning to make sense of something unfamiliar, will use new and different ways of doing this. We often make sense by 'telling the story', which is dependent on language. If we need to tell a story for which we don't have the language (the vocabulary and the concepts) we may have to find different ways of making meaning. When it comes to making sense of something in the natural world Bruner suggests we need to find logical or categorical ways of doing this. Instead of telling the story we organise our thinking in order to find the feature that objects or events have in common, for example. So both narrative and logical-categorical ways of making sense are important since they prepare learners for the different domains of learning.

Pramling and Samuelsson (2001) looked at how a teacher was able to move children into a new domain by a careful and respectful focus on the role of specific language in building meaning-making tools. A group of 3-year-old children were playing with water, making sense of 'floating'. To suggest this the teacher had placed an array of objects on a table beside the bowl of water. The ten objects included a cork with a hole in it, a metal screw and nut, a pine cone, paper, fabric and wood splinters. The teacher, in a rather more formal manner than perhaps one might expect, asked a child if each object would float or sink and why. The child then put the object in the water to see what happened. The first object chosen by the child was the cork. He put it in the water and when asked by the teacher said that it floated and when asked why, said ''Cause it lays there.' The teacher did not correct the child but asked 'Why does it float there?' (hence modelling the correct terminology). The child's response was, ''Cause it is so very heavy.' This is a deceptively correct response. I love this answer, which shows that the ever-inventive child offers an alternative hypothesis. He has arrived at a tentative theory. Presented with a cork with a hole in it he thinks it will float until the water comes in, fills it up so that it will then sink. The experiment went on with the child shifting both explanations and thinking, replacing one hypothesis with another as his existing knowledge was challenged and then adjusted. Pramling and Samuelsson believe that the child develops a discourse, which is a systematic process of inclusion and exclusion regarding what to say and what not to say, how it should be said and how not. They argue that the adult in this situation has allowed the child to make and test hypotheses and in this way introduced the children to how scientific knowledge can be discovered.

Here is one of Ingrid Pramling Samuelsson's stories, found online, illustrating the importance of really listening to what children say.

> For a time, the photograph below was standing on my kitchen table. It is a photo of two macaw parrots, and one of these parrots is now living in a huge cage in my kitchen. One of my granddaughters, who was 5 years old, saw the photo, and the following conversation took place:
>
> *Hjördis:* This is a boy and a girl, isn't it? [points at the parrots]
> *Ingrid:* Yes!
> *Hjördis:* And which one do you want to buy?
> *Ingrid:* The boy.
> *Hjördis:* I thought so.

[For a few seconds, I had a conversation in my mind about gender questions and what kind of message I gave to her by choosing the male.]

Ingrid: I took a deep breath and asked, 'Why did you think I would choose the boy?'

Hjördis: Well, because if you have a girl parrot, other birds will come flittering, and you will get baby parrots, and I do not think you want a whole bunch of them!

(Ingrid Pramling Samuelsson, 2004)

Imitation and elaboration

Our twenty-first century child, as an active meaning maker, has been engaged in making intentional actions from before the end of her first year of life. In this way she demonstrates understanding before she is able to vocalise an idea or thought. Shirley Brice Heath (1983) tracked what a small child called Vilgot did in coming to understand what a book is and what it is used for. His initial actions and interactions depended to a large extent on imitation:

- At the age of 14 months he came across a book in his collection of toys, opened it, turned the pages and made sounds that were very like talk. In doing this he demonstrated an awareness of how adults sometimes make speech sounds as they turn pages.
- At 22 months he responded to an adult's suggestion that they should read a book and chose a large novel. The adult sat with him on the floor, turned the pages and made up a story. The child listened, looked at the pages every so often and was quite satisfied with the whole event. Here his actions indicated that he knew that a book carried a story that he could listen to.
- Four months later he picked one of his own books and handed it to his grandmother. She could not read without her glasses so she started telling the story from memory. Vilgot stopped her and instructed her to 'read it properly'. At that point he knew that there is an invariant pattern to the book. So he was aware of the text itself, what it was and what purpose it served, although he did not yet know the word 'text'.
- At 30 months he chose a book for an older child and brought it to an adult who offered to read it to him. He turned the pages back and forth and then declined the offer, saying 'No, there is too much text in this book'. An extraordinary moment indicating that he had understood what the word text meant and made a judgement that too much text meant that the book might be boring for him.
- Just before his third birthday he asked the adult to write all the names of his family members and some other words using alphabet blocks. Whilst the adult was doing this he picked out and pointed to the letters of his own name, saying 'It's in my name' every time the adult used that letter. His awareness now included a recognition of individual letters.

Children focus their intention on what interests them. That is why play – the ability to explore in depth the things that interest the child – is so important. When a child displays an interest in something it is likely that their existing knowledge or understanding about an aspect of the object or situation has been challenged and thus raised some questions in the mind of the child. What do you think Vilgot in the example above might have been interested in? What questions did his interactions around books raise in his mind? Perhaps he asked what the black marks on the page were for. Maybe he wanted to know what they were called. Or perhaps he asked why there were spaces between groups of black marks. *Learning is the way in which children move from what is still unknown by using what is known.* Each example of Vilgot's interaction with books shows him building on what he has learned in order to answer a question he has set himself about what he still does not understand. He shows us that learning requires the ability to transfer a skill or a memory for use in a different situation or context.

Much of Vilgot's learning has come about through imitation, which may be one of the most important ways in which young learners learn before spoken language develops. A child can imitate an action; internalise that in the form of a memory and repeat it in a different context. Hay *et al.* (1991) believed that imitation in young children is more than copying since it requires reflection on the whole meaning of the actions involved. So imitation itself has meaning because it reflects the child's abilities to understanding the intentions of others. But is imitation enough to account for learning? In order to imitate someone or something the child has to both be able to identify and elaborate. Let's go back to Vilgot to try and analyse what he did when he was imitating reading. The first thing he did was make sounds as he turned the pages. He must have been copying and elaborating on what he had seen a reader do with a book. So, as Vilgot imitated the saying-out-aloud-as-turning-the-pages behaviour of an expert reader, he began to act like and possibly identify himself as a reader. He moved on from that to reveal how much more sophisticated was his understanding of what reading involves as he knew enough to reject a book with too much text and possibly no pictures; to differentiate between a story told and a story read; and to know that his name contained individual letters.

We see elaboration most clearly in role play, where children coordinate and sequence what were originally imitations into elaborate continuous performances of a chosen role. In this context elaboration means doing something personal with the intention of transforming it into something innovative. Since learning and development always take place within a context and a cultural setting the fact that these differ accounts for variation. The child, exposed to different situations, objects, interactions and problems must first be able to distinguish one thing from another. In other words, the child must become *conscious of difference*. Stern (1991), who worked with young children and their mothers, noted that all the small variations a mother exhibits when she interacts with her child strengthen the child's development of variation. Children learn what is appropriate where, with whom and so on. Variation is regarded by some as a key variable in learning (Lindahl, 1996). You may remember the work done by Chris Athey on schemas, which are repeated patterns of behaviour. It is likely that children's repetitive exploration of patterns that interest them indicate their awareness of variation and it appears that the questions they ask could include such things as 'Will it remain the same if I . . .?' To help understand this consider Harry's behaviour:

> Harry has an interest in rotation. He draws lots of circles and spirals. He chooses round shapes when making models. He spins round in the playgroup. He holds a long ribbon in one hand and moves it in a circular pattern in the air. Perhaps he asks himself if something round will be round on the ground as well as in the air.

Or perhaps he asks if it will remain round when made with his arm or with a pen held in his hand or with a ribbon held up high above his head. Maybe he asks if a small movement will make a small circle whilst a big movement will make a big one.

(Personal observation notes, 2005)

This is a very straightforward example where Harry's interest in circularity or rotation is very evident in his play. Here is another drawn from Lindahl and Samuelsson (2002: 35) that relates to a much younger child, Wataru, who was 14 months old at the time of the observation and had an interest in spinning, which is close to a schema of rotation:

> Wataru had just started at day care. One day he approached one of the teachers with a circular plastic ring in his hand. The teacher took the ring and spun it on the floor with her fingers. The child imitated the adult's actions, but not successfully. He then put the ring on the table and tried to spin it there. It did spin a little. Later he crawled away leaving the ring on the floor but returned a little later with a ring with a larger diameter. He crawled with the ring in front of him to show the teacher and he held it in the air to get her attention. She did not do anything with the ring at first but offered the child another toy, which he ignored. The teacher made the big ring spin and Wataru took the small ring and succeeded in getting it to spin. At which point he hooted with delight. Still later he found a white tray which was circular and tried to get it to spin and when he was successful the teacher clapped her hands to confirm his success. Later still a little girl picked up the tray and ran off with it. Wataru tried to run after her but could not. The little girl teased him with the tray. A few days later he had a ring in his hand and the teacher had a tray and they were sitting in front of a mirror. He started spinning the ring on the floor with great skill and then moved on to spinning the tray. Later he managed to get a thick wooden ring to spin too.

The learning process started with Wataru imitating the teacher spinning a plastic ring he had given her on her finger. It was his evident passion for what would spin that made him persist in his search for answers to his unvoiced questions. On the basis of trial and error and watching what others did, he was able to compile a mental list of 'spinnable' objects.

Dealing with the problems in the real world

The problems children encounter in their everyday lives range in complexity according to where in the world the child is. We tend to think that the lives of all children in the developed world are safe and secure and whilst this is true for some of these children the real facts are horrifying. In the 2005 review of child poverty in rich countries (UNICEF, 2005) it was stated that there had been a rise in poverty in 17 out of the 24 OECD nations for which data was available. At the top of the league table (meaning where there is the least poverty) were Denmark and Finland, where less than 3 per cent of children were living in poverty. At the bottom were the United States (the richest country in the world!) and Mexico, where child poverty rates were higher than 20 per cent. In 2006 it was consoling to learn that child poverty rates in the UK had fallen.

Today, in 2012, after years of deep recession in much of the developed world, things have changed. At the top of the latest UNICEF report card are Finland and Iceland and amongst the worst are Italy, Greece, the UK and the United States (UNICEF, 2012a). The figures relate to the percentage of children under the age of 17 living in relative poverty, which is defined as a household where disposable income, when adjusted for family size and composition, is less than the national median income.

In *The Guardian* Amelia Gentleman (2012) wrote a disturbing article about child poverty in the UK, based on the findings of UNICEF reported above. It is quoted here since the findings are relevant for all of us involved in the lives of young children:

UNICEF's Report Card 10, *Measuring Child Poverty*, argues that the UK's success in reducing child poverty over the last decade was the result of the previous government's drive to increase household incomes by introducing tax credits and improving public services for children.

Although the UK missed the target set by Tony Blair to cut the number of children in poverty to 1.7 million by 2010, the country still saw a large reduction in child poverty as a result of government intervention, UNICEF said. (In 2009–10, the last year for which figures are available, 2.6 million children in the UK were below this poverty line, according to the definition in the target.)

The report notes that in a downturn children are first to drop off the policy agenda, and says it is evident that 'frontline services for families are everywhere under strain as austerity measures increase the numbers in need while depleting the services available. It is also clear that the worst is yet to come.'

The report states: 'Many families, even those on low incomes, have some form of "cushion" – whether in the form of savings, assets or help from other family members – by which to maintain spending during difficult times. There is therefore almost always a time lag between the onset of an economic crisis and the full extent of its impact.

'Failure to protect children from poverty is one of the most costly mistakes a society can make. The heaviest cost of all is borne by the children themselves. But their nations must also pay a very significant price – in reduced skills and productivity, in lower levels of health and educational achievement, in increased likelihood of unemployment and welfare dependence, in the higher costs of judicial and social protection systems, and in the loss of social cohesion. The economic argument, in anything but the shortest term, is therefore heavily on the side of protecting children from poverty.'

. . . The report includes detailed discussion of the best way to measure child poverty and includes a new child deprivation index, which classifies children as deprived if they lack two or more items from a list of 14 basic requirements (which include three meals a day, fresh fruit and vegetables every day, outdoor leisure equipment such as a bicycle, two pairs of properly fitting shoes, an internet connection and money to participate in school trips and events). The UK fares better on this index (with 5.5% of children deemed to be deprived, and ranked ninth out of 29 economically advanced nations) than it does on the more conventional relative poverty rate, which Unicef defines as the percentage of children in households with income lower than 50% of the national median. On this measure the UK is ranked 22nd out of 35 nations, with 12.1% of children classified as living in poverty.

Children, even very young children, are aware of what is happening to them and to their families, and sometimes become aware of what is happening to other people, far and near. Here are some comments made by children to illustrate this.

It's so unfair! Since my mum lost her job we can't do any of the nice things we used to do. We go to the park, but my bike is much too small for me and when I ride it my knees bash into the handlebars but we can't afford a new one. And we didn't have a summer holiday this year. And my shoes are tight but my mum says they will have to do until Christmas.

(Aliya, aged 6: personal communication, 2012)

And it's like what my mum told me about Ireland. When the English people went there they said 'You have to speak English and you can't speak your own language anymore.'

(Fiona, aged 7: in Smidt, 1988)

You have to go to the supermarket and fill your trolley with tins and things that have come from South Africa. Then, when you get to the pay desk you have to take them out one at a time . . . slowly . . . and you have to look at each one and go 'Oh! I don't want this. This comes from South Africa'. You have to do it really slowly so the girl on the desk gets cross 'cos you're taking so long and then she will go 'We won't sell these things from South Africa anymore and that's because people won't buy them'. And then that supermarket won't have things from South Africa anymore. We really like red apples in my house but we won't buy them if they come from South Africa and my mum says it won't kill me to eat other apples instead.

(Sam, aged 6: in Smidt, 1988)

These children are expressing their thoughts and ideas about what seems just and unjust, fair and unfair personally and for other people. The latter two comments were made many years ago but give evidence that where children are invited to reflect on their own thoughts they are able to use language (written or spoken) to help them communicate, clarify and sharpen up their ideas. This only happens where children are invited to think about issues of some substance. Bruner (1986) said that if the language of education is to allow children to reflect on issues as part of creating culture, the language used cannot be the bland and anonymous language of fact but must express a point of view and invite others to either agree with or adopt a different stance. This, as you can imagine, is a somewhat contentious stance because it allows children to think for themselves. To do this they have to reflect on their own thinking. This is known as metacognition. Katz (1998) believed that what she called high-quality learning experiences in the early years were only possible if those involved with young children were prepared to address the real issues that interest or affect children. An overemphasis on exploring meaningless and bland topics like colour, for example, denies children the opportunities to explore the things that matter to them. These might include death, loss, fear, war, illness, loneliness, being outside of the group, the dark, unhappiness and so on.

In 1989, governments throughout the world promised all children the same rights by adopting the UN Convention on the Rights of the Child (CRC). The rights are based on what a child needs to survive, grow, participate and fulfill their potential. They apply equally to every child, regardless of who they are, or where they are from.

Human rights are founded on respect for the dignity and worth of each individual, regardless of race, gender, language, religion, opinions, wealth or ability and therefore apply to every human being everywhere. The Convention recognises the human rights of children, defined as any person under the age of 18. It is the only international human rights treaty that includes civil, political, economic, social and cultural rights. It sets out in detail what every child needs to have for a safe, happy and fulfilled childhood. It is said to be the most complete statement of children's rights ever produced and is the most widely ratified international human rights treaty in history. It enshrines specific child rights in international law, defining universal principles and standards for the status and treatment of children worldwide.

The Convention spells out a specific role for UNICEF, in its capacity as the UN body responsible for the rights of children. UNICEF is required to promote the effective implementation of the Convention and to encourage international cooperation for the benefit of children.

You may like to know that, to date, all UN member states except for the United States and Somalia have now formally approved the Convention. The UK signed it on 19 April 1990 and ratified it on 16 December 1991. It came into force in the UK on 15 January 1992.

So children do have rights to life, good health care, free primary education and more that could not be questioned by anybody, but one right that requires adults to negotiate with children is sometimes regarded with suspicion. Many claim that children cannot participate fully until they are capable of exercising responsibility and there is a general theory that young children are not able to express their own ideas. But look at a piece of research carried out by Sheridan and Samuelsson with 5-year-old children in Swedish preschools in 2001. They were looking at how well these very young children could use difficult terms such as 'decide'. The research was detailed and we will focus only on some selected issues.

The children were asked a number of questions relating to decision making. The researchers were interested in the responses given by the children and categorised them into groups. When the children were asked what they would like to do at school if they could decide, the majority of them responded by saying 'Play'. This is, in fact, what most children do in Swedish preschools. The children were then asked if they thought that the teachers knew what they, the children, would like to do. To answer this the children had to have a theory of mind which means knowing that other people (in this case the teachers) also had views that might not be the same as theirs. Most children initially said that the teachers did not know what the children liked to do and when challenged and asked how they knew that the teacher did not know their preferences they gave a range of answers from 'she can't see us' to 'she isn't with us' to 'she is too busy' and so on (Sheridan and Samuelsson, 2001).

The children were then asked, 'What do you do when you decide something?' Their answers fell into several categories as follows:

- *To decide what you want to do* was the most common use of the word 'decide'. The children said things like 'Well, we all decide we want to go outside' or 'We just start playing something and all our friends join'. Within the agreed play there were almost always rules and the children said that they either just accepted rules as given or agreed them together.

- *What is allowed or forbidden* was another thing that involved children in decision making. So one child might say to another, 'You are not allowed to play with my doll' or explain 'We must walk in the corridor'. In the first example one child has decided what is forbidden: in the second the decision has been taken more remotely.
- *Aspects of power* are involved, where children decide things like who is to do what and decide what is involved. So, for example, a child decides to play a leading role and then has the right to decide the rules – who can play, what part they play, when the play needs changing and so on.
- *Thinking out* or *inventing* clearly involves deciding what to do and how. Children talk of deciding that players or characters should reveal characteristics, saying things like 'He needs to be strong' or 'The leader should be good at talking'.
- *To do what the majority wants to do* was the last category of the meaning of 'decide'. It was given by only one child and came closest to a crucial aspect of democracy.

The theories of the very young

We have talked about how questions arise in the minds of children as they explore things that interest or excite them. From a very young age children seek to understand, interpret and later explain responses to the questions they have asked. Some people are happy to call the questions children ask and answer 'theories' and Rinaldi defines a theory as a satisfactory, if provisional, answer. The important point is that the answer is satisfactory to the child at the time. Through experience and interactions and more exploration some challenges may arise and then the child has to come up with a different answer. Rinaldi gives a wonderful theory given by a 3-year-old girl, who said 'The sea is born from the mother wave'. Rinaldi analyses this theory like this: 'The child has conceptualised and is developing the idea that everything has an origin. Putting together all the elements in her possession in a creative way, the child formulates a satisfactory explanation, and while she is conceptualising it, she shares it with others' (Rinaldi, 2006: 114).

Here are some other theories:

> Sandra, at the age of 2, was taken to the docks by her parents and saw one of the metal structures that the boats were tied up to. She was intrigued by this unfamiliar object and set about exploring it – touching it, smelling it and walking round it. Then she announced 'I seed it and I felt it and it's not a dog'.
>
> (From a verbal account by Sandra's mother, 1963)

The child's theory was that it was only through investigation, using all possible means, that she found out that something she had first thought was a dog was not. A very complex cognitive task!

> When Hannah was in the reception class one of the adults in the school wrote on the blackboard 'Maths is hard'. When Hannah's mother said 'I wonder why the teacher wrote that maths is hard?' the 5-year-old child replied 'She only speaks a little English so she doesn't know that it should say maths are hard.' Here the child's theory is that only fluent speakers of English will know that maths (because it ends with the letter 's') must be a plural and so the verb should match that!
>
> (From a verbal account by Hannah's mother, 2000)

Hannah's theory involves the process of overgeneralising rules. The word maths has an 's' on the end and that means it must be a plural. Someone who speaks English will know this and will then use 'are' instead of 'is'. So her theory is that the teacher involved must have made that error because she was not a fluent speaker of English. Another incredibly complex series of thoughts.

There are theorists and educators who are uncomfortable with talking about children's thoughts or questions as theories. But it seems evident that what the children are doing is so cognitively challenging and complex that it has to be taken seriously. Those educators who respect and pay attention to these theories can utilise the windows they offer into the cognitive processes children are going through as they come to generate theories and change them. As they pose questions and try to answer them they are exploring what is not yet known through what is already known. And what is already known comes from all their experience and their interactions. So their knowledge, which has been socially and culturally constructed through interaction and exploration, provides them with a set of internal representations that they then use to allow them to explore more deeply. Bruner talked of learning as following a *spiral curriculum* and what he meant by that was that any learner will revisit something over and over again: the representations that follow will change with experience. Early *enactive explorations* will be dominated by senses and movement. Later *iconic explorations* will involve images and pictures. Finally, *symbolic learning* involves symbolic systems like language. So the child moves from exploring a personal interest using movement and all the senses, to making some sort of image or picture, mental or actual. This involves the process of memory, so essential in learning. Questions arise and answers constructed, but with more experience the answers may come to be seen as flawed so new questions are raised. Over time the learner becomes able to use symbolic systems as short cuts or elaborations to explanations.

Summing up

We have tried to pull together some of the themes of this book in looking at how children learn. We have looked at some ideas on how children make sense of symbolic systems and use these to transform their understanding of aspects of the world. We have looked at how children develop their own theories and refine these as their understandings develop. We have looked at how seriously children can talk about important issues in their lives. In general the focus in this chapter has been on children as creative constructors and profound thinkers. Our twenty-first century child adds to her repertoire the essential competencies of questioning, hypothesising, testing, analysing, generating rules, identifying patterns, making conclusions and starting again.

Things to think about

- Can you find examples of children's theories? If so do these surprise you in any way?
- How might you change what you do in your work with children to ensure that you know that they can discuss anything with you?

Chapter 9

The role of neuroscience

This final chapter has been totally re-written for this new edition, to reflect just how much the rapidly developing field of neuroscience is beginning to contribute to our understanding of how young children develop and learn. We look at some of the findings and the underpinning theories and assess how these affect our understanding.

The human brain

We all hold some everyday or common-sense understanding of what the brain is and does. Let us start by looking at what I wrote about the brain in the first edition:

> The brain is an organ that is hungry for oxygen and it is divided up into different sections. The cerebral cortex of the brain is the one that is most associated with thinking and reasoning and it, itself, is divided into two hemispheres that are interconnected. There is an ongoing debate about the different functions governed by each of these hemispheres. The cerebrum itself is divided in two halves and each of these is further divided into four lobes, each associated with particular activities as follows:
>
> - At the rear of the brain is the occipital lobe, which is concerned with sight or vision.
> - Above this is the parietal lobe, which deals with movement, number and orientation.
> - The temporal lobe is associated with hearing and language.
> - The frontal lobe deals with feelings, emotions, planning and decision making as well as with short-term memory and attention.
>
> The brain consists of neurons, which are sometimes described as the building blocks of the brain. These are so numerous that they have been compared to the number of stars in the galaxy. They are supported and serviced and repaired by an even more numerous set of cells called glial cells and these form a type of glue. What neurons do is to form connections or networks and the way in which they appear to do this is by sending tiny electrical signals along the axon (the body of the neuron) to be received by the dendrites (the arms of the neuron). Synapses are the connections through which nerve impulses travel from one neuron to another. The number of synapses relative to the volume of tissue is called synaptic density. There is some feeling that it is the laying down of these neural connections that constitutes learning.
>
> (Smidt, 2006: 125)

That was then. Now, we still perceive of the brain as being the seat of our intellect, reason and feelings. If I asked you to describe or draw the human brain what would probably emerge would be something resembling a dirty cauliflower.

In an astonishing new study, scientists at the National Institutes of Health (NIH) in the United States imaged human and monkey brains and found that the pathways or connections between neurons are almost perfectly grid-like. The emerging images of the brain have been compared to what you would see in a computer ribbon cable. This is the thin, flat, multiconductor cable that is widely used for internal peripheral connections in electronic systems. The NIH researchers note that the brain is made up of an enormous collection of these 'ribbons', all running parallel or perpendicular to one another. They don't run diagonal to one another and there is no evidence of single neurons straying away from these neural pathways. It is said to resemble a three-dimensional map of Manhattan.

In short, as the brain gets wired up in early development, its *connections form along perpendicular pathways*, running horizontally, vertically and transversely. This grid structure appears to guide connectivity in a similar fashion to how lanes for cars on motorways can channel traffic. They can limit the options for growing nerve fibres to change direction during development. They can turn in just four directions: left, right, up or down, and this may enforce a more efficient and orderly way for them to find their proper connections. The researchers suggest that this enables the structure to *adapt through evolution*. As you can imagine, getting detailed images of these pathways in the human brain had long eluded researchers, in part because the human cortex, or the outer mantle, develops many folds, nooks and crannies that obscure the structure of its connections.

It was, in part, the knowledge gained from the study that helped shape design specifications for the most powerful brain scanner of its kind known as the *Connectom diffusion magnetic resonance imaging scanner*, which can visualise the networks of criss-crossing fibres – by which different parts of the brain communicate with each other – in 10-fold higher detail than conventional images.

Did you know that a genome is the complete set of genes in an organism? Researchers call the visual map of the brain now apparent through imaging the neuronal version of your DNA genome.

The group of researchers largely responsible for the new information emerging from the Martinos Centre for Biomedical Imaging and the Harvard Medical School about the structure of the brain is led by Jan Van Wedeen (Van Wedeen *et al.*, 2012). 'Before, we had just driving directions. Now, we have a map showing how all the highways and byways are interconnected,' says Van Wedeen. 'Brain wiring is not like the wiring in your basement, where it just needs to connect the right endpoints. Rather, the grid is the language of the brain and wiring and re-wiring work by modifying it.'

It is clear that the development of sophisticated imaging devices are responsible for much of what we now know about the human brain (Asher, 2012).

Understanding the role of experience in the development of the brain

For us, one of the key factors emerging from recent and current research is the light it sheds on the importance of experience in shaping the developing brain. To fully appreciate the findings it is important to understand what is meant by the term *'plasticity'*. This can be used for two different but related meanings. The first refers to how experience shapes the brain and how changes in brain structure and function accompany learning and memory throughout life. The second refers to the brain's responses to traumatic events such as loss of sight or hearing, the amputation of a limb, the ingestion of toxic or addictive substances or other forms of brain damage.

Let us now begin to examine what is known about what happens whilst the foetus is developing in utero. We know that development before birth is affected by experiences with the outside world primarily through what the mother does or experiences. So what the mother eats and drinks, the stresses and emotional difficulties she encounters, any illnesses she has and what she takes into her body in the form of alcohol or drugs can all affect the developing brain. The implications in terms of poverty, deprivation, poor health, trauma and illnesses like maternal diabetes are important to remember.

Almost all of any individual's estimated 100 billion neurons develop early in the prenatal period. They derive from neural stem cells in a process that involves both *overproduction of cells* and *cell death*. Some researchers believe that about twice as many neurons are produced as will survive. In the outer layer of the brain, which, you remember, is the cerebral cortex which deals with perception, cognition and behaviour, the newly born neurons migrate along cells called support or *radial glial* cells to form six layers, each with a different function. So first the neurons differentiate into the cells that make up the cerebral cortex and then form *axons* (which are projections that send information to other neurons) and *dendrites* (which are projections that receive information from other neurons). These axons and dendrites are then able to connect to one another. The connections are called *synapses* and some of them develop during the latter part of the prenatal period, but most only develop after birth. Another process that starts at the end of the prenatal period is *myelination*, which is where axons are encased in a fatty coating that makes communication among neurons more efficient (Stiles, 2008).

The environment in utero is primarily a protected and safe place, although this is not always the case. It is evident that the more complex post partum environment is going to play a vital role in development of the brain after birth. There are two models for exploring the relationships of experience to plasticity and we will examine both, briefly.

Experience-expectant plasticity

The first is known as *experience-expectant plasticity* and refers to the overproduction of synapses in specific areas of the brain at specific times. In the language of neuroscience these are then organised and pruned by experiences that are expected or common to the human species. In everyday language this means that some connections are either lost or arranged differently according to things that happen to all human infants. We know that almost all human infants experience changes in light and dark, hear sounds and language, have opportunities to touch and feel and move objects and learn to relate to caregivers and others. As a result of evolution neural systems in human beings expect to encounter certain stimuli in the environment in order to fine-tune their performance.

To make this clear think about the *visual system*. If the infant, through some kind of defect in the eye, cannot perceive light and dark, the development of vision will not follow the normal path. This is the result of a physical defect rather than any sort of environmental deprivation. It is important to remember that the kinds of stimuli expected vary widely so, for example, children will learn to speak their first language under a huge range of cultural conditions. Western mothers tend to talk 'motherese' to their infants; in other cultures mother-to-child speech is very limited. Yet babies from both systems learn to speak.

These experiences help build the structures of the brain in a way that supports particularly human physical abilities – for example, *binocular vision, upright locomotion, eye–hand coordination, language* and *emotional relationships*.

It is becoming apparent that human infants need to have such experiences to enable them to use both eyes when looking, walk upright, use their hands in a way that is coordinated with what they see, communicate with others and experience a wide range of emotions through their interactions with others.

You may almost certainly have heard of *critical periods*, which are times when particular experience is thought to be essential for development. Thomas and Johnson (2008) prefer to use the term *sensitive periods*, which are times when specific parts of the brain require and are responsive to particular experience. You will be familiar with the argument that adults find it more difficult to learn a second or additional language than children do. It was thought that this was because there was a critical period for the learning of a second language. Recent evidence shows that this is not necessarily the case. Adults, in fact, learn a second language more quickly than children, although their final level of attainment may not be as high. Learning a language involves many complex and often related skills and there is growing evidence that the sensitive periods differ for the various components of language. Evidence is now suggesting that learning new words or vocabulary as a late learner is easier than learning new sounds or new grammar. In the language of neuroscience this may be because plasticity may show greater or earlier reductions for phonology (or word sounds) and morphosyntax (the rules binding words) than for lexical semantics (the meaning).[1] It is tempting to conclude that human beings can and do continue to learn throughout their lives.

To illustrate this we can cite an example of perceptual narrowing. This is the term used to describe the improvement in the infants' ability to discriminate among auditory (and visual) stimuli that they encounter in their environment, accompanied by a decrease in their previous ability to do so for stimuli they do not encounter. Let's unpick this to make it clear. We know that infants can produce the sounds of all languages in their earliest babbling: the sounds that are not related to their home language or languages drop out after a while in the absence of the child hearing those sounds. Theorists suggest it is the *overproduction and then pruning of synapses* that explain this.

In short, we can define experience-expectant plasticity as follows:

> A particular experience that is expected in the environment contributes to the wiring of the system. Most members of the species have that experience. Examples include the learning of language, the ability to use ocular vision and more. What happens is that, in the absence of a particular experience, some brain connections become redundant.

Experience-expectant plasticity and critical period constraints apply only to species-wide and species-typical traits like vision or language in human infants, or imprinting in geese.

Did you know that newborn geese will follow the first moving object they see after birth? This is known as imprinting.

Experience-dependent plasticity: learning and memory

Twardosz (2012) talks of *experience-dependent plasticity*, which involves the modification of existing synapses or the generation of new ones on the basis of individually specific experience. This is what enables individuals to become members of their own culture. So a child in Hanoi might eat using chop sticks, whilst a child in a village in the Sudan might eat with her fingers. Spanish children learn to read text from left to right whilst children learning Arabic learn to read from right to left. You can see from these examples how learning and memory work. Any child is born into a context of a community, a society, a set of values and customs and beliefs and traditions. The child experiences what exists within her culture. The connections in her brain are affected by what she sees and does. This experience-dependent plasticity occurs throughout life and there are no sensitive or critical periods.

Bruer (1999) tells us that behaviours unique to human individuals, social groups and cultures are acquired through experience-dependent brain plasticity and it is that which accounts for most of our learning. This plasticity stays with us through life. Rutter (2002) says that the distinction between expectant and dependent plasticity is possibly the most important distinction to keep in mind when reading about brain development and early childhood. The implication is that there is not really a window of opportunity, biologically determined, where learning is both efficient and retained.

This brings us to the tricky issue of *enriched environments* and early learning.

Did you know that studies have been made on rats that were then extrapolated to young children? The rats were originally housed in sterile environments, then were given things more like those they might find in the wild (which were given the label of enriched environments). The rats appeared to show some changes in brain development, and some attempts were made to extrapolate from these findings to environments for young children.

It will not surprise you that the way in which this research was interpreted led to people in the developed world making judgements about the environments of children from poorer homes in terms of these being able to provide the children with what was deemed 'worthwhile educational experience'. It is important to remember that we cannot and should not apply findings from research on non-human species to human beings. Moreover, we should always remember that what is defined as a worthwhile educational environment for the rich developed world, equipped as it will be with toys and man-made things, does not necessarily offer more worthwhile or engaging and challenging experiences than an environment set in rural or pastoral or poorer communities. We will return to this issue later in the chapter.

Neuroscience and early development

The last decade of the twentieth century is sometimes called *The Decade of the Brain*, primarily because of the excitement created in and by the media about the potential implications of the findings coming from magnetic resonance imaging and other imaging systems about early childhood education. Think back and you might remember reading articles or attending conferences on themes such as school readiness, how to achieve quality childcare, the importance of the first three years of life, how to be a good parent, Mozart for babies, brain gym for school pupils and much more. There were, and continue to be, some innovations, some advances in understanding and some funding initiatives. In the UK, for example, some funding went into provision for our very young children and there were advances in our understanding of what those working with young children need to know. But alongside the positives were many negative outcomes mainly in the form of persistent oversimplifications and misunderstandings that began to influence recommendations for parents and teachers.

Perhaps the most significant of these was intent focus on *the importance of the first three years of life* as a critical period during which, it was claimed, most brain development took place. Parents and educators were regarded as those with the responsibility to stimulate the child appropriately during this window of opportunity. It was as though the adults in the child's life were in a race against time. What a gift this was for the manufacturers of educational toys and materials!

More recently there has been much work dealing with such misconceptions and what is emerging is a growing body of knowledge, research and literature. If you are interested in this you might seek out the work of Bailey *et al.* (2001) and Jones and Zigler (2002) amongst others.

In summary we can now say the following:

- *The human brain can be modified by experience throughout life*, not just in the early years or through sensitive periods. There is continued and highly significant brain development during childhood and adolescence. The implications of this are to ensure that funding and research are not limited to the first three years of life but extended both to the prenatal stage and to childhood and adolescence. More than that, there is no need to force feed children during these early years, as seems to be happening in many places where parents seem to think that early formal learning will produce more successful adults.
- Bailey (*ibid.*) found that that there was much to learn about the very concept of sensitive periods in early development. In fact, Bruer, in the same book, said that *it is very difficult to even demonstrate the existence of these sensitive periods for some aspects of human development*, most notably music. There is also the fact that there is not just one such sensitive period for the whole brain.
- Very concerning to many was the *emphasis placed on seeing brain development in the early years as being so dependent on the interaction between the young children and the primary caregiver* – usually the mother. We have no doubts that these interactions are extremely significant but there are factors that impact on the lives of millions of people who are unable, for one reason or another, to give their undivided attention to their infants. These might include the devastating and long-term effects of other extremely significant variables related to poverty, poor nutrition, migration, ill health, war, trauma and stress. Little or no attention is paid to these factors.

Did you know that the relatively new science of epigenetics, which is finding that genes can be switched on and off by nutrition, drugs and also by physical and psychological events, may offer new insights into some behavioural and mental health conditions like autism, attention deficit hyperactivity syndrome and more? The research is just being reported and since the findings add to the nature/nurture debates care needs to be taken in just accepting the early findings as they are reported in the media (see, for example, Weinhold, 2012).

Music and brain development

Music has played a significant role in my life and in the lives of my children and grandchildren. Through my interest and involvement in both listening to and making music I have had many opportunities to observe the effects of music making on people as individuals but also on people as members of groups. My observations are backed up by what is emerging both from studies of the brain and from the societal changes brought about by the extraordinary national music making education programmes such as *Il Sistema* in Venezuela.

There, as you may know, a national system for introducing all children to classical music has been in place for more than three decades. In 1975, an amateur Venezuelan musician, José Antonio Abreu, founded what was called *Social Action for Music*, and became its director. The goal of the scheme was to use an orchestra as a model for an ideal society and to involve children from all over the country, ensuring that those from the most impoverished regions were enabled to participate. Children were given musical instruments to play. Initially they were given classical stringed instruments like violins or cellos, but the range of instrument was later broadened. A set of standards and rules were agreed. These included that all the children found time to practice their instrument daily and agreed to join in with local musical events on a regular basis. Importantly the model was supported by different administrations, including the government of Hugo Chavez, who remained a dedicated and committed supporter. This experiment is a wonderful example of using something creative – in this case music – to work towards *social change*. The children who, without the programme, would have had limited educational experiences and options, end up now being part of a group that is celebrated publicly by others in the community and more widely. Music requires a strict discipline. An orchestra cannot play unless each member respects all other members. Hence it is an example of a functioning collaborative approach that would not work without cooperation and negotiation: an excellent model for any society.

In terms of thinking more deeply about what we learn from neuroscience and music, are the studies involving children and adults looking to see if there are cognitive advantages evident in the brain when people engage in learning music? Hyde *et al.* (2009) measured behavioural responses and structural changes in the brain after children had had 15 months of weekly half-hour keyboard lessons. The children were aged 6 when they started learning to play and there was both an experimental group and a control group that participated solely in school music activities. The researchers used a specialised imaging technique to look at the size of the brain and the changes within it. This technique is known as *deformation-based morphometry*. What they found was that the children having regular weekly keyboard lessons had a greater relative size both in the corpus callosum (which controls motor development) and in the region of the brain controlling hearing. They performed better than the control group on melody and rhythm tests and on a four-finger sequencing task. There seemed to be no differences in visual-spatial or verbal measures between the two groups. Twardosz (2012) concludes that the research throws some light on the effectiveness of learning to play an instrument on general cognitive development.

Kraus and Chandrasekaran (2010), in their review of the literature relating to the impact of intense musical training on professional musicians, noted that there was evidence of improvement in speech and emotional processing, which suggests that musical training, which by its very nature requires intensive listening, improves a person's ability to extract information. Their recommendation pleases me: they think that there should be substantial investment in promoting the learning of music in schools and settings: music should hold a prominent place on all early years curricula and those working with young children should be alert to cognitive developments as a result of these programmes.

A personal account of the brain and learning

Pamela Poulson (2011) has talked about her personal experience of watching her middle son, brain-damaged from the age of 6 months, become able not only to talk and walk and run and swim but also to dance and achieve a black belt in karate. As an infant he had a cyst next to his cerebellum and the surgeons initially feared that he might have poor balance and motor control, possibly affecting his walking. The child had to have surgery, but because of the resilience of the brain and its very plasticity new pathways were formed and the child continued to learn. With use and activity the dendrites – or connections – continue to grow. Poulson found that, in dance, students can be helped to develop new neural pathways as they learn new skills, practise existing skills, memorise complicated sequences of steps and reproduce or elaborate these. So activity and action seem to be essential. There is a danger here of falling into the trap of thinking a highly developed specialised enriched environment is essential whereas the truth is that action can take place anywhere, activity is not confined to middle-class pursuits – all experience is valuable.

Myths and claims to think about

It is very possible that those involved in the care and education of young children will still be persuaded by seeing words like 'research has shown' or 'brain studies reveal', followed by sweeping statements about what it is that you, the teacher, or parent or educator, should be doing to ensure that your child or the children you care for or teach will develop and learn. Here is a list of so-called facts (or perhaps myths and claims) downloaded from the internet. Read them and think about how rigorous the science is, how sweeping the claims are, how recognised the researchers seem to be and whether you will go along with the proposals. Some of these have already been mentioned earlier in this chapter. I am inviting you to use the knowledge you have acquired through reading this chapter be become more critical in your reading and appraisal.

Claim 1: the wonders of Brain Gym

The examples come from *The Brain Gym: Teacher's Edition* (Dennison and Dennison, 1989), where the promoters of the Brain Gym explain the programme and its advantages. After each item is a comment from a recognised scientist critiquing the item and that is followed by the words of Paul and Gail Dennison, who are commenting on criticisms made about the scientific validity of the claims. You may find it interesting to consider the language used by the brain gym teachers (BGTE) and by the reviewers. Both use language like 'lateral midline', 'inhibited learning challenge' and more. Your response to this may well be like mine. What on earth do these terms mean? Here is what some scientists have said about the language and how much it can be depended on to be accurate:

In 2008 Sense About Science published a briefing document in which 13 British scientists responded to statements taken from the 'Brain Gym Guide (Teacher's Edition)'. Each of them entirely rejected the statements that were put to them. Brain Gym's scientific content was described as 'pseudo-scientific'. One of the scientists, Professor of Neuroscience Colin Blakemore, said that 'there have been a few peer reviewed scientific studies into the methods of Brain Gym, but none of them found a significant improvement in general academic skills.'

(Sense about Science, n.d.)

In addition, in 2007 Dr Keith Hyatt of Western Washington University wrote a paper in which he carefully analysed the available research into Brain Gym, as well as its theoretical basis. His conclusion was that Brain Gym is not supported by research, and that its theoretical basis does not stand up. Importantly his paper also encouraged teachers to learn how to read and understand research, to avoid teaching material that has no rational or accepted scientific basis (Hyatt, 2007: 117–124).

Try reading some of the claims made by the BGTE below to see what you think.

- BGTE: 'Brain Gym activities . . . enable students to access those parts of the brain previously inaccessible to them.'
- Dr Beth Losiewicz, cognitive scientist: 'There is no evidence whatsoever that any part of the brain goes "unused".'
- The Dennisons: 'Our clinical research shows that the whole-brain performance of students with learning challenges is inhibited. We usually understand this as their inability to process at the lateral midline or to express what they know. The Brain Gym activities are intended to help such students process comfortably at the midline, and that is indeed what the movements appear to do. We see our students as normal individuals with learned, ineffective movement patterns, known as specific language disabilities. We do not claim to change their brains, only to help them learn new movement patterns that will more successfully access corresponding skills and functions.'
- BGTE: 'The student touches above each eye with the fingertips of each hand . . . halfway between the hairline and the eyebrows. The Positive Points bring blood flow from the hypothalamus to the frontal lobes, where rational thought occurs.'
- Professor David Attwell, neuroscientist: 'Rational thought does not occur in the frontal lobes, and there is no evidence that touching these points can alter blood flow within the brain.'
- The Dennisons: 'Recent opinion (such as the work of neuroscientist Dr Elkonen Goldberg, author of *The Executive Brain*) asserts that the frontal lobes are involved in reasoning, high-order functioning, judgment, and rational behavior. And most physiology books support the premise that touch stimulates circulation to the area of the body touched – a principle used in such modalities as acupressure and massage. Hence we theorize that holding the Positive Points improves circulation to the frontal area of the brain. Our students report that, after holding the Positive Points, they are better able to think clearly, make choices, consider consequences, and let go of emotional overlay from past experiences.'

And now we come to my favourite bit:

- BGTE: 'The Brain Buttons . . . are massaged deeply with one hand while holding the navel with the other hand . . . They activate the brain for . . . sending messages from the right brain hemisphere to the left side of the body, and vice versa; receiving increased oxygen; stimulation of the carotid artery for increased blood supply to the brain; an increased flow of electromagnetic energy.'
- Professor David Atwell, neuroscientist: 'There is no evidence that rubbing these areas promotes signalling from the right brain to the left side of the body. The brain would only receive increased oxygen if its blood flow increased, but stimulating receptors in the carotid sinus leads to a fall of cardiac output and potentially a decreased oxygen flow to the brain. Massage of these points does not generate electromagnetic energy in the form of radiated light, heat or radio waves.'

There is much more of this and if you want to read it just search for Brain Gym International online.

Claim 2: the Mozart effect

We all know that Mozart was a musical genius who composed and performed classical music from when he was about 5 years old. In 1993 Rauscher *et al.* made an extraordinary claim that after individuals listened to Mozart for 10 minutes there were improvements in their spatial reasoning skills. The results were difficult to replicate. Many findings showed no effect whatsoever. Some reported findings showing a small increase in spatial reasoning skills, lasting for a short period. The *Journal of the Royal Society of Medicine* followed this up but their article was as elusive as their findings. The article did try and link what they thought happened within the brains of those listening to the music but it seems that they found little brain activity that was regular, predictable, significant or worth commenting on. But the producers of audio CDs were ready to jump on the bandwagon and began to promote classical music CDs for babies to listen to. As you can imagine, parents were more than willing to invest in these in the hope that their babies would instantly become more clever and successful.

Claim 3: BrainU

This is an introductory course in neuroscience designed especially to meet the needs of teachers. It came about because a group of academics believed that many teachers were interested in the findings coming from neuroscience but felt unable to assess them because of their own lack of knowledge about the subject. In the newly developed programme teachers learn neuroscience in the ways in which they are expected to teach their students. The programme, developed and carried out by the University of Minnesota together with experts in pedagogy, is new and has not yet been thoroughly investigated. It seems that one of the positive things to emerge is a growing confidence in the teachers to evaluate claims made by researchers and hence to be more critical in what they were prepared to accept. If nothing else, teachers having been through the programme might have access to some of the specialist language emerging from neuroscience. To my mind there is nothing wrong with teachers learning more about neuroscience and it is too early in the life if this programme to assess it.

My concern is that it might be extended into training parents on the proliferating programmes in the developed world that set out to teach people how to be 'good' parents. You will appreciate that the definition of what makes a good parent in these programmes is totally rooted in Western concepts of children, childhood, learning, development and more. Having read this book I hope you feel able to challenge this view.

Claim 4: the myth of the first three years

We have already touched on this but it is important to revisit it because the arguments are critical. Loosely, it was initially claimed that from birth to the age of 3 is the period of high synaptic density. This is when more neural connections are formed than are pruned. The implication was that this is the critical or sensitive period for brain development – the time when children learn most easily and effectively and during which experiences result in largely irreversible neural changes. This myth grew out of earlier neuroscientific studies, but much has been disputed. For example, we now know that brain development is not uniform. Huttenlocher and Dabholkar (1997) found that peak synaptic densities and elimination vary according to brain area. For example, neural links are formed rapidly in the auditory cortext at around 3 months of age, but this is not so in the frontal cortex where these peak at the age of about 3½ years. So although our very eyes and experience tell us how much children do learn in those early years (to sit, to walk, to speak their own language), what is clear is that learning continues well beyond the age of 3, beyond the age of 7, beyond the age of 11 and so on. We are, as a species, lifelong learners.

Claim 5: the myth of enriched environments

Early neuroscience research, looking at experiments on rats being placed in specially enhanced environments, extrapolated to saying that young children, in these crucial three years, needed access to enriched environments. The positive outcome was that many preschool facilities were able to invest in expensive equipment and this resulted in some improvements in the everyday experiences of already fortunate children. The negative outcome was the insistence that learning could only take place in the presence of 'things'. But lived life tells us this is not so. Do you remember Hung in Ho Chi Minh City? The little boy selling his wares at the airport? And how he wanted to buy his mother a mobile phone, and learned English from the tourists? The realities of his life are as valid as the realities of any person's life and he learns from everything that happens to him. From negative experiences, like being hounded by the police, he has developed life skills to help him be safe. From the opportunities he discovered from observing tourists and what they are interested in, he developed economic knowledge to help him better his life and that of his family. Mark Rosenzweig and his colleagues, scientists interested in the concept of enriched environments, cautioned, 'It is difficult to extrapolate from an experiment with rats under one set of conditions to the behaviour of rats under another set of conditions, and it is much riskier to extrapolate from a rat to a mouse to a monkey to a human' (1972).

Many of the books written about the education and care of young children adopt a tone that is determinedly middle-class, stating all the things children need to encounter in the playgroups, nursery classes, crèches, toddler groups, with their parents or carers, with their childminders and peers. Yet in the wider world the majority of children learn through what happens to them in their everyday lives and since some of them grow up to become poets and architects, doctors and builders, imams and painters, musicians and writers, cooks and entrepreneurs, teachers and taxi drivers, we must assume that they have managed to learn despite the absence of 'things'. Consumerism dominates most aspects of our lives and the notion of the enriched environment, whilst applicable to rats in cages, is not relevant to how children and adults learn.

Things to think about

- What, if anything, have you learned about how to critically review innovations in education and care as they arise?
- Would you be able to explain how your thinking about what we are learning from developments in neuroscience might affect your teaching or interactions with young learners?
- If you were in a position of power would you rather give a laptop computer to each child in the first year of school in a village in a developing country or use the money to pay for an additional teacher in that year group?

Note

1   My thanks to my dear friend Raymonde Sneddon for helping me decode my own words which I could not make sense of when re-reading!

In conclusion

The world seems to have become even more polarised and divided during the writing of this second edition. Again we have had horrific natural disasters, almost certainly attributable to the effects of global warming. We have seen wars and revolutions over much of the Arab world, changes of government accompanied by worldwide recession engulfing swathes of the developed world. Today it is Greek children who are experiencing hunger, witnessing almost daily street battles and facing horrific racism; Syrian children who are dying in a civil war; English children finding there are no after-school places to go to and, when leaving school, no jobs to be had. The funding for Sure Start programmes has been withdrawn. But the picture is not universally bleak. In Reggio Emilia the state-funded preschool provision continues to flourish and in South Africa, India, China and Brazil children are being offered experiences that they could not have dreamed of ten years ago.

In the UK there are beginning to be opportunities for 2-year-olds to benefit from preschool provision. This may well be a boon for working parents and can offer very young children opportunities for forming relationships and communicating with others, learning with and from them. The Sure Start programme for 2-year-olds focuses on the potential of young children, which we have been examining throughout this book. It recognises the importance of a play-based approach where children's interests are taken note of and respected. Children choose what to do. In this way there is not an interest in preparing them for the next stage. They are trusted to initiate learning in a safe and cognitively challenging environment and form relationships with other children and adults. What they say and do is documented and shared with parents, who are vital partners in the enterprise. This project is in its infancy.

To end this book you are invited to think about a different context and a different set of cultures, languages, religions and societies. Doing this will enable you to move away from a Eurocentric view of development and begin to be able to think about other ways of doing things. Do you remember how we talked of an African context where children are believed to play a critical role in their own development, and have a responsibility for their own 'self-education'? Toddlers and youngsters learn in the participatory and regular processes in the home, community, and through all their interactions. There is no divide between work and play and little or no explicit teaching or didactic support. Children are expected to develop and demonstrate competence and learning throughout life through what might be termed *participatory pedagogy*. They learn from and alongside peers and adults in everyday activities. It will be worth your while to think about how this way of thinking about a different style of learning might impact on you.

Bibliography

Aarons, V. (1996) 'Telling history: inventing identity in Jewish American fiction', in A. Singh, J.T. Skerrit, Jr. and R. Hogan (eds), *Memory and Cultural Politics: New Approaches to American Ethnic Literature*, Boston: North Eastern University Press.

Abbott, L. and Nutbrown, C. (eds) (2001) *Experiencing Reggio Emilia: Implications for Pre-School Provision*, Buckingham and Philadelphia: Open University Press.

Allery, G. (2010) 'Observing symbolic play', in S. Smidt (ed.), *Key Issues in Early Years Education: A Guide for Students and Practitioners* (second edition), London and New York: Routledge.

Anning, A. (2002) 'Conversations around young children's drawing: the impact of the beliefs of significant others at home and school', *International Journal of Art and Design Education*, 21 (3): 197–208.

Anning, A. and Edwards, A. (eds) (1999) *Promoting Children's Learning from Birth to Five: Developing the New Early Years Professional*, Buckingham and Philadelphia: Open University Press.

Ansell, N. (2008) 'Childhood and the politics of scale: descaling children's geographies?' *Progress in Human Geography*, 33: 190–209, first published 2 September 2008.

Arbib, M., Conklin, E.J. and Hill, J.C. (1987) *From Schema Theory to Language*, Oxford: Oxford University Press.

Aries, P. (1962) *Centuries of Childhood: A Social History of Family Life*, London: Jonathan Cape.

Asher, J. (Press Officer) (2012) 'Brain wiring a no-brainer?', *NIH News*. Online at: www.nih.gov/news/health/mar2012/nimh-29.htm (accessed 11 January 2013).

Athey, C. (1990) *Extending Thought in Young Children*, London: PCP.

Bai, L. (2005) 'Children at play: a childhood beyond the Confucian shadow', *Childhood*, 12 (1): 9–32.

Bailey, D.B., Bruer, J.T., Symons, F.J. and Lichtman, J.W. (eds) (2001) *Critical Thinking About Critical Periods*, Baltimore: Brooks Publishing Co.

Bakhtin, M. (1981) 'Discourse in the novel', in C. Emerson and M. Holquist (eds), *The Dialogic Imagination: Four Essays by Bakhtin*, Austin, TX: University of Texas Press.

Bakhtin, M. (1986) *Speech Genres and Other Late Essays*, Austin, TX: University of Texas Press.

Barbarin, O.A. and Richter, L. (2001) *Mandela's Children: Growing Up in Post-Apartheid South Africa*, London: Routledge.

Barrs, M. (ed.) (1998) *Part to Whole Phonics*. Portsmouth, NH: Heinemann.

Beetlestone, F. (1998) *Creative Children, Imaginative Teaching*, Buckingham: Open University Press.

Bellamy, C. (1999) *The State of the World's Children 1999*, New York: UNICEF.

Bergen, D. (2002) 'The role of pretend play in children's cognitive development', *Early Childhood Research and Practice*, 4 (1). Online at: http://ecrp.uiuc.edu/v4n1/bergen.html (accessed 13 January 2013).

Bialystock, E. (1992) 'Symbolic representation of letters and numbers', *Cognitive Development*, 7 (3): 301–316.

Bissell, S. (2002) 'Big or small, child labour and the right to education', in N. Kabeer, G. Nambissan and R. Subrahmanian (eds) *Child Labour and the Right to Education in South Asia: Needs versus Rights?* New Delhi: SAGE Publications Pvt Ltd.

Blaise, M. (2005) *Playing it Straight: Uncovering Gender Discourses in the Early Childhood Classroom*, New York and London: Routledge.

Blenkin, G.M. and Kelly, A.V. (eds) (1987) *Early Childhood Education: A Developmental Curriculum*, London: Paul Chapman Publications.

Bolle de Ball, M. (1987) 'Aspiration au travail et experience du chomage: crise, deliance et paradoxes', *Revue Suisse de Sociologie*, 1: 63–83.

Bolloten, B. and Spafford, T. (1998) 'Supporting refugee children in East London primary schools', in J. Rutter and C. Jones (eds), *Refugee Education: Mapping the Field*, Stoke on Trent: Trentham Books.

Bond, T. (2004) *A Study on Street Children in Ho Chi Minh City, conducted by Terre Des Hommes Foundation*, Lausanne: National Political Publisher.

Bornstein, M.H., Haynes, O.M., Pascual, L., Painter, K.M. and Galperín, C. (1999) 'Play in two societies: pervasiveness of process, specificity of structure', *Child Development*, 70 (2): 317–331.

Bourdieu, P. (1977) *Outline of a Theory in Practice*, Cambridge: Cambridge University Press.

Bourgois, P. (1998) 'Just another night at the shooting gallery', *Theory, Culture and Society*, 15: 37–66.

Bowlby, J. (1953) *Child Care and the Growth of Love*, Harmondsworth: Penguin.

Bråten, S. (2009) *The Intersubjective Mirror in Infant Learning and Evolution of Speech*, Philadelphia: John Benjamins Publishing.

Bretherton, I. (ed.) (1984) *Symbolic Play*, London: Academic Press.

Brierley, J. (1987) *Give Me a Child Until He is Seven: Brain Studies and Early Childhood Education*, London: Routledge/Falmer.

Brittain, V. and Minty, A.S. (1988) *Children of Resistance: On Children, Repression and the Law in Apartheid South Africa*, Kliptown Books Ltd in collaboration with Canon Collins: London.

Bronfenbrenner, E. (1979) *The Ecology of Human Development: Experiments by Nature and Design*, Cambridge, MA: Harvard University Press.

Brooker, L. (2002) *Starting School: Young Children Learning Cultures*, Buckingham and Philadelphia: Open University Press.

Brooker, L. and Woodhead, M. (eds) (2008) *Developing Positive Identities. Early Childhood in Focus 3: Diversity and Young Children*, Milton Keynes: Open University Press.

Bruce, T. (1991) *Time to Play in Early Childhood Education*, Sevenoaks: Hodder and Stoughton.

Bruer, J. (1997) 'Education and the brain: a bridge too far', *Educational Researcher*, 26 (8): 4–16.

Bruer, J. (1998) 'Brain science, brain fiction', *Educational Leadership*, 56 (3): 14.

Bruer, J. (1999) *The Myth of the First Three Years*, New York: Free Press.

Bruer, J.T. (2001) 'A critical and sensitive period primer', in D.B. Bailey, J.T. Bruer, F.J. Symons and J.W. Lichtman (eds) *Critical Thinking about Critical Periods*, Baltimore: Brooks Publishing Co.

Bruner, J. (1996) *The Culture of Education*, Cambridge, MA: Harvard University Press.

Bruner, J.S. (1978) 'On prelinguistic prerequisites of speech', in R.N. Campbell and P.T. Smith (eds), *Recent Advances in the Psychology of Language: Language Development and Mother-Child Interaction*, New York: Plenum.

Bruner, J.S. (1982) 'Formats of language acquisition', *American Journal of Semiotics*, 1 (3): 1–16.

Bruner, J.S. (1983) *Child's Talk: Learning to Use Language*, Oxford: Oxford University Press.

Bruner, J.S. (1986) *Actual Minds, Possible Worlds*, Cambridge, MA: Harvard University Press.

Butterworth, G. and Harris, M. (1994) *Principles of Developmental Psychology*, Hove: Lawrence Erlbaum Associates Ltd.

Cannella, G.S. and Viruru, R. (2004) *Childhood and Postcolonization*, New York: Routledge Falmer.

Carraher, T.N., Carraher, D.W. and Schliemann, A.D. (1985) 'Mathematics in the streets and in school', *British Journal of Development Psychology*, 3 (1): 21–29.

Chomsky, N. (1965) *Aspects of the Theory of Syntax*, Cambridge, MA: MIT Press.

Chomsky, N. (1972) *Language and Mind*, New York: Harcourt Brace Jovanovich.

Chomsky, N. (1975) *Reflections on Language*, New York: Random House.

Christensen, P. (1999) 'Towards an anthropology of childhood sickness: an ethnographic study of Danish school children', Ph.D. thesis, University of Hull.

Chukovsky, K. (1925/1963) *From Two to Five*, Berkeley and Los Angeles: University of California Press.

Clay, M. (1973) *Reading: The Patterning of Complex Behaviour*, Auckland: Heinemann.

Cohen, R.N. (2001) 'Foreword', in A. Njenga and M. Kabiru, *The Web of Cultural Transition: A Tracer Study of Children in Embu District of Kenya*, The Hague: Bernard van Leer Foundation.

Cole, M. (1996) *Culture in Mind*, Cambridge, MA: Harvard University Press.

Cox, S. (2005) 'Intention and meaning in young children's drawing', *International Journal of Art and Design Education*, 24 (2): 115–125.

Craig, G. (2003) 'Children's participation through community development: assessing the lessons from international experience', in C. Hallett and A. Prout (eds), *Hearing the Voices of Children: Social Policy for a New Century*, London and New York: RoutledgeFalmer.

Cross, G. (2004) 'Wondrous innocence: print advertising and the origins of permissive child rearing in the US', *Journal of Consumer Culture*, 4 (2): 183–201.

D'Arcy, C. (2002) 'Children teach languages at Birmingham University', *Community Languages Bulletin*, Autumn, London: Centre for Information on Language Teaching.

Dahlberg, G., Moss, P. and Pence, A. (1999) *Beyond Quality in Early Childhood Education and Care*, London and New York: RoutledgeFalmer.

Darwin, C. (1872) *The Expression of the Emotions in Man and Animals*, London: Murray.

Datta, M. (ed.) (2000) *Bilinguality and Literacy: Principles and Practice*, London and New York: Continuum.

Davidson, B. (1951) 'The arts in Italy', *New Statesman*, 14 April.

Davies, B. (1997) 'Constructing and deconstructing masculinities through critical literacy', *Gender in Education*, 9 (1): 9–30.

Dennison, G. and Dennison, P. (1989) *The Brain Gym: Teacher's Edition*, Ventura, CA: Edu Kinesthetics.

Derrida, J. (1972) *Speech and Phenomena and Other Essays on Husserl's Theory of Signs* (translated by Allison), Evanston, IL: Northwest University Press.

Donaldson, M. (1978) *Children's Minds*, London: Fontana.

Dunn, J. (1988) *The Beginnings of Social Understanding*, Oxford: Blackwell.

Dunn, J. and Hughes, C. (2001) '"I got some swords and you're dead": violent fantasy, antisocial behaviour, friendship and moral sensibility in young children', *Child Development*, 72 (2): 491–505.

Dyson, A.H. (1993) *The Social Worlds of Children Learning to Write in an Urban Primary School*, New York: Teacher's College Press.

Dyson, A.H. (1997) *Writing Superheroes: Contemporary Childhood, Popular Culture, and Classroom Literacy*, New York and London: Teachers College Press.

Ebbeck, F.N. (1972) 'Learning from play in other cultures', *Childhood Education*, 48 (2): 69–72.

Ebbeck, M. (1998) 'Gender in early childhood revisited', *Australian Journal of Early Childhood*, 23 (1): 29–32.

Egan, K. (1988) *Primary Understanding: Education in Early Childhood*, New York: Routledge.

Ellis, J. (1978) *West African Families in Great Britain*, London: Routledge.

Ennew, J. (2000) 'Why the Convention is not about street children', in D. Fottrell (ed.), *Revisiting Children's Rights: 10 Years of the UN Convention on the Rights of the Child*, The Hague: Kluwer Law International.

Ennew, J. and Swart-Kruger, J. (2003) 'Introduction: homes, places and spaces in the construction of street children and street youth', *Children, Youth and Environments*, 13 (1), Spring. Online at: www.colorado.edu/journals/cye/13_1/Vol13_1Articles/CYE_CurrentIssue_ArticleIntro_ Kruger_Ennew.htm (accessed 11 January 2013).

Erickson, F. and Schultz, J. (1982) *The Counsellor as Gatekeeper: Social Interaction in Interviews*, New York: Academic Press.

Faulkner, F. (2001) 'Kindergarten killers: morality, murder and the child soldier problem', *Third World Quarterly*, 22 (4): 491–504.

Ferreiro, E. and Teberosky, A. (1979, English edition 1982) *Literacy Before Schooling*, Exeter, New Hampshire and London: Heinemann Educational Books.

Figueiredo, M. (1998) 'Tricks', in S. Smidt (ed.) *The Early Years: A Reader*, London: Routledge.

Flavell, J.H. (1992) 'Cognitive development: past, present and future', *Developmental Psychology*, 28 (6): 998–1005.

Foucault, M. (1979) *The History of Sexuality, Vol. 1: An Introduction*, London: Allen Lane and Penguin.

Fox, C. (1993) *At the Very Edge of the Forest: The Influence of Literature on Storytelling by Children*, London and New York: Cassell.

Francis, B. (1998) *Power Plays: Primary School Children's Constructions of Gender, Power and Adult Work*, Stoke on Trent: Trentham Books.

Freire, P. (n.d.) 'Quotes'. Online at: www.goodreads.com/author/quotes/41108.Paulo_Freire (accessed 11 January 2013).

Freud, A. (1966) *Normality and Psychopathology in Childhood*, Madison, CT: International Universities Press.

Gardner, H. (1973) *The Arts and Human Development*, New York: Wiley.

Geertz, C. (1983) *Local Knowledge*, New York: Basic Books.

Gelman, R. (1990) 'Structural constraints on cognitive development', *Cognitive Science*, 14 (39).

Gentleman, A. (2012) 'Child poverty in UK set to increase as result of austerity drive, says UNICEF', *Guardian*, 29 May. Online at: http://www.guardian.co.uk/society/2012/may/29/child- poverty-increase-unicef-austerity (accessed 11 January 2013).

Glasser, I. (1994) *Homelessness in a Global Perspective*, New York: Maxwell.

Gauser, B. (1997) 'Street children: deconstructing a construct', in A. James and A. Prout (eds), *Constructing and Reconstructing Childhood: Contemporary Issues in the Sociological Study of Childhood* (2nd edition, revised), Basingstoke and London: Falmer Press.

Goldschmied, E. and Jackson, S. (1994) *People Under Three*, London and New York: Routledge.

Goldstein, D. (1998) 'Nothing bad intended: child discipline, punishment, and survival in a shantytown in Rio de Janeiro', in N. Scheper-Hughes and C. Sargeant (eds), *Small Wars: The Cultural Politics of Childhood*, Berkeley: University of California – Berkeley Press.

Göncü, A. (1998) 'Development of intersubjectivity in social pretend play', in M. Woodhead, D. Faulkner and K. Littleton (eds), *Cultural Worlds of Early Childhood*, London and New York: Routledge and Open University.

Göncü, A. and Mosier, C. (1991) 'Cultural variation in the play of toddlers', paper presented at the biennial meeting of the Society for Research in Child Development, Seattle, WA.

Goswami, U. (2001) 'Cognitive development: No stages please – we're British', *British Journal of Psychology*, 92: 257–277.

Goswami, U. and Brown, A. (1989) 'Melting chocolate and melting snowmen: analogical reasoning and causal relations', *Cognition*, 35: 69–95.

Gottlieb, A. (2004) *The After-life is Where We Come From: The Culture of Infancy in West Africa*, Chicago: Chicago University Press.

Greenough, W.T., Withers, G.S. and Anderson, B.J. (1992) 'Experience-dependent synaptogenesis as a plausible memory mechanism', in I. Gormezano and E.A. Wasserman (eds), *Learning and Memory: the Behavioural and Biological Substrates*, Hillsdale, NJ: Lawrence Erlbaum.

Gregory, E., Long, S. and Volk, D. (eds) (2004) *Many Pathways to Literacy: Young Children Learning With Siblings, Grandparents, Peers and Communities*, London and New York: RoutledgeFalmer.

Gupta, P.K. (2005) 'India', in H. Penn, *Unequal Childhoods: Young Children's Lives in Poor Countries*, London and New York: Routledge.

Hall, S. (1992) 'What is this "black" in popular culture?', in G. Dent (ed.), *Black Popular Culture*, Seattle: Bay Press.

Hallett, C. and Prout, A. (eds), (2003) *Hearing the Voices of Children: Social Policy for a New Century*, London and New York: RoutledgeFalmer.

Halliday, M.A.K. (1978) *Language as Social Semiotic*, London: Edward Arnold.

Halliday, M.A.K. (1993) *Explorations in the Functions of Language*, London: Edward Arnold.

Hardy, B. (1968) 'Towards a poetic of fiction: an approach through narrative', in B. Hardy (ed.), *Novel: A Forum on Fiction*, Providence, RI: Brown University.

Hargreaves, D.J. (1986) *The Developmental Psychology of Music*, Cambridge: Cambridge University Press.

Harris, P.L. and Kavanaugh, R.D. (1993) 'Young children's understanding of pretence', *Monograph of the Society for Research in Child Development*, 58 (1), Serial No. 231.

Harste, J., Burke, C. and Woodward, V. (1984) *Language Stories and Literacy Lessons*, Portsmouth, NH: Heinemann.

Hay, D., Stimson, C. and Castle, J. (1991) 'A meeting of minds in infancy: imitation and desire', in D. Frye and C. Moore (eds), *Children's Theories of Mind*, Hillsdale, NJ: Erlbaum.

Health Exchange News (2009) 'Early childhood development: a local priority in Brazil'. Online at: http://healthexchangenews.com/2009/06/18/early-childhood-development-a-local-priority-in-brazil (accessed 8 January 2013).

Heath, S.B. (1983) *Ways with Words: Language, Life and Work in Communities and Classrooms*, Cambridge, MA: Cambridge University Press.

Hebb, D.O. (1958) *A Textbook of Psychology*, Philadelphia and London: W.B. Saunders.

Hendrick, H. (1997) 'Constructions and reconstructions of British childhood: an interpretative survey, 1800 to the present', in A. James and A. Prout (eds), *Constructing and Reconstructing Childhood: Contemporary Issues in the Sociological Study of Childhood* (2nd edition, revised), Basingstoke and London: Falmer Press.

Heywood, C. (2001) *A History of Childhood*, Cambridge: Polity Press.

Higonnet, A. (1998) *Pictures of Innocence: the History and Crisis of Ideal Childhood*, London: Thames & Hudson.

Hochschild, A. (2001) 'Global care chains and emotional surplus value', in W. Hutton and A. Giddens (eds), *On the Edge*, London: Vintage.

Holland, P. (2003) *We Don't Play With Guns Here: War, Weapon and Superhero Play in The Early Years*, Maidenhead and Philadelphia: Open University Press.

Hubel, D.H. and Weisel, T.N. (1977) 'Functional architecture of the Macaque monkey visual cortex', *Proceedings of the Royal Society of London*, B 198: 1–59.

Hughes, F.P. (1995) *Children, Play and Development* (3rd edition), Needham Heights, MA: Allyn and Bacon.

Hunt, J. McVicker (1961) *Intelligence and Experience*, New York: The Ronald Press.

Hutt, S.J., Tyler, S., Hutt, C. and Christopherson, H. (1989) *Play, Exploration and Learning: A Natural History of Pre-School*, London and New York: Routledge.

Huttenlocher, P.R. and Dabholkar, A.S. (1997) 'Regional differences in synaptogenesis in human cerebral cortex', *The Journal of Comparative Neurology*, 387: 167–178.

Hyatt, K.J. (2007) 'Brain gym: building stronger brains or wishful thinking?', *Remedial and Special Education*, 28 (2): 117–124.

Hyde, K.L, Lerch, J. Norton, A, Forgeard, M., Winner, E., Evans, A.C. and Schlaug, G. (2009) 'Musical training shapes brain structural development', *Journal of Neuroscience*, 29, 3019–3025.

Ilari, B.S. (2002) 'Music perception and cognition in the first year of life', *Early Child Development and Care*, 172 (3): 311–322.

Invernizzi, A. (2003) 'Street-working children and adolescents in Lima: work as an agent of socialization', *Childhood*, 10 (3): 319–341.

Invernizzi, A. and Williams, J. (eds) (2008) *Children and Citizenship*, London: Sage.

Jalava, A. (1988) 'Nobody could see that I was a Finn', in T. Skutnabb-Kangas and J. Cummins (eds), *Minority Education: From Shame to Struggle*, Clevedon: Multilingual Matters.

Jamieson, L. and Dikwankwetla, W.M. (2010) 'Children in action: children's participation in the law reform process in South Africa', in B. Percy-Smith and N. Thomas (eds), *A Handbook of Children and Young People's Participation: Perspectives from Theory and Practice*, London and New York: Routledge.

Johnson, M.H. (1990) 'Cortical maturation and the development of visual attention in early infancy', *Journal of Cognitive Neuroscience*, 2: 81–95.

Jones, S.M. and Zigler, E. (2002)' The Mozart effect: not learning from history', *Applied Developmental Psychology*, 23: 355–372.

Kagan, J. (1998) *Three Seductive Ideas*, Cambridge, MA: Harvard University Press.

Karmiloff-Smith, A. (1992) *Beyond Modularity: A Developmental Perspective on Cognitive Science*, Cambridge, MA and London: MIT Press.

Karmiloff-Smith, A. (1994) *Baby, It's You*, London: Random House.

Katz, L.G. (1998) 'Introduction: what is basic for young children', in S. Smidt (ed.), *The Early Years: A Reader*, London: Routledge.

Kearney, C. (2003) *The Monkey's Mask: Identity, Memory, Narrative and Voice*, Stoke on Trent: Trentham Books.

Kenner, C. (2000) 'Symbols make text: a social semiotic analysis of writing in a multilingual nursery', *Written Language and Literacy*, 3 (2): 235–266.

Kenner, C. (2004a) 'Community school pupils reinterpret their knowledge of Chinese and Arabic for primary school peers', in E. Gregory, S. Long and D. Volk (eds), *Many Pathways to Literacy: Young Children Learning With Siblings, Grandparents, Peers and Communities*, London and New York: RoutledgeFalmer.

Kenner, C. (2004b) *Becoming Biliterate: Young Children Learning Different Writing Systems*, Stoke on Trent: Trentham Books.

Kenner, C. and Kress, G. (2003) 'The multisemiotic resources of biliterate children', *Journal of Early Childhood Literacy*, 3 (2): 179–202.

Kenner, C., Kress, G., Al-Khatib, H., Kam, R. and Tsai, K.-C. (2004) 'Finding the keys to biliteracy: how young children interpret different writing systems', *Language and Education*, 18 (2): 124–144.

Kramsch, C. (ed.) (2002) *Language Acquisition and Language Socialization: Ecological Perspectives*, London and New York: Continuum.

Kränzl-Nagl, R. and Zartler, U. (2010) 'Children's participation in school and community: European perspectives', in B. Percy-Smith and N. Thomas (eds) *A Handbook of Children and Young People's Participation: Perspectives from Theory and Practice*, London and New York: Routledge.

Kraus, N. and Chandrasekaran, B. (2010) 'Music training for the development of auditory skills', *Nature Reviews Neuroscience*, 11: 599–605.

Kress, G. (1997) *Before Writing: Rethinking the Paths to Literacy*, London: Routledge.

Kress, G. (2000) *Early Spelling: Between Convention and Creativity*, London: Routledge.

Lamb, M. (1999) *Parenting and Child Development in 'Non-Traditional' Families*, New Jersey: Lawrence Erlbaum.

Lansdown, G. (2005) *The Evolving Capacities of the Child*, New York: UNICEF Innocenti Research Centre.

Lash, S. and Urry, J. (1994) *Economies of Sign and Space*, London: Sage.

Lave, J. and Wenger, E. (1991) *Situated Learning: Legitimate Peripheral Participation*, Cambridge: Cambridge University Press.

Levi, P. (1979/1991) *The Truce*, London: Abacus.

Levi, P. (1989) *The Drowned and the Saved*, London: Michael Joseph.

LeVine, R. (2003) *Childhood Socialization: Comparative Studies of Parenting, Learning and Educational Change*, Hong Kong: Comparative Education Research Centre.

LeVine, R.A., LeVine, S., Liedermann, P.H., Brazelton, T.B., Dixon, S., Richman, A. and Keffer, C.H. (1994) *Child Care and Culture: Lessons from Africa*, Cambridge: Cambridge University Press.

Lindahl, M. (1996) *Experience and Learning, Gothenburg* (in Swedish). Cited in M. Lindahl and I.P. Samuelsson, 'Imitation and variation: reflections on toddlers' strategies for learning', *Scandinavian Journal of Education Research*, 46 (1): 25–45.

Lindahl, M. and Samuelsson, I.P. (2002) 'Imitation and variation: reflections on toddlers' strategies for learning', *Scandinavian Journal of Education Research*, 46 (1): 25–45.

Lloyd, B. and Duveen, G. (1990) 'A semiotic analysis of the development of social representations of gender', in B. Lloyd and G. Duveen (eds), *Social Representations and the Development of Knowledge*, Cambridge: Cambridge University Press.

Lofdahl, A. (2005) 'The funeral: a study of children's shared meaning-making and its developmental significance', *Early Years*, 25 (1), March: 5–16.

Lorenz, K. (1981) *The Foundations of Ethnology*, New York: Springer-Verlag.

Luo, Y., Baillargeon, R., Brueckner, L. and Munakata, Y. (2003) 'Reasoning about a hidden object after a delay: evidence for robust representations in 5-month-old infants', *Cognition*, 878 (3): 23–32.

Mahbub ul Haq (1999) *Human Development in South Asia*, Oxford: Oxford University Press.

Marsh, J. and Millard, E. (2000) *Literacy and Popular Culture: Using Children's Culture in the Classroom*, London: PCO.

Matthews, J. (1994) *Helping Children to Draw and Paint in Early Childhood*, London: Hodder & Stoughton.

Matthews, J. (1997) 'The 4 dimensional language of infancy: the interpersonal basis of art practice', in *Journal of Art and Design Education*, 16 (3): 285–293.

Mayall, B. (2000) *Negotiating Childhoods*, ESRC Children 5–16 Research Briefing, London.

Mayall, B. (2002) *Towards a Sociology for Childhood: Thinking from Children's Lives*, Buckingham: OUP.

Mayall, B. (2007) 'Children's lives outside school', *Primary Review Research Survey 8/1*, Cambridge: University of Cambridge Faculty of Education.

Mayall, B., Bendelow, G., Storey, P. and Veltman, M. (1996) *Children's Health in Primary Schools*, London: Falmer Press.

Mayall, B. (1999) 'Children in action at home and in school', in M. Woodhead, D. Faulkner and K. Littleton (eds), *Making Sense of Social Development*, London: Routledge.

McIvor, C. (1995) 'Children and disability: rights and participation', in *Save the Children, In Our Own Words: Disability and Integration in Morocco*, London: Save the Children.

Meadows, S. (1993) *The Child as Thinker: The Development and Acquisition of Cognition in Childhood*, London and New York: Routledge.

Meltzoff, A.N. and Gopnick, A. (1993) 'The role of imitation in understanding persons and developing theories of mind', in S. Baron-Cohen, H. Tager-Flusberg and D. Cohen (eds), *Understanding Other Minds: Perspectives From Autism*, New York: Oxford University Press.

Mitra, S. (2012) *Beyond the Hole in the Wall: Discover the Power of Self-Organized Learning*, Kindle Single, TED Books. Online at: www.ted.com/talks/sugata_mitra_the_child_driven_education.html (accessed 11 January 2013).

Moog, H. (1968/English translation 1976) *The Musical Experience of the Pre-school Child*, London: Schott Music.

Moyles, J. (1988) *Just Playing? The Role and Status in Play in Early Childhood Education*, Milton Keynes: Open University Press.

Moyles, J. (1998) 'To play or not to play? That is the question!', in S. Smidt (ed.), *The Early Years: A Reader*, London: Routledge.

Nelson, C.A. and Bloom, F.E. (1997) 'Child development and neuroscience', *Child Development*, 68 (5): 970–987.

Nelson, K. (2000) 'Narrative, time and the emergence of the encultured self', *Culture and Psychology*, 6 (2): 183–196.

Nsamenang, A.B. (2004) *Cultures of Human Development and Education: Challenge to growing up African*, New York, NY: Nova.

Nsamenang, A.B. and Lamb, M.E. (1994) 'Socialization of Nso children in the Bamenda Grassfields of Northwest Cameroon', in D. Faulkner, K. Littleton and M. Woodhead (eds), *Cultural Worlds of Early Childhood*, London and New York: Routledge and Open University.

OECD (2011) *Education at a Glance 2011: OECD Indicators*, Paris: OECD. Online at: www.oecd.org/education/preschoolandschool/educationataglance2011oecdindicators.htm (accessed 15 January 2013).

O'Kane, C. (2002) 'Marginalized children as social actors for social justice in South Asia', *British Journal of Social Work*, 32: 697–710.

O'Kane, C. (2003) 'Street and working children's participation in programming for their rights: conflicts arising from diverse perspectives and directions for convergence', *Children, Youth and Environments*, 13 (1) Spring.

Oates, J. (ed.) (1994) *The Foundations of Child Development*, Milton Keynes and Oxford: Open University with Blackwell Publishing.

Observer (2012) 'We must not abandon the battle against child poverty', 10 June. Online at: www.guardian.co.uk/commentisfree/2012/jun/10/observer-leader-eradicating-child-poverty (accessed 8 January 2013).

Oxley, H., Dang, T.T. and Antolín, P. (2001) 'Poverty dynamics in 6 OECD countries', *OECD Studies*, 30 (8).

Pahl, K. (1999) *Transformation: Meaning Making In Nursery Education*, Stoke on Trent: Trentham Books.

Painter, C. (1999) *Learning Through Language in Early Childhood*, London and New York: Cassell.

Paley, V.G. (1984) *Boys and Girls: Superheroes in the Doll Corner*, Chicago, IL: University of Chicago Press.

Paley, V.G. (1988) *Bad Guys Don't Have Birthdays: Fantasy Play at Four*, Chicago and London: University of Chicago Press.

Penn, H. (2001) 'Research in the majority world', in T. David (ed.), *Promoting Evidence Based Practice in Early Childhood Education: Research and its Implications*, London: JAI.

Penn, H. (2004) *Understanding Early Childhood: Issues and Controversies*, London and Oxford: Oxford University Press.

Penn, H. (2005) *Unequal Childhoods: Young Children's Lives in Poor Countries*, London and New York: Routledge.

Percy-Smith, B. and Thomas, N. (eds) (2010) *A Handbook of Children and Young People's Participation: Perspectives from Theory and Practice*, London and New York: Routledge.

Piaget, J. (1962) *Play, Dreams and Imitation in Childhood*, London: Routledge and Kegan Paul.

Piaget, J. (1970) *Structuralism*, New York: Basic Books.

Pinker, S. (2002) *The Blank Slate: The Modern Denial Of Human Nature*, London: Penguin Press.

Pinker, S. (1994) *The Language Instinct*, London: Penguin.

Poulson, P. (2011) 'The brain and learning', *The Journal of Dance Education*, 2 (3): 81–83.

Pramling, N. and Samuelsson, I.G. (2001) '"It is floating 'cause there is a hole": a young child's experience of natural science', *Early Years*, 21 (2): 139–149.

Pramling Samuelsson, I.G. (2004) 'How do children tell us about their childhoods?' *Early Childhood Research and Practice*, 6 (1). Online at: http://ecrp.uiuc.edu/v6n1/pramling.html (accessed 11 January 2013).

Prout, A. and James, A. (1990/1997) 'A new paradigm for the sociology of childhood, provenance, promise and problems', in A. James and A. Prout (eds), *Constructing and Reconstructing Childhood: Contemporary Issues in the Sociological Study of Childhood* (2nd edition, revised), Basingstoke and London: Falmer Press.

Prout, J. (2005) *The Future of Childhood*, Abingdon and New York: RoutledgeFalmer.

Raffaelli, M. (1999) 'Homeless and working street youth in Latin America: a developmental review', *Inter American Journal of Psychology*, 33: 7–28.

Rahnema, M. and Bawtree, V. (eds) (1997) *The Post-Development Reader*, London and New York: Zed Books.

Raman, V. (2000) *Childhood – Western and Indian: An Exploratory Essay*, New Delhi: Centre for Women's Development Studies.

Rauscher, F., Shaw, G.L. and Ky, K.N. (1993) 'Music and spatial task performance', *Nature*, 365.611.

Reddy, N. (2000) 'Children as partners in change: children, citizenship and governance', unpublished keynote address at the Bapscan Congress, York, September 2002.

Richards, P. (1996) *Fighting in the Rain Forest: War, Youth and Resources in Sierra Leone*, Oxford: International Association of African Affairs.

Richter, L. and Griesel, R. (1994) 'Malnutrition, low birth weight and related influences on psychological development', in A. Dawes and D. Donald (eds), *Childhood and Adversity: Psychological Perspectives From South African Research*, Cape Town: David Philip.

Rinaldi, C. (2006) *In Dialogue with Reggio Emilia: Listening, researching and learning*, London and New York: Routledge.

Rogoff, B. (1990) *Apprenticeship in Thinking: Cognitive Development in Social Context*, Oxford: Oxford University Press.

Rogoff, B. (2003) *The Cultural Nature of Development*, Oxford: Oxford University Press.

Rogoff, B., Mistry, J., Göncü, A. and Mosier, C. (1993) 'Guided participation in cultural activities by toddlers and caregivers', *Monogram Social Research, Child Development*, 58 (8), Serial no. 236.

Romero, M.E. (2004) 'Cultural literacy in the world of Pueblo children', in E. Gregory, S. Long and D. Volk (eds), *Many Pathways to Literacy: Young Children Learning With Siblings, Grandparents, Peers and Communities*, London and New York: RoutledgeFalmer.

Roopnarine, J.L., Johnson, J.E. and Hooper, F.H. (eds) (1994) *Children's Play in Diverse Cultures*, Albany, NY: State University of New York Press.

Rose, S. (ed.) (1998) *From Brains to Consciousness? Essays on the New Science of the Mind*, London: Penguin.

Rosemberg, F. (2005) 'Ruthless rhetoric: child and youth prostitution in Brazil in childhood', *Childhood*, 6 (1): 113–131.

Rosen, H. (1984) *Stories and Meanings*, Kettering: National Association for the Teaching of English Papers in Education.

Rosenzweig, M.R., Bennett, E.L and Diamond, M.C. (1972) 'Brain changes in response to experience', *Scientific American*, 226: 22–29.

Roskos, K.A. and Christie, J.F. (eds) (2000) *Play and Literacy in Early Childhood: Research from Multiple Perspectives*, Mahwah, NJ: Lawrence Erlbaum Associates Ltd.

Rousseau, J.J. (1762/2000) *Emile*, London: Penguin.

Russ, S.W. and Kaugars, A.S. (1999) 'Emotion in children's play and creative problem solving', *Creativity Research Journal*, 13 (2): 211–219.

Rutter, J. and Jones, C. (eds) (1998) *Refugee Education: Mapping the Field*, Stoke on Trent: Trentham Books.

Rutter, M. (2002) 'Nature, nurture and development: from evangelism through science toward policy and practice', *Child Development*, 73 (1): 1–21.

Sarangi, S. and Roberts, C. (2002) 'Discourse (mis)alignments in professional gatekeeping encounters' in C. Candlin and S. Sarangi (ed.), *Language Acquisition and Language Socialization: Ecological Perspectives*, London and New York: Continuum.

Sassoon, A.S. (1987) *Gramsci's Politics* (2nd edition), London: Hutchinson.

Sayeed, Z. and Guerin, E. (2000) *Early Years Play: A Happy Medium for Assessment and Intervention*, London: David Fulton.

Scheper-Hughes, M. (1993) *Death Without Weeping: The Violence of Everyday Life in Brazil*, Berkeley, CA: University of California Press.

Schmidt, M.F.H., Rakoczy, H. and Tomasello, M. (2012) 'Young children enforce social norms selectively depending on the violator's group affiliation', *Cognition*, 124 (3): 325–333.

Segall, M.H., Dasen, P.R., Berry, J.W. and Poortinga, Y.H. (1990) *Human Behaviour in Global Perspectives*, New York: Pergamon.

Sense about Science (n.d.) 'Brain gym'. Online at: http://www.senseaboutscience.org/data/files/resources/55/braingym_final.pdf (accessed 14 January 2013).

Shahar, S. (1990) *Childhood in the Middle Ages*, London: Routledge.

Sheridan, S. and Samuelsson, I.P. (2001) 'Children's conceptions of participation and influence in pre-school: a perspective on pedagogical quality', *Contemporary Issues in Early Childhood*, 2 (2): 169–194.

Silin, J.G. (1995) *Sex, Death and the Education of Children: Our Passion for Ignorance in the Age of AIDS*, New York: Teachers College Press.

Skutnabb-Kangas, T. and Cummins, J. (eds) (1988) *Minority Education: From Shame to Struggle*, Clevedon: Multilingual Matters.

Smidt, S. (2001) '"All stories that have happy endings, have a bad character": a young child responds to televisual texts', *English in Education*, 35 (2): 25–33. National Association for the Teaching of English.

Smidt, S. (1988) 'Making links: children talking about reality', *English in Education*, 22 (1). National Association for the Teaching of English.

Smidt, S. (ed.) (1998) *The Early Years: A Reader*, London: Routledge.

Smidt, S. (2004) 'Sinister storytellers, magic flutes and spinning tops: the links between play and "popular" culture', *Early Years*, 24 (1): 75–86.

Smidt, S. (2006) *The Developing Child in the 21st Century: A Global Perspective on Child Development*, London and New York: Routledge.

Smidt, S. (2009) *Introducing Vygotsky: A Guide For Practitioners and Students in Early Years Education*, London and New York: Routledge.

Smidt, S. (ed.) (2010) *Key Issues in Early Years Education: A Guide For Students and Practitioners* (2nd edition), London and New York: Routledge.

Smidt, S. (2013) *Introducing Malaguzzi*, London and New York: Routledge.

Smilansky, S. (1968) *The Effects of Sociodramatic Play on Preschool Children*, New York: John Wiley and Sons, Inc.

Smilansky, S. and Shefataya, L. (1990) *Facilitating Play: A Medium for Promoting Cognitive, Socio-emotional and Economic Development in Young Children*, Silver Springs, Maryland: Psychosocial and Educational Publications.

Stern, D. (1991) 'Ett Litet Barns Dagbok [A young child's diary]', Stockholm: Natur & Kultur. Cited in M. Lindahl and I.P. Samuelsson, 'Imitation and variation: reflections on toddlers' strategies for learning', *Scandinavian Journal of Educational Research*, 46 (1).

Stiles, J. (2008) *The Fundamentals of Brain Development: Integrating Nature and Nurture*, Cambridge, MA: Harvard University Press.

Sulzby, E. (1986) 'Writing and reading: signs of written and oral language organization in the young child', in W. Teale and E.L. Sulzby (eds), *Emergent Literacy: Writing and Reading*, Norwood, NJ: Ablex.

Super, C.M. and Harkness, S. (1986) 'The developmental niche: a conceptualisation at the inter-face of child and culture', *International Journal of Behavioural Development*, 9: 545–569.

Observer (2012) 'Leader: eradicating child poverty', 10 June. Online at: www.guardian.co.uk/commentisfree/2012/jun/10/observer-leader-eradicating-child-poverty (accessed 11 January 2013).

Theis, J. (2001) *Tools for Child Rights Programming: A Training Manual*, Save the Children (unpublished).

Thomas, M.S.C. and Johnson, M.H. (2008) 'New advances in understanding sensitive periods in brain development', *Current Directions in Psychological Science*, 17: 1–5.

Tizard, B. (1991) 'Working mothers and the care of young children', in A. Phoenix and A. Woollett (eds), *Social Construction of Motherhood*, London: Sage.

Tobin, J.J. (1997) *Playing Doctors in Two Cultures: The United States and Ireland*, New Haven, CT: Yale University Press.

Tomasello, M. (1997) 'Joint attention as social cognition', in C.D. Moore and P. Dunham (eds), *Joint Attention: Its Origins and Role in Development*, Hillsdale: Erlbaum.

Tomasello, M. and Rakoczy, H. (2003) 'What makes human cognition unique? From individual to shared to collective intentionality', *Mind and Language*, 18 (2): 121–147.

Tomasello, M., Striano, T. and Rochat, P. (1999) 'Do young children use objects as symbols?', *British Journal of Developmental Psychology*, 17: 563–584.

Trevarthen, C. (1977) 'Descriptive analyses of infant communicative behaviour', in H.R. Schaffer (ed.), *Studies in Mother-Infant Interaction*, London: Academic Press.

Trevarthen, C. (1998/1995) 'The child's need to learn a culture', in M. Woodhead, D. Faulkner and K. Littleton (eds), *Cultural Worlds of Early Childhood*, London and New York: Routledge and Open University.

Tse, D., Langston, R., Kakeyama, M., Bethus, I., Spooner, P., Wood, E., Witter, M. and Morris, R. (2007) 'Schemas and memory consolidation', *Science*, 316 (5821): 76–82.

Twardosz, S. (2012) 'Effects of experience on the brain: the role of neuroscience in early development and education', *Early Education and Development*, 23 (1): 96–119.

UNCHS (United Nations Centre for Human Settlements) (Habitat) (2000) *Strategies to Combat Homelessness*, Nairobi: UNCHS.

UNICEF (2005) *Child Poverty in Rich Countries 2005*, Florence: UNICEF Innocenti Research Centre.

UNICEF (2012a) 'Report Card 10', Child Poverty and Child Deprivation Across the Industrialised World. Online at: www.unicef.org/media/media_62521.html (accessed 11 January 2013).

UNICEF (2012b) *The State of the World's Children 2012*, New York: UNICEF.

Van Wedeen, J., Rosene, D., Wang, R., Dai, G., Mortazavi, F., Hagmann, P., Kaas, J. and Tseng, W. (2012) 'The geometric structure of the brain fiber pathways', *Science*, 335 (6067): 1628–1634.

Viruru, R. (2001) *Early Childhood Education: Postcolonial Perspectives from India*, London: Sage.

Volosinov, B. (1973) *Marxism and the Philosophy of Language*, New York: Seminar Press.

Vygotsky, L.S. (1962) *Thought and Language*, Cambridge, MA: MIT Press.

Vygotsky, L.S. (1966) 'Play and its role in the mental development of the child', *Soviet Psychology*, 12 (6): 62–76.

Vygotsky, L.S. (1978) *Mind in Society: The Development of Higher Psychological Processes*, Cambridge, MA: Harvard University Press.

Vygotsky, L.S. (1981) 'The instrumental method in psychology', in J.V. Wertsch (ed.), *The Concept of Activity in Soviet Psychology*, Armonk, NY.

Waage, T. (2005) *Modern Childhood: The Image of the Child in Our Society, The Seventh Kilbrandon Lecture*. Online at: www.scotland.gov.uk/Resource/Doc/136953/0034036.pdf (accessed 11 January 2013).

Walkerdine, V. (1984) 'Developmental psychology and the child-centred pedagogy: the insertion of Piaget's theory into primary school practice', in J. Henriques (ed.) *Changing the Subject*, London: Methuen.

Walkerdine, V. (1988) *The Mastery of Reason: Cognitive Development and the Production of Rationality*, London: Routledge.

Weinhold, B. (2012) 'A steep learning curve: decoding epigenetic influence on behavior and mental health', *Environmental Health Perspectives*, 1 October. Online at: http://ehp.niehs.nih.gov/2012/10/a-steep-learning-curve-decoding-epigenetic-influence-on-behavior-and-mental-health/ (accessed 11 January 2013).

Wertsch, J.V. and Stone, C.A. (1985) 'The concept of internalisation in Vygotsky's account of the genesis of higher mental functions', in J.V. Wertsch (ed.), *Culture, Communication and Cognition*, Cambridge: Cambridge University Press.

Wertsch, J.V. and Stone, C.A. (1979) 'A social interactional analysis of learning disabilities remediation', paper presented at International Conference of Assessment for Children with Learning Difficulties, San Francisco.

White, S. (2001) *Child Brigade: An Organisation of Street Working Children in Bangladesh*, Sweden: Save the Children.

Whitehead, M. (1997) *Language and Literacy in the Early Years* (second edition), London: Paul Chapman.

Williams, A. (2004) 'Playing school in multiethnic London', in E. Gregory, S. Long and D. Volk (eds), *Many Pathways to Literacy: Young Children Learning With Siblings, Grandparents, Peers and Communities*, London and New York: RoutledgeFalmer.

Williams, C. and Kamii, C. (1986) 'How do children learn by handling objects?', *Young Children*, November: 23–26.

Winterson, J. (1985) *Oranges are Not the Only Fruit*. London, Boston, Melbourne and Henley: Pandora Press.

Woodhead, M. (1997) 'Psychology and the cultural construction of children's needs', in A. James and A. Prout (eds), *Constructing and Reconstructing Childhood: Contemporary Issues in the Sociological Study of Childhood* (2nd edition, revised), Basingstoke and London: Falmer Press.

Woodhead, M., Faulkner, D. and Littleton, K. (eds) (1998) *Cultural Worlds of Early Childhood*, London: Routledge with Open University.

Zimba, R.F. (2002) 'Indigenous conceptions of childhood development and social realities in southern Africa', in H. Keller, Y.P. Poortinga and A. Scholmerish (eds), *Between Cultures and Biology: Perspectives on Ontogenetic Development*, Cambridge: Cambridge University Press.

Index